THE POLITICS OF MONEY

The
Politics of Money

BRIAN JOHNSON

McGRAW-HILL BOOK COMPANY
New York   St. Louis   San Francisco

Library of Congress Catalog Card Number: 71-133847

32640

Printed in Great Britain

TO THE MEMORY OF
MY FATHER

1624126

Contents

Author's Note   xiii

Introduction   1

MONEY'S POLITICAL PAST

1 The Money of Monarchy   11
2 The Age of Oligarchic Money   23

WELFARE VERSUS GOLD

3 The Crisis of Oligarchic Money   53
4 The Scissor Blades of Welfare and Nationalism   70
5 Tales from Bretton Woods   103
6 Forging Fetters for the Future   121

ATLANTIC POLITICS AND GOLD

7 Onto the Dollar Standard   139
8 The New Monetary Nationalism   159
9 Anglo-Saxon Profligates, Continental Conservatives   166
10 Gold War   198

INTERNATIONAL CURRENCIES AND NATIONAL POLITICS

11 Sterling's International Twilight—A Dawn of Hope   227
12 The Price of the Dollar's Defence   249

LAST BARRIER TO WORLD GOVERNMENT OR FIRST STEP

13 Development Aid and the Monetary Bottleneck   267

Contents

14 Reforming the World Monetary System: Political
     Choices and Prospects   283

     A Short Glossary of Terms   310

     References   315

     Bibliography   321

     Index   331

Illustrations

The first known official coin, from the Kingdom of Lydia, *c*. 600 BC. *Reproduced by courtesy of the Trustees of the British Museum* *facing page* 34

1272 gold florin. *Reproduced by courtesy of the Trustees of the British Museum* 34

Henry VIII silver shilling of 1543. *Reproduced by courtesy of the Trustees of the British Museum* 34

Gold sovereign of 1890. *Reproduced by courtesy of the Trustees of the British Museum* 34

'Assignat' paper money that financed the French Revolution 35

'Continental' dollars, theoretically convertible into Spanish 'Pieces of Eight'. *Reproduced by kind permission of the Greenwich, Conn., Historical Society* 35

Banknote of the Russian Revolutionary inflation. *Chase Manhattan Money Museum* 50

A 500,000,000 Reichsmark note of 1923. *Reproduced by kind permission of Mrs. Guy Johnson* 50

The highest denomination banknote ever printed, the 100,000,000,000,000,000 pengo note. *Reproduced by kind permission of the National Bank of Hungary, B.P.* 50

Montagu Norman, Governor of the Bank of England, 1920–44. *Photo: Topix* 51

Hjalmar Horace Greeley Schacht, President of the Reichsbank, 1924–30 and Hitler's Finance Minister, 1933–7. *Copyright: Wiener Library* 98

Emile Moreau, Governor of the Bank of France, 1922–8. *Copyright: Radio Times Hulton Picture Library* 98

ix

Benjamin Strong, Governor of the Federal Reserve Bank of New York, 1920–8. *Copyright: United Press International (UK) Ltd.*   98

Harry Dexter White chatting with Keynes at the inaugural meeting of the IMF and World Bank, Savannah, Georgia, shortly before Keynes's death. *Photo: IMF*   99

The Federal Reserve Bank of New York, which handles foreign exchange dealings on behalf of the United States government. *Photo: Ezra Stoller Associates. Reproduced by permission of the Federal Reserve Bank of New York*   114

The New York Federal Reserve Bank's gold vaults, the world's largest store of monetary gold. *Reproduced by permission of the Federal Reserve Bank of New York*   114

The dollar's defenders of the 60's. William McChesney Martin, Chairman of the Federal Reserve Board, 1953–1970, and President Johnson's Secretary of the Treasury, Henry Fowler. *Photo: The New York Times*   115

The dollar's defenders of the 70's? National governors of the IMF voting on September 29, 1969, to approve the creation of Special Drawing Rights or 'paper gold'. *Photo: IMF*   115

IN TEXT

The young lady of Threadneedle Street in her first premises, from *London and Its Environs*, 1761. *Reproduced by courtesy of the Bank of England*   *page* 29

"Trade follows the flag, but democrats follow the fool." *From The Ungentlemanly Art reproduced by arrangement with the Collier–Macmillan Co.*   45

"Please, teacher, what do we do next?". *From the Labour Party Leaflet*, Banking is So Simple, *1931*   73

"Phew! That's a nasty leak. Thank goodness it's not at our end of the boat." *Cartoon by David Low, March 1932, reproduced by arrangement with the Trustees and the London* Evening Standard   93

"It can't be ours! It's got golden hair!" *Cartoon by David Low, May 1944, reproduced by arrangement with the Trustees and the London* Evening Standard   122

"Make the hole a bit bigger and you can bury me too." *Cartoon by David Low, September 1952, reproduced by arrangement with the Trustees and the London* Evening Standard   181

"Vive la France! Vive le General! Vive la gloire!—And don't forget to buy me as many Deutschmarks as you can lay your hands on before the market closes!" 19.xi.68. *From a* Daily Express *Pocket Cartoon by Osbert Lancaster*   207

"Now suppose we drop the term 'overdraft' altogether and start talking about 'a new facility for sterling'?" 10.vii.68. *From a* Daily Express *Pocket Cartoon by Osbert Lancaster*   246

Top-heavy world. *Reproduced by arrangement with the* New York Times   281

Author's Note

Many people helped me in writing this book. I owe a particular debt to Dr. Gordon Bjork, whose friendship and enthusiasm did much to get the project started, and whose comments at every stage encouraged and guided me. I must also record my debt to Mr. Paul G. Hoffman, Administrator of the United Nations Development Programme, whose interest in the book encouraged me to take a leave of absence from the UNDP to complete it. Valuable research help and guidance was given me by Mr. David Damant and Mr. Dominick Harrod, while Mr. William Bruce Basset and Mr. Dudley Freeman were generous with their time in reading and commenting on much of the manuscript. Sir Robert Jackson, Sir Frank Lee, Dr. H. W. Singer, Mr. George Eddy and Mr. William Pomerance, among many other people, helped me in handling the severe problems of selection and emphasis that any such broad-ranging book must face. My thanks are also due to Mr. John Murray for his keen personal involvement from the first glimmerings of the idea to the final product. I am grateful to Mr. Robin de Beaumont, for permission to photograph a sample from his collection of French Revolutionary paper-money. Finally, Mrs. Christine Vernetti, Miss Michiko Sakata and Miss Patricia Traynor have my sincere gratitude for their fast and efficient typing of successive drafts. Beyond all practical help, however, the understanding and encouragement of my wife Pamela brought this book to birth.

Cecily, you will read your Political Economy in my absence. The Chapter on the Fall of the Rupee you may omit. It is somewhat too sensational. Even these metallic problems have their melodramatic side.

OSCAR WILDE
The Importance of Being Earnest

A change in prices . . . affects different classes unequally, transfers wealth from one to another, bestows affluence here and embarrassment there, and redistributes Fortune's favours so as to frustrate design and disappoint expectation.

J. M. KEYNES
Essays in Persuasion

Introduction

"Money doesn't talk," a New York mayoral candidate complained recently, "it screams." Shouting or whispering, however, no one doubts its effectiveness in achieving or influencing political power. But money also *listens*. The 'listening' side of money is unfamiliar to most of us. This is because money does not listen to the individual but to the actions of government and the community as a whole. This book is about the 'listening' aspect of money. It is not about the spending of money as such, but about who or what influences money's buying power when it is spent; and about the effect that changes in money's value have upon the distribution of wealth and power.

THE POLITICS OF PRICES

After an epoch during which eyeball-to-eyeball confrontation between national currencies made almost daily headlines, with the Perils of the Pound continuing as the longest running melodrama in modern financial history, with foreign holidays and investment curbed by currency controls, and spending habits changed by sky-high interest rates, credit squeezes and inflation, who needs to read about the political influences on, and repercussions of, the management of a currency? The newspapers are daily filled with the political effects of monetary crisis. But how much do people know about the root causes of the problem, of the origins of different national monetary attitudes, preferences and mechanisms which lie behind a currency crunch?

Today many people are aware that the facts of monetary life—that inflation of the money supply in excess of the supply of purchasable goods and services spells price rise, while a slower expansion of money than of such goods and services produces a decline in prices—are as universal as the laws of physics. Fewer people, however, comprehend the extent to which the effects of inflation and deflation differ between economic

sectors, social classes, and, most important today, between
entire nations and groups of nations.

Yet it is precisely the different impact of changes in the
monetary supply on different groups, rewarding some while
penalizing others, which produces the politics of money. Inflation blesses the spender and embarrasses the saver. In doing
so it strikes at the moral basis of the capitalist system. This is
why Lenin prescribed debauch of the currency as the best way
to destroy capitalism. On the other hand, when governments
expand the money supply more slowly than business activity
demands so as to raise the value of money, saving is encouraged
at the expense of spending, and capitalist morality rides high.
But this road also leads to the abyss. For by stifling enterprise
with declining prices, and throwing people out of jobs while
rewarding all those with an assured money income from rents
or pensions, extreme deflation fulfils Marx's prescription for
revolution.

Since earliest economic times, governments have been pressed
by different interests to steer closer to Marx's deflationary
Scylla, or Lenin's inflationary Charybdis. In early times these
interests were reasonably clear-cut, and the issues relatively
simple. But as economic and social organization grew more
complex and became centred on the nation state, monetary
group interests based on economic role—the rentier landlord
and investor, the earning tenant and entrepreneur—became
overlaid with the political character and aspirations of the
nation as such. Nations, in response to the pressures of their
most powerful economic groups, have long possessed characteristically different attitudes to money which in turn influence
national outlooks on other parts of the political arena. The
Frenchman's scorn of paper money and his preference for gold
is proverbial. But why do the French differ so much from the
British, the Germans and the Italians in this respect? This book
attempts to explain how such preferences came about, what
influence they have had in shaping the present world monetary
system and what influence they may continue to exert on the
politics of monetary change.

Today, with the emergence of regional economies, monetary interests are again becoming transformed. The basic

stress-planes of group and national interest—debtor *versus* creditor, Frenchman *versus* German—now feel the power-interest tug of supra-national economic classes. These new groupings may find themselves at odds with nations' traditional monetary outlook. How will they interact?

THE MORALITY OF SPECULATION

Perhaps the most visible political issue raised by money's capacity to listen is the conflict in time of financial crisis between the individual rich and the government that supposedly protects the security of the money contract. It was a familiar conflict of the sixties. The owners of wealth may flee from the down-going cash escalator to the up-escalator of real property, whether it be shares in a company, land, gold or paintings.

Speculative money bears the stamp of its owner. It therefore appears in many different guises. There is the political 'funk' money, like the billions* in gold that crossed the Atlantic in 1937–39, fleeing from Hitler, or the British capital that fled to South Africa after World War II, and to Australia in the last decade, to avoid the results of a Labour government. Then there is funk money's exotic first cousin, the 'hot' money of oil sheiks, South American millionaires and other rich individuals and companies, which restlessly scours the earth in search of the best combination of high interest and low risk. There is also the enormous volume of 'legitimate' international cash, or 'liquidity', used to settle international trade debts or for corporate international investment which, in time of monetary crisis, will join the gambling money being bet on a parity change, and which, too, can help force the parity shift to occur, a self-fulfilling expectation.

Part of the fascination of such money movements lies in the nice questions of political philosophy that lurk just below the surface turmoil of apprehension and greed. Does the Frenchman who, fearing devaluation, rushes his suitcase full of francs over the Swiss or German border to turn them into marks or Swiss francs, have the 'right' to do so because his government

* The American billion (1,000 million) is used throughout as today it has wide currency in Europe.

had not fulfilled its side of the social contract by defending the purchasing power of his money? If so, is this 'right' any different from the 'right' of the Frenchman or Englishman who threatens the international strength of his own national currency by buying marks with his francs or pounds, not in response to his government's own weakness but so as to benefit from another government's strength? If one defends such behaviour, as conservative owners of such liquid wealth naturally do, as imposing discipline on the managers of national currencies, was the action of French businessmen, who in 1968 were using industrial reorganization credits given them by their government to gamble against the franc, essentially different on a moral level? Where you draw the line on such questions defines your monetary–political standpoint.

THE THRESHOLD OF SUPRA-NATIONALISM

Nations cling to their separate currencies not simply as badges of national individuality, but as means of ensuring that the big political–financial choices remain in the hands of the people they primarily affect. Should there be more emphasis on price stability than output? Should the nation invest more in social amenities such as health, education and welfare so as to raise the enjoyment and well-being of the mass, or should it regard as 'valid' investment only that put into production of goods and commercial services? Whichever the path chosen, more socialist and redistributive, or more capitalist and accretive, the community whose property and welfare is principally at stake must surely, it is believed, reserve to itself such fundamental choices.

Yet valid as this principle may appear, the international economy is today sufficiently integrated to make it impossibly costly to insist upon it. The state of Britain today, her loss of economic and political independence, is ample evidence of this. There has been no formal change in the *outward* forms of Britain's sovereign power, the right to choose the nation's exchange rate and the right to create the nation's legal tender money. Yet, as one can scarcely be unaware, very severe constraints upon her sovereignty are today applied to Britain by her creditors, both individually, and jointly through the International Monetary Fund.

Today, in fact, the more that nations struggle to free themselves from outside constraints—whether refusing to adjust their currency's parity to a level in line with international prices, or attempting to build up balance of payments surpluses and thus amass the reserves that spell financial independence—the more self-defeating the process becomes. For one nation's surplus is another nation's deficit. And if the nations that normally run a surplus refuse, through various measures of fiscal and monetary control, to permit that surplus ever to become a deficit, then nations like Britain, which are frequently in deficit, may find themselves unable to get back into surplus, no matter how frantically they plunge into sackcloth and ashes.

The danger that some nations' puritanical insistence on the virtues of a foreign payments surplus might produce universal competition in restraint of demand, and thus lead to universal depression, seemed almost as real in the mid-1960's as it was in the 30's. So did a mood of resentment that a handful of conservative surplus countries should be able to dictate social priorities to their neighbours. The only effective solution to this problem of the orthodoxly virtuous few imposing their own life styles on the more liberal majority, is for *political* ties between countries to be brought more closely into line with existing economic reality. But the prejudices of traditional nationalism, amplified and extended by the processes of democracy, make that day still appear far off. Indeed the Common Market countries, who share the avowed goal of full economic integration, insist on autonomous currency management as strongly, and resist other members' pressure as bitterly, as anyone. Yet, as this book attempts to explain, such insistence costs the world every year hundreds of billions of dollars' worth of unfulfilled potential growth and unrealized economic development.

UNNECESSARY INTERNATIONAL CRISIS—AN INFRINGEMENT OF RIGHTS?

International financial crises of the past occurred quite largely because of the rudimentary state of knowledge of the real working of the monetary system and the consequent lack of effective technical and governmental machinery to check, steer and control. But our experience of, and equipment for, economic management is such today as to make the international monetary crises of the 60's unjustified on technical and economic grounds. Thus this last decade of flirting with catastrophe, which has hindered advanced nations—particularly Britain— in carrying out fundamental structural adjustments to their economies and has bottle-necked the flow of international aid, can be justified and explained solely at the political level.

If ever there was an example of politically denied opportunities begging for militant protest, this, surely, is it. For dry-as-dust though monetary reform may appear, the sheer quantity of human well-being or suffering at issue is perhaps greater than with almost any of the more widely recognized and protested issues. This must be so simply because the decisions of those who operate the central monetary controls directly affect the options, and therefore outcome, of all the other debates. Yet no one sits down on the steps of the Bank for International Settlements in Basle, nobody pickets the International Monetary Fund building in Washington, or mobs finance ministers. The idea is laughable. But why?

The reason is of considerable importance. Apart from what I suspect to be a widely held belief that finance ministers and central bankers are not actually human beings, their subject is protected by technical complexity and an impressive, impenetrable jargon. Opposition to narrowness and conservatism is thus often stifled in the fog of mystification that surrounds the management of money. The result is that few outside the tiny circle of those directly involved in monetary decision-making, and the orbiting crowd of (often politically conservative) financial journalists who interpret their actions to the financial and business world, have a broad picture of the issues and the solutions offered. So perhaps no one sits-in or confronts because no one knows where to sit, or who to confront with what. This book, a liberal polemic on the issues involved, is intended to show them.

Technical complexity, and the real need for secrecy as a

shield against the darts of the speculator, has subjected the politics of money to a powerful, and probably unavoidable, conspiracy of silence. But the conspiracy has been joined by politicians who, often with dire results, have tended to veer between driving head-on against the facts and preferring to leave the politics of money, along with its technical aspect, to the professionals. General de Gaulle is an adequate example of the first extreme; Britain's Labour governments have all perfectly exemplified the second. The classic example of the latter is surely Sidney Webb's protest when the National Government, formed in 1931 to defend the pound, promptly devalued it off gold, thus sharply reducing the level of unemployment: "No one told us we could do this!"

If this was the level of information of a cabinet minister during what remains Britain's greatest currency crisis of the century, it is scarcely surprising that the informed member of the public has generally remained in the dark.

But today people are somehow aware that the issues are more open, and the alternatives to rigid orthodoxy less frightening than they seemed in the past. In large measure, this is because they have heard of Keynes: they know that national tools of economic management are today capable of ironing out the more disastrous excesses of boom and bust. It is equally, perhaps, a function of witnessing so many last-gasp financial rescue operations. Today even the most unquestioning among us must have come to the realization that international financial co-operation which was able to go as far as it has recently gone, must be able, given greater political will, to undertake more constructive projects than simply battling to avert ever-imminent catastrophe in a system which the bankers then declare to be incapable of improvement by reform.

Monetary drama, the spectacle of grey-faced central bankers converging on Basle, of last-minute currency swaps and a split-level gold price, indicate conflict but also compromise. Talk of world monetary reform and 'paper gold' suggests that the recent torment of the international financial community may have been the travail of a new international order, that deadlock *is* giving way to agreement on the general direction of future change. But how significant will the change be when it comes? How will it affect the daily lives of humbler mortals than central bankers and finance ministers?

Despite a persistent atmosphere of crisis, the 1960's saw international monetary arrangements enter an era of high hopes. Indeed the true fascination of this subject in terms of world history arises from the possibility that achievement of a supra-national world authority, the solid basis for an ultimate world state, may even now be being forced upon greedy and suspicious humanity. If such a development does occur, it may arise not so much from the pressures of political idealism, nor from the threat of nuclear suicide, but from the desire to protect our cosy, habit-forming, 20-year prosperity, by underpinning our international economy with international monetary order.

Today there exists the real possibility that broader public understanding of monetary problems, and popular pressure for political solutions, can budge politicians and financiers from the automatic placing of national prestige and group advantage before international prosperity. This short history of the political dynamics of monetary change may, I hope, help the layman to assess recent progress in this direction and clarify the broad choices with which the world public is still faced.

MONEY'S POLITICAL PAST

1

The Money of Monarchy

1. THE COIN OF THE KING

Who decides what money is, and how much to create? Long before kings and kingdoms arose, money was created by common consent. Any prized commodity—seashells, furs or cattle, for example—could be used to measure and store value for the purpose of trade. From early times, however, metals, and especially silver and gold, proved the most convenient commodities to serve as money. The earliest governmental control of money that the archaeologist's spade has so far revealed was around 600 BC appropriately enough in the Lydian kingdom of King Croesus. Monarchical money might be dated from this earliest recorded official currency: the first known bargain between ruler and people in which monopoly control of the coinage became a service for which the ruler extracted a price.

From that time, for two thousand years, merchants would bring their silver and gold to the moneyers because they wanted it in a form readily acceptable in cash transactions. The moneyer would turn the merchant's metal into coin, keeping a small portion back for his own profit—the 'mint charge'—and also for seigneurage, the due that he owed to the king for the use of the royal dies which gave the coin its 'face' value, and enforced its acceptance at that value wherever the king's writ ran.

Right up until the 17th century, this service, backed by dire penalties for invasion of the royal monopoly, was the total extent of central monetary control, and as such proved more or less adequate to economic needs. But with the revolution of trade and technologies that grew in the wake of the Renaissance, such crude and casual control began to fail to meet the more exacting requirements of money.

Until the mid-17th century, minting methods remained so

simple that any moderately skilled rogue could counterfeit coins.* The standard royal penalty for counterfeiting (surprisingly mild according to the tariffs of the times) was the loss of a hand, though some legal codes called for more drastic punishments, including boiling alive. King Henry I of England, in a move which might find some sympathy today, castrated his mint officials for surreptitiously debasing the coinage and thus ruining the country with base coin. The practice of debasement, however, continued throughout history unabated, forcing merchants to cut or scratch the coin that they received to assay its metal content, and always to have about them a pair of scales to check the weight of coins that had been 'debased'—drilled or clipped—by private (or official) profiteers.

Late mediaeval commerce was also becoming seriously hampered by the chaotic variety of currencies in circulation. In Europe, every king, most princes and many nobles, bishops and cities possessed the right to issue coins. During the decline of the Frankish Empire, no less than three hundred vassals claimed coinage rights; in 15th-century Germany there were 600 coinage authorities, while in Italy every major city had its own currency. By 1300, France had reduced the number of her currencies to thirty. England, however, unified by the Norman conquest, could boast a centralized coinage four centuries before any other major kingdom. But even in England, during

* The method of making coins until the Frenchman Blondeau invented a machine for milling (serrating) a coin's edge, was known as hammering, i.e., putting a blank disc between two dies and hitting the top die with a hammer. With great skill, very fine coins could be produced by this process, but the vast majority were crude. Furthermore, the method was so slow and labour-intensive that output per man (two men when Blondeau's screwpress came in) was low, and the cost of coining high. Making a gold piece might cost 5 per cent of its face value, a silver coin 25 per cent, and copper coins were so relatively expensive to produce that moneyers rarely had either the time or the desire to make them.

These high costs, plus the seigneurage charge, both encouraged people to withhold their precious metals from the mints, and encouraged counterfeiting. Not until 1800 was steam power linked to coin-making machinery (in London) to resolve this problem; but by that time the era of monarchical money was over, bank credit having removed much of the pressure from the coinage.

the anarchy under Stephen and Matilda, the barons resorted to their own private currencies. Thus, not only when it listened to its creator and his echoing counterfeiters did money's value become confused, but when it talked it often chattered in the gibberish of Babel.

As if these impediments did not provide enough confusion to marketer and merchant, the king's seigneurage charges were often used as a major source of revenue. Kings invariably reserved the right to remint, or raise—'cry up'—the value of existing coins as often as they pleased.* If the new coins contained less precious metal than the old ones, their value fell and prices rose. However, the increase in prices of local goods and services often would not reflect the change in precious metal content. If trade were on the increase, the demand for money to make cash payments could readily offset the apparently diminished acceptability of the coinage. Indeed, in the principalities of Northern Italy, where trade was growing most rapidly in late mediaeval times, merchants often petitioned the authorities to debase the coinage.[1] For as trade grew, the demand for money in which to settle trade debts constantly outstripped the supply of gold and silver, forcing the value of money to rise and prices and profits to fall. The prosperity of the early Renaissance in the Italian cities was thus consciously encouraged by 'stretching' the gold and silver supply at the mint. But these debasements rarely kept pace with the

* Though coinage debasement by clipping or straight devaluation (crying up the coin's face value) was practised long before, Ancient Rome can claim the doubtful honour of inventing debasement by fiddling with the coinage's metal content. Between AD 301 and 323 the number of Roman *denarii* asked in exchange for a (constant value) solid gold piece (the *solidus*) rose from 50,000 to 160,000 even though in that twenty-two-year period the silver content of the *denarius* was only halved (from 4 per cent to 2 per cent). Simple arithmetic and his furnace for assaying metal fineness must therefore have told the enquiring trader that this scale of depreciation had little to do with the *denarius*' silver content. But if this monetary insight was ever grasped, it became lost again until thirteen hundred years later. Only after 1526, when Copernicus wrote his *Treatise on Debasement* did men begin to realize that as coins were in daily practice merely tokens of value, it was the *number* of coins in circulation which determined the coinage's buying power, rather than how much of any particular metal they happened to contain.

increasing need for money, so as to maintain a stable price level. In practice, money's depreciation forced up prices, but the rising prices themselves served to increase the profitability of trade, drawing more goods to the cities.

While debasement was in progress in one state, goods bought from outside did tend to mount in cost in full proportion to the decrease in precious content in the coinage. This was because once a political frontier was crossed, and the coin issuer's authority was ended, a coin's value was determined by its precious metal content alone. With a plethora of different monetary authorities, cross-boundary cash transactions, which could occur every few miles in many parts of Europe, continued into the 17th and even 18th centuries to be made by metal weight.

The needs of a more active commerce produced a much faster rate of depreciation of money in the Italian cities than in relatively stagnant agricultural England. Nevertheless in England, as elsewhere in Christendom, the need for money to finance growing commerce tended to reinforce a natural monetary alliance between king and bourgeoisie against the rentier aristocracy's dead hand. When the spendthrift Henry VIII reduced the precious metal content of the English coinage by 60 per cent between 1543 and 1551, the chief sufferers were landowners living off fixed money rents. The massive debasement caused singularly little disruption of trade; in fact it almost certainly helped to alleviate the persistent trade depression of the first half of the 16th century. Unwittingly but inexorably, money was thus being managed to promote a shift in political power, and to help build a new political order.

THE INSOLUBLE PROBLEM OF THE STANDARD

The greatest and most persistent problem of monarchical currencies was that of the standard. Man's tinkering with the money supply was the most important single reason for variations in its buying power and problems with its exchange, but not the only one. Chance discoveries of metal deposits, aided by technical improvements in mining and metallurgy, caused the natural supply of monetary metals to vary greatly from time to time.

From early on there were attempts to regulate the basic source of supply—precious metal mining. In early China, for example, the official ban on private metal mining was lifted when economic activity was flagging and prices were depressed. But official efforts to control these natural tides of new discovery were sporadic and generally about as effective as Canute's control over the sea. Yet despite periodic dearth or overabundance in the supply of silver and gold, men clung to those two metals because their availability did keep roughly in step with economic need. Indeed, the relationship between demand and supply had a crude but definite link. Technological improvements in transport and navigation, which encouraged the expansion of trade and of markets and increased the need for money, also tended to reveal deposits of monetary metal.

The trouble was, however, that over the centuries no one of these metals stayed just sufficiently rare (or common) to remain irremovably entrenched as the standard. The Persian Empire solved the problem of varying metallic scarcity with a double (bimetallic) standard—gold and silver in the ratio of $13\frac{1}{2}$ units of silver to one of gold. But when Alexander the Great dispersed the gold hoards of the Persian temples into everyday circulation, gold's sudden abundance upset the relative scarcities of the two metals and forced down the silver/gold ratio from $13\frac{1}{2}/1$ to $10/1$. For most of money's early history, however—except when gold briefly predominated in Roman Constantinople—the world reckoned its wealth and settled its debts mainly in silver.

But in 1272 the Florentines coined their renowned gold florin. And in the following century, as the florin found its way through trade all over Europe, a ratio was automatically established between it and silver coin. Bimetallism was reborn. It was to have a long life: almost exactly 500 years in fact, during which time the relatively greater natural scarcity of gold slowly reasserted itself, pushing the ratio from about $11/1$ in the 13th century to $16/1$ in the 19th.

The silver/gold ratio provided increasing headaches for the

keepers of kingly coin currencies, because each ruler fixed and changed his own figure.* The merchant bankers who were emerging in the early 16th century were thus able to make great profits from 'arbitrage'—moving metal around the map to take advantage of different relative scarcities, and foreign traders, especially those with the Levant where silver was much scarcer, and the silver/gold ratio as low as 9/1, exported vast quantities of silver, hence upsetting European standards and, in the case of England, which gained early predominance in the Levant trade, denuding the country of silver.

In order to defend their metal supply and thus to maintain the royal income from a flow of metal through the mint, rulers placed bans upon the export of both coin and bullion in trade. The English Parliament placed bans upon gold and silver export no less than seven times in the 15th century, and clamped close restrictions on foreign trade, insisting that foreign merchants spend at least part of their receipts on English goods. But such controls were at best ineffective, and foreign commerce continued to prosper while the English kings of the 15th and 16th centuries increasingly resorted to debasement to supply the growing needs both of central government and commerce.

2. THE DEFEAT OF MONARCHICAL MONEY

England not only developed the first major example of a centralized coinage, but her early political development ensured that it was among the best maintained.† This same political precosity, however, also ensured that their kingly monetary system, like their absolute monarchy, would be the first to fall.

---

* At the end of the 15th century, for instance, 10 units of gold were equivalent to 98 units of silver in Spain, 105 in Italy, 110 in France, 111½ in England.

† William the Conqueror's feudal council forced him to abjure the profitable debasements by which he had financed the government in his Duchy of Normandy, in return for a hearth tax: a notable example of successful pressure by an economic group on the monarch's monetary freedom. His successors on the English throne were generally granted taxes by Parliament on the same condition: that they refrained from tampering with the coinage, though the later Norman kings often overlooked this stipulation.

Queen Elizabeth I's celebrated restoration of the currency had been made possible by the capture of treasure from the Spanish Main. But in the 1620's and 30's that source began to dry up. Yet England's commerce, and hence her thirst for money, was growing faster than ever. Meanwhile opposition to the king prevented the Stuarts from reforming the coinage so as to maintain the sterling silver standard. The squirearchy and burgher Parliamentarians were in no mood to allow the government to deflate the coinage to its bullion value and hence deprive them of a large part of their capital: if recoinage were to take place, the cost would have to be borne by the exchequer, but the exchequer of the early Stuarts, indeed of Cromwell, too, was in no position to bear such expense.*

So England's silver money continued for most of the 17th century without a recoinage. Yet, with commercial revolution in full swing, the demand for cash was so strong that right until the 1690's, worn, debased, clipped and counterfeited coins, including virtually unrecognizable pieces in circulation since the time of Elizabeth I, were freely accepted in exchange: indeed fine, full-weight coins were the ones that, obeying Gresham's Law,† disappeared from circulation into private hoards or to be melted for export. Nothing could have shown more clearly than the English coinage's century of deterioration without depreciation that the value of the unit of account did *not* depend on the quantity of the precious metal in the coin. Yet despite this staringly obvious fact, and the writings of numerous theorists who pointed it out, identification of a coin's

---

* Charles I did strike back at his burgher opposition. In 1640, at his wits' end for money, he seized between £100,000 and £120,000 in silver, deposited for coinage at the mint. Henry VIII had taken similar action a century before, and got away with it. But times had changed. Charles was forced to strike a bargain with the merchants, returning their capital in exchange for a six-month loan at 8 per cent, which he duly repaid. But the incident was a nail in the coffin of monarchical control of money. Long after the Civil War was over, and a more limited monarchy restored, Charles I's 'stop' on the mint was used as an argument to prove how unsafe a great national bank, such as the Bank of Amsterdam, would be under a monarchy.

† 'Gresham's Law' (that bad money drives out good) was a phrase coined by Henry Dunning Macleod in 1857 in the mistaken impression that Elizabeth I's astute financial counsellor, Sir Thomas Gresham, had explained it in 1558.

value with its metal content, and the desire for a return to the old standard, remained.

Unable either to lay their hands upon sufficient bullion to reform the coinage without reducing the coinage's volume, or to enforce the capital levy involved in recoining from the precious metal in the coinage, English kings had even before the Civil War lost the political power necessary to maintain their money. The restored monarchy rapidly lost the remnants of its coinage control. From 1666, the seigneurage charge was abolished by Act of Parliament along with other mint charges, and the mints became free, the cost of minting being met thereafter by a duty of 10 shillings a ton on wines, vinegar, cider and beer, and 20 shillings on spirits.* Meanwhile, the production of milled coin, begun under Cromwell, restricted illegal private enterprise coinage to manageable proportions.

A still more significant blow to royal monetary control was the abolition, in 1660, of all prohibition on the export of bullion. This was a great victory for the now powerful foreign trading interest of the City of London. The City's able spokesman, Thomas Mun, had argued in his celebrated book, *England's Treasure by Foreign Trade*, that restraint of bullion export could only hamper the growth of national wealth by restricting foreign trade, and causing other nations to retaliate with their own bullion export restrictions. Mun's alternative proposal, the classic exposition of 'mercantilism', was to protect individual industries which were without competitive advantage of skill (technology) or natural resources, and thus artificially to create, by protection, a favourable balance of trade which would bring bullion into the realm.†

* Free assay and coinage of bullion at the mint for all-comers was continued until the Gold Standard Act of 1925.

† Such restrictions were, of course, equally open to retaliatory action, and, to the extent that his case for freeing bullion rested upon tariffs and bounties (subsidies), it was as specious as that of his 'bullionist' opponents. Removal of the restrictions on bullion export simply showed the ascendancy to economic, and thus political, power of the great Charter companies which profited by the export of bullion, rather than any early flowering of Free Trade doctrine related to gold and silver.

3. THE FALL OF MONARCHICAL MONEY

England's restored monarchy was also curbed in its power to raise money without parliamentary consent. Gone forever were the forced loans, the sales of monopolies, the Ship Money and other devices by which Charles I had contrived to rule without Parliament for eleven years. Yet the restored monarchy still made no distinction between the royal exchequer and the king's privy purse—the expenses of the kingdom and those of the royal household. Thus, in the second half of the 17th century, with costly mercantile wars to finance, rapidly escalating costs of domestic government, and basic income only from the excise, royal credit deteriorated hopelessly.

Charles II, who faced the Dutch War of 1672 with an empty exchequer, was reduced to borrowing cash in personal loans of fifty and a hundred pounds, paying, in addition to exorbitant rates of interest, a finder's commission of 2 per cent to anyone who introduced a lender. Such hand-to-mouth financing in the face of vaulting expenses could not possibly continue and, in the same year, Charles stopped all exchequer payments, the suspension lasting two years. As a result of the stop, scores of royal suppliers went bankrupt, as did several of the largest goldsmiths of the City who had placed too many eggs in the royal basket. Royal credit thereafter descended to a new low. But it was the French War of 1689 that gave England's monarchical money its *coup de grâce*. Charles's debts had been £2¼ million and his annual income a little over £1½ million when he slammed the exchequer window. By 1694, King William was spending annually the total amount of Charles's debt on maintaining the army alone, and by 1697 had run up total debts of over £20 million. By 1694, therefore, with taxation as high as Parliament dared, the excise mortgaged for years to come and a million raised from a state lottery, the king was finally forced to abdicate his right to control the money supply. In return for a loan of £1,200,000 from a consortium of wealthy speculators and merchants, the Bank of England was chartered as a joint stock banking monopoly with the right to issue currency and receive deposits.

At once the Bank, by taking over the royal debts in exchange for banknotes, produced a roaring currency inflation. Prices soared, and the value of all currency—both Bank paper and the long-debased coinage—depreciated rapidly. The oligarchy who now controlled the currency had taken the bit between their teeth and run away with it. The market price of gold and silver soared far above the face value of the coinage, which promptly began to disappear into goldsmiths' melting pots for export or to back their own issue of paper notes. Formal royal abdication of monetary control came with William's address to the Lords and Commons in November 1695. The Bank of England's inflation had at last made a recoinage essential, and William declared that he proposed to leave the whole matter in the hands of Parliament.

Fierce dispute immediately broke out as to what the causes of depreciation had been, and what should be the remedy. The issues, though straightforward to us today, were not seen clearly at the time. To return to the good old standard of Elizabeth would mean a massive diminution of the money in circulation, a collapse of prices, the bankruptcy of many in trade and the enrichment of all creditors. Devaluation of the coinage, on the other hand, i.e., 'crying up' coins' face value so that their bullion value would at least match the market price of that bullion, would protect and stabilize domestic trade, though (by lowering the money's purchasing power abroad) initially hit the foreign trader.

In his *Further Considerations Concerning Raising the Value of Money*, John Locke, that high priest of the rights of property, and gentle philosopher of bourgeois revolution, became the champion of the old standard, and hence the great authority for 'sound money' men for all time to come. Behind him, in enthusiastic array, ranged the Court Party and the landed interest, gleeful at the prospect of a raising and stabilization of the purchasing power of their rents. Opposing him was William Lowndes, Secretary of the Treasury, who proposed recoinage at the *de facto* standard, and was backed by goldsmiths, bankers and many commercial men who owed debts measured in the debased coinage.

With landed property predominant in Parliament, the issue was never in doubt. The recoinage of 1697-98 returned the money of England to Elizabeth's silver standard. Part of the bullion for the new coinage was raised by a window tax,* payable in the old coin, but the bulk came from the fact that the old coinage still held by poorer people who could not pay off debts or taxes with it in time, or turn it in to the mint by a fixed date, was only accepted at a heavy discount thereafter. The resultant deflation produced a great crash of prices, including that of labour, and 'great hardship upon the labourers and poorer sort of people', so that a proclamation of July 1698 commanded local justices to meet frequently to keep the peace. Nevertheless, rioting broke out in several parts of the country.

Neither Lowndes nor Locke, nor any of the multitudinous pamphleteers offering more or less quack monetary remedies, understood that paper banknote inflation had caused the depreciation of *all* 'face-value' money. Locke thought that the decline in money's buying power was due to the appalling state of the coinage, but never stopped to ask why the price rise had happened so suddenly, and not over a century of gradual debasement. Lowndes thought money had lost value because so much silver bullion had gone abroad in trade and to pay for the war, its scarceness making it rise in price.

All such arguments were, however, irrelevant. The more fundamental point at issue was clearly grasped by Locke and his friends. Public finance was no longer a matter of one untrustworthy individual endowed with the divine right to change the law at will, and to shift money's value in his favour. The notes of the Bank of England represented 'the public credit'—the wealthy of the land lending to the state to finance the prosecution of commercial wars abroad, and a government at home that worked in their interest. As Locke put it:

> It will weaken, if not fatally destroy, the public faith, when all that have trusted the public, and assisted in present necessities . . . shall be defrauded of 20 per cent of what Acts of Parliament were security for.[2]

From now on, men of influence believed that the mint weights, removed from the hand of the king, should be untouchable and sacrosanct, fulfilling the basic condition behind an

* Which resulted in the bricking-up of many 17th century windows.

automatic metallic monetary standard, which Locke and his followers, above all the great Adam Smith, saw as the best possible monetary system for support of the rights of property and the promotion of trade.

2

The Age of Oligarchic Money

1. THE ORIGINS OF OLIGARCHIC MONEY

Oligarchic, or bank-managed, money first emerged in the burgher-ruled states of North Italy and the Low Countries. Genoa, governed by a merchant council, had developed the world's first modern-style banking system by the end of the 15th century. Bank-created money was also in wide use among the merchants and traders of the Netherlands even while they were still under Spanish colonial rule. In fact Dutch banking had its origins in loans made on deposits of New World treasure, privately deposited with Dutch merchants to avoid the heavy seigneurage charges of the Spanish mint.[1] By contrast, kingly control over England's money supply, like prerogative power in other spheres, was only gradually replaced by that of the propertied and merchant classes.

The Civil War and Commonwealth period laid the groundwork for oligarchic monetary rule in England. Like the Spanish in the Netherlands, the early Stuarts forced as much bullion as they could through the mints, so as to reap the profits of seigneurage. In doing so they were in effect subsidizing anyone who, as a holder of bullion, could establish a bank. The Civil War hastened this trend. Not only merchants, but many country landowners, especially those on the side of Parliament, being fearful for their plate and treasure, sent it for safekeeping to London, and were issued with notes based on its security in return. Paper money, whose use was thus expanded during the emergency, had, however, long been in use in commerce in England, as elsewhere* and had given merchants a degree of

---

* The earliest paper money, the bill of exchange, was a credit to finance the movement of goods, which worked as follows. Let us say that John of Ipswich was exporting a consignment of wool worth 10 gold florins to Giovanni of Florence. Instead of paying the 10 florins promptly (which was often difficult to arrange), Giovanni would write a 'bill', promising to pay John the equivalent of 10 florins in sterling at a specified place and date. The

independence from the vagaries of the king's coinage.* But it was the notes which goldsmiths and silversmiths offered in return for safekeeping of plate, jewellery and bullion that were the precursors both of today's banknote and cheque. Their notes, which at first were signed and discounted by every payee, later, as the practice grew, circulated at par (face value) and were the means by which unneeded reserves came to be pooled for communal benefit, one man's assets financing another man's business.

---

bill would represent the sterling exchange value of the 10 florins plus interest for the risk and the wait involved. Such bills counteracted long delays between payment for, and receipt of, goods, since the bill writer did not have to raise the money to pay for the goods until closer to the time when the goods would arrive, or even until after they had been resold by him, thus providing him with the wherewithal to pay.

In the meantime, these bills could be used as money. John could use Giovanni's bill to finance other trade or, as markets became more sophisticated, he could even sell it at a discount for cash. One act of trade could therefore provide the 'money' for several transactions during the time between promise and delivery. When the three months were up, Giovanni's banker friend in London would pay John the promised sterling and Giovanni would pay florins to the banker's office or correspondent in Florence.

Transactions in such bills had an added attraction in mediaeval times. If they were payable in a currency other than that of the issuer they were a means of lending money, yet avoiding the laws against usury. Bills of exchange generally fell due for settlement at the great fairs held regularly in important trade centres, where the authorities turned a blind eye on financial transactions carried out amid the hubbub of worldly intercourse. In the Middle Ages, bills of exchange were financed throughout Europe by a network of Italian merchants and financiers, who centred their London activities in Lombard Street, which remains a world banking centre today.

Gradually, bills of exchange began to be issued without the backing of actual goods, simply as promises to pay. Such 'credit' bills (as distinct from 'real' or 'commodity' bills) were the equivalent of paper credit or 'fiduciary' currency, as opposed to 'commodity' (metal) currency, or paper currency fully backed by a fixed amount of metal.

* Only a degree, though, because kings maintained the *standard* of payment in which bills must ultimately be settled. However, bills could be settled in currencies whose standard was well maintained, or even, as was the case during much of the middle ages, in abstract 'units of account', somewhat comparable to the notionally dollar-based 'paper gold' which the IMF began to issue in 1970. These abstract units served as a non-national means of international settlement at mediaeval fairs. (See Paul Einzig, *A History of Foreign Exchange*, p. 24.)

Official paper money, as opposed to private goldsmiths' notes, was already current in Holland and parts of Italy, when it spread simultaneously in France and England in the 1680's to finance their military struggles for the upper hand in foreign trade. But its use spread fastest in England. This was not so much because English trade was growing much more rapidly than that of other countries—in the 17th century it wasn't—as because of the strain put on the English coinage by trade with India.

During the reigns of Charles II and James II (1660–85) imports from India multiplied thirtyfold. So great was the outflow of English silver to pay for them that the East India Company started shipping gold to England from Europe to buy silver for export. As this practice continued, England's gold supply steadily increased while silver became desperately short. A comparable modern situation would be if change were to become scarcer than banknotes. By 1700, England's traditional silver standard was threatened. Sir Isaac Newton, Master of the Royal Mint from 1699, busied himself in its defence.* Newton's efforts as monetary manager were worthy of the father of modern physics. His gold parity for the pound sterling survived to 1931, and during this 232-year interval, was to become the keystone of an international monetary system. But as a measure to protect England's silver currency, it failed completely. In the year 1717 alone, the East India Company exported over three million ounces of silver, much of which came from the coinage. The great profitability of trade with the East was still pushing inexorably toward a gold standard.

THE CREDIT NETWORK: FOUNDATION OF OLIGARCHIC
CONTROL

England's gradual shift to a gold from a silver standard was made possible by paper money. But it was the need to mobilize

---

* After 'delving into the curious lore of gold and silver parities, degrees of fineness, mint changes and the like' (see Sir Roy Harrod, *The Dollar*, Norton Library, 1963, p. 4), Newton reduced the mint's buying price for gold guineas so as to bring the price of gold in England back to the level of the rest of Europe. The gold guinea was consequently reduced in value from 22 to 21 silver shillings in the year 1717, and the price of an ounce of gold was fixed at £3 17s. 10½d.

credit for industrialization that gave banknotes their greatest boost. A whole new scale of investment was required for factory machinery. With it grew new financing techniques. The immobility of factory plant also had its influence; for it tied down the wandering merchant, who had previously used the spare cash of other City merchants to finance handicraft production as he wended his way. He thus began to tap local sources of credit and, above all, earnings from the land. Farmers earned their income in a lump sum, i.e., when they sold their harvest. If a farmer deposited his cash with a local merchant, the merchant could then make him regular remittances (with interest) meanwhile having the use of the money. In using these agrarian savings, more and more 18th-century English merchants took on a banking role.

Up to the mid-18th century, however, English banking was almost entirely restricted to London, and mainly concerned with financing foreign trade. When Edmund Burke arrived there in 1750 he noted that there were no more than twelve bankers shops outside the metropolis.

By 1793 there were almost 400. Soon collection of agricultural earnings to finance industry began to take place on a national scale, with London bankers acting as middlemen between specializing areas of the country. Local banks who collected the savings of agricultural East Anglia, Sussex and Somerset built up large credits with their London agents, their deposits enabling London bankers to discount* Northern industrialists' 'inland' bills of exchange. The London market in bills of exchange thus served to finance inter-regional trade, while at the same time the local banks, with their London deposits behind them, were able to provide capital for local investment. In economic terms, this reciprocal relationship between country banks, their clients and the City, began to unleash the potential of the nation as a whole. In terms of monetary politics it solidified both debtors and creditors in support of wider use of credit-money.

* Thus a merchant might give a producer £900 cash in exchange for a bill of exchange which promised £1,000 in three months' time. The £100 being his profit in return for the service and risk-bearing involved.

THE BANK OF ENGLAND: HIGH COURT OF THE MONETARY
OLIGARCHS

When the Bank of England received its Charter there was considerable consternation as to the political dangers of the Crown's granting these monopoly privileges to its creditors. Indeed the Bank's first Deputy Governor, Michael Godfrey, felt constrained to write a pamphlet denying that the Bank would 'hereafter joyn with the prince to make him absolute, and so render parliaments useless'.[2] Such fears were to prove groundless. Far from the Bank allying with the king against the influence of Parliament, its directors cultivated all possible contacts with parliamentarians, on whom they relied for periodic renewal of their Charter, clearly realizing, in the aftermath of the Glorious Revolution of 1688, where ultimate sovereignty now lay.

In practice, opposition to the Bank's monopoly position was to come largely from its competitors in the City of London, and from the grassroots financial establishment—the country banks. These banks resented the Bank's monopoly position which restricted their own growth and indeed threatened their stability.* Held back as they were by the obviously limited capacity of any six-man partnership to accumulate idle reserves, the country banks were highly prone to failure in bad times. Literally hundreds of them were wiped out in the post-Napoleonic War depression. Yet not until 1833 was the Bank of England's joint-stock monopoly limited, and provincial banks more than 65 miles from London allowed to issue stock and thus grow in size and solidity.

As the most broadly based bank, and manager of the government's debt, the Bank of England had at its disposal more than one means of influencing the country's money supply. From the Bank's foundation, much of its business was in discounting or re-discounting bills. By raising or lowering its discount charge, the Bank could influence the amount of money available in the

---

* Under its Charter, the Bank of England was to be the only banknote issuer that could share the burden of maintaining its note-backing gold reserve among a large number of stockholders. All other note issuers were forced by law to be partnerships limited to six persons or less.

City, and thus business activity generally. Lowering the Bank's discount rate (bank rate) would make money cheaper to raise and thus spur productive enterprise: raising it would have the opposite effect. A second source of control which developed much later, at least partly at the constant urging of Walter Bagehot, then leader-writer for *The Economist*, stemmed from the Bank's ability to 'manage' the public debt. In times of great strain, where a sudden and direct effect on the money market was called for, the Bank could scoop in or gush forth money by buying or selling 'government paper'.*

Gradually, as the Bank's shareholders found that their own interest was threatened in a financial panic, the Bank emerged as a 'lender of last resort' to sound firms faced with failure in a credit crisis. At first its help was to individual firms in trouble. Only as the mechanisms of the money market became ground smooth with use and experience and therefore responsive to changes in interest rates were the Bank of England's directors able to gauge the effectiveness of calculated intervention. Nevertheless, almost every major financial crisis from the mid-18th century saw the Bank progress in developing its regulatory role.

Naturally this authoritative governmental role attracted political opposition. There was fierce argument as to where the Bank should draw the line in giving help. Borderline cases were bound to occur, which made the Bank enemies. In 1717 the Bank was subjected to a politically inspired speculative attack from which it was only saved by direct government intervention. In the panic that followed the bursting of the South Sea Bubble in 1720 and again twenty-five years later, during

* Owners of government stock (shares in the national debt, often referred to as gilt-edged because it is government guaranteed) can obviously be persuaded to sell it to the Bank if it offers a favourable enough price, or what is technically called 'strong enough support in the gilt-edged market'. As they do so, the Bank creates money to pay them for it, thus directly expanding the money supply. Conversely, if the Bank offers a low price—'weak support'—for government paper, people will be inclined to buy gilt-edged from the Government Broker, their payments to the Bank for it thus shrinking the money supply. (A more detailed discussion of this process of monetary creation and its implications for present-day politics will be found in Chapter 9, pp. 171–77).

S.Wale delin. J.Green sc. Oxon.

The Bank

The young lady of Threadneedle Street in her first premises, 1761

the '45 Rebellion, when Bonnie Prince Charlie was marching South and French invasion was feared, the Bank only saved itself by a ruse. It paid out gold for its notes to individuals who agreed to return the coins by the back door, thus giving the anxious line of would-be note redeemers a reassuring impression of the Bank's cash position.

As the Young Lady of Threadneedle Street emerged from her adolescent exploits, growing confidence increased her interventions. Up to the mid-19th century, however, her control of credit was still very crude. Indeed, she only attempted to use it to regulate domestic business activity in the direst emergency, for the device of varying bank rate was far from an electronic-age knob to be twiddled for fine adjustment and tuning, but a heavy, steam-age lever only showing results on being pulled with great vigour.

One reason for this apparent insensitivity was simply that, until the 1830's at least, the Bank still behaved first and foremost as a profit-motivated private concern. It competed in the market over the discount rate for bills. But gradually the City elders came to realize that competition in the market place often caused the Bank to apply the brakes too gently and too late. As a concession, therefore, to ensure the continuation of its Charter by Parliament, the Bank allowed its discount rate to become 'high and dry' above the going market price. The Young Lady of Threadneedle Street was coming of age. She was beginning to accept full-time responsibility for the operation of the monetary system as a whole. She was becoming a modern central bank.

THE GREAT 'BANKING-CURRENCY' DEBATE

But the Young Lady was not to emerge fully into her modern guise as supreme money manager until the greatest intellectual battle in British monetary politics had been fought and won.

From its first appearance on the scene, paper currency confused the thinking of monetary theorists by blurring their clear mental division between coin and credit. Because it was inconceivable—except in unforeseeable moments of total panic—that everyone would want to convert their paper banknotes into gold at the same time, paper circulation had from early on been allowed to increase beyond the value of metal into which it was supposedly convertible. Debate thus inevitably centred around the 'unbacked' part of the note issue. Should the money supply be tied rigidly to gold, or should there be flexibility? The 1830's had seen two banking crises in England (1836 and 1839) which demonstrated clearly that the banking system had grave problems defining, let alone controlling, the money supply. During this time, a few sophisticated individuals had noticed that prices did *not* move parallel to the volume of metal money and banknotes in circulation. Realizing that this was because credit is, after all, money, and acts in the same way as any other money in influencing prices, they proposed to take credit into account when controlling the money supply.*

These men, representatives of a new liberal economic intelligentsia, intent upon scientific examination of the facts of economic life, and interested, above all, in applying reason so as to maximize general prosperity, in many respects foreshadowed the monetary ideas of Keynes. Looking at the role of credit in the monetary system, they realized that to control the level of business activity effectively, spending *as a whole* would have to be influenced, and that this could only be done by regulating money in all its guises. To achieve this control, they believed that bankers should be given a free hand, and the Bank of England's note issue and credit control should *not* be rigidly tied to the gold reserve but be considered complementary parts of its money-controlling function.

Strange though it may at first appear, this concept was bitterly opposed by most bankers of the day, including the directors of the Bank of England. The banking community disliked the Banking School's ideas because they saddled them with public responsibility for management of the economy, and threatened to nail them down in the very centre of the political

---

* Known as the 'Banking School', this group included James Wilson, founder of *The Economist* newspaper, and father-in-law of Walter Bagehot (also Editor of *The Economist*, who was later to explain and codify the operations of the London money market in his classic *Lombard Street*), John Fullerton, a self-made financier, and Thomas Tooke, author of a celebrated *History of Prices*.

arena. Thus while the Banking School said 'Trust the Bankers', the bankers themselves were strenuous in avoiding the implications of such trust. They much preferred to look to the world market, as expressed in the international flow of gold, to regulate the money supply. The majority of them, therefore, supported the opposite monetary theory, the so-called 'Currency School'.

According to the Currency School, paper currency was simply a convenience and should not be used to expand the money supply. Credit money was simply ignored in this theory. George Warde Norman, a director of the Bank of England for more than half the 19th century and a leading exponent of the Currency School, described credit simply as a 'means of economizing the use of money'.[3] The Bank of England's control of the money supply through bill discounting and debt management operations did not therefore have any place in the monetary theory of the Currency School. It was an adjunct to the system but not part of it.*

The Currency School had the most influence and adherents, even though it generally had the worst of the argument. Its exponents won the ear of Sir Robert Peel's government, and

* Though there was never any serious doubt as to the ability of national central banks to create national money, the ideas of the Currency School lingered on in commercial banking theory until well into the present century. Edwin Cannan, in an article entitled 'The Meaning of Bank Deposits', which appeared in the journal *Economica* in 1921, spelled out what he called the 'cloakroom theory' of commercial banking. Bankers, in Cannan's analogy, were similar to cloakroom attendants, receiving deposits of their clients' paraphernalia and obliged to return them on demand. The difference consisted only in the fact that 'money is more homogeneous than bags and their contents', so that, whilst cloakroom depositors insist on the *same* bag, depositors in a bank are willing to accept other pieces of money in lieu of those they deposited. However, just as 'the most abandoned cloakroom attendant cannot lend out more umbrellas or bicycles than have been entrusted to him, the most reckless banker cannot lend out more money than he has of his own plus what he has of other peoples' (pp. 258–59, quoted in Fritz Matchlup, *The Quarterly Journal of Economics*, vol. LXXIX, August 1965). The cloakroom theory, in fact, persists in many bankers' views as to how international credit must be operated. However, the breakthrough of Special Drawing Rights creation by the IMF agreed in 1969 probably signals the final closure of the Currency School's long and persistent career.

the Bank Act of 1844 marked their official triumph. This Act sanctioned oligarchic control of the money supply by officially denying the existence of that control. It did this by separating the Bank of England's functions into two watertight compartments: the Issue Department and the Banking Department, and it prescribed that from henceforth the Bank publish two distinct and separate balance sheets. The Issue Department sheet would show the number of notes outstanding, and against this the total number covered by gold. The amount not so covered (the fiduciary issue, as it was called), was fixed to a rigid maximum of £14 million. Meanwhile the Banking Department was to be entirely independent, freed from all official responsibilities.

So much for theory. In practice, however, the principle behind the 1844 Bank Act was largely ignored and the Banking School's ideas prevailed. Despite the technical separation of the two functions of the Bank, credit control was regularly used to support the reserves. It was simply not possible in practice to ensure a rigid relationship between issued paper and gold in the vault. What happened, for instance, when sudden emergencies produced an outflow of gold abroad? Notes in the public's hands could not be called in at will to respond to the diminished gold backing. Clearly it would take time to restrain the note issue so as to correspond exactly with the diminished gold supply. However, the use of bank rate could anticipate a sudden flow of gold abroad—for instance, to pay for unexpected grain imports. A rise in bank rate would mean higher interest earnings on deposits by foreigners and bring gold in from abroad. For 19th century London was not merely a commercial mecca where money could be put to maximum use, it was also the safest haven of much of the world's 'funk money'— the Switzerland of the day. According to Bagehot, 7 per cent would bring gold to London from the North Pole, 10 per cent from the moon. Shifts of bank rate, therefore, by influencing the flow of short-term foreign funds, removed the necessity of restricting the note issue, and thus of continually checking the growth of Britain's economy. But the monetary crises of 1847, '57 and '66 were too much for bank rate alone, and Parliament was forced to suspend the £14 million rule, the extra note issue in each case saving the British banking system from collapse.

London's focal role internationally thus sidestepped the 1844 Bank Act. It permitted oligarchic monetary government—the men of 'high commercial standing' on the Court of Directors of the Bank—to shield themselves from monetary politics, while wielding the substance of monetary control.

2. MONEY, REVOLUTION, AND REACTION

England's revolt against absolute monarchy had come too early either for proletarian upheaval, or financing by paper inflation. Neither Royalists nor Roundheads made major political use of the mob: while in lieu of central financing, both sides melted their plate and delved into their coffers. Prices, therefore, made no horrendous leap in England even at the height of the Civil War, and no great monetary transfer of real wealth occurred.

The monetary politics of Europe's and America's bourgeois revolutions, however, were altogether different. For the forty years' conflict which opened with a ragged fusillade on the bridge at Concord, Massachusetts, and closed to waltz music at the Congress of Vienna, occurred when both wage-earning masses and paper currencies in which to pay them were comparatively widespread.

Floods of inconvertible banknotes financed defeat of the British in their North American colonies, and the *ancien regime* in France. Resorted to by Britain, after 1797, they also helped topple Napoleon. The upward surge of prices which these paper inflations produced, redistributed wealth toward the manufacturing and commercial classes in each society, though the price rises were often so severe, rapid and uncertain that they benefited most the sharper element among financiers, lawyers, millers and brewers who made fortunes speculating in land or, in the case of France, in *assignats*, the French Revolutionary money, convertible (theoretically) into confiscated church lands.[4]

But unlike the American colonists' settlement of 1789, the European settlement of 1815 produced not defeat of the old

The first known official coin. A stamped lump of electrum — an alloy of gold and silver used by the ancients — from the Kingdom of Lydia, *c.* 600 BC

1272 gold florin. This beautiful coin, the first of fine gold to circulate since the time of Constantine almost a millennium earlier, restored the bimetallic standard on which the world continued to base its money values for another half-millennium

Henry VIII silver shilling of 1543 so debased that the copper soon showed through. Known as the Red Nosed Harry, it was the last full-face portrait of a monarch on English coinage

Gold sovereign of 1890. The British gold sovereign, fixed at Sir Isaac Newton's parity of £3 17*s*. 10½*d*. an ounce of gold, was the anchor of the 19th-century international monetary system, performing the international role that the United States dollar plays today

The paper money that financed the French Revolution. These banknotes were inconvertible and printed by the revolutionary government in any quantities needed to finance France's 'wars of liberation'

Continental dollars, theoretically convertible into Spanish 'Pieces of Eight', became so inflated that by the American Declaration of Independence they were already dubbed 'shin-plasters'. The phrase 'not worth a Continental' persists in the United States today order but reaction: a compromise between aristocrat and oligarch in which landowners once again generally came out on top.

Both England and France (and their client states in Europe and beyond) deflated their currencies in a return to their pre-war parities.

In France the paper *assignat* had by 1803 depreciated into almost total discredit. Bonaparte, in a move to favour his Napoleonic aristocracy,* had fixed the new franc currency at the parity arrived at by Louis XVI's finance minister Colonne in 1785. Return to Colonne's and Bonaparte's metal parity after an inflationary decade of revolution and war greatly exacerbated the chronic post-war deflation in France and elsewhere in Europe, making the difficult adjustment from wartime to peacetime production more onerous still. Industry and commerce struggled under the money dearth and unemployment soared. Meanwhile, landlords, both *ancien* and *nouveau* (by 1820 the old nobility had made good half its land losses), and wage earners who could find employment, enjoyed a fat bonus in spending power.

Britain's return to gold convertibility in 1819 at the pre-war sterling parity was a similar gesture to the landed rentier.† In returning Britain to the gold standard the reactionary Tory government of Liverpool, Wellington and Castlereagh caused savage deflation at a critical moment of post-war readjustment. The ensuing price collapse, bankruptcies and unemployment produced a flood of social misery and discontent which, climaxing in the Peterloo Massacre, brought England to the verge of class war.

Ex-colonial America, however, with no entrenched landed rentier class, chose a very different settlement. During the struggle for independence, monetary chaos had reigned. 'Continental' paper currency became so inflated (the notes were

---

* When Napoleon came to power he had found large stocks of confiscated land still not sold or granted away. With them he endowed a new 'middle class' aristocracy of soldiers, lawyers and bureaucrats who had served his dictatorship.

† So was passage of the Corn Law Act of 1815, which prevented the entry of cheap grain, an injurious measure not only to the poor, but also to the manufacturing classes, who had no wish to see the poor spending all their money on bread.

dubbed 'shin-plasters') that it soon cost more to print than it would buy. Foreign coin was the only currency to be trusted, the best available being the Spanish milled dollar—the 'piece of eight'. This, then, became the national coinage *de facto*, though the government's accounts were kept in sterling until 1785, when dollars became the official currency.

But with unlimited needs and pressures for growth, Americans were in no hurry for monetary discipline. True, Alexander Hamilton's official gold valuation of the dollar at just over $\frac{1}{20}$ ounce, made upon the establishment of the United States mint in 1791, survived with one slight change as the standard of value until 1933. But continual inflation of the paper currency drove all the early American silver dollars abroad, so that foreign currencies continued to circulate. Indeed, more than sixty years were to pass before Americans had even a token silver coinage of their own.[5]

Thus from American independence until 1879, Federal currency issues continued inflationary and often inconvertible, because the political weight of cash-crop farmers with mortgaged land, who were in urgent need of buoyant prices for their tobacco, corn and cotton, and of speculators of every hue, was strong enough to keep the monetary restrainers at bay. Opposition to banking and the 'money power' welled also from deeper psychological springs—an aspect of the ex-colonists' hostility to monopoly and privilege which had led to the Boston Tea Party and the Revolution itself. This powerful suspicion of bankers found its personification in President Jackson. "Ever since I read the history of the South Sea Bubble", Jackson told Nicholas Biddle, President of the Bank of the United States, "I have been afraid of banks." Jackson vetoed extension of the Bank of the United States' Charter in 1832 as unconstitutional. It constituted a monopoly, he declared, which would permit "the prostitution of our Government to the advancement of the few at the expense of the many".[6] Jackson's suspicion of America's first central bank caused the nation to lurch along without one until as late as 1913. Even today, Federal law prevents American banks from branching outside the state or locality where they were established, though the later establishment by banks of holding companies, and the move of major clients to the great banking centres has almost completely nullified this regulation's size-limiting effect.

The 'money power' was not to be contained. Jackson's destruction of the Philadelphia-based Bank of the United States was the cue for New York's Wall Street bankers to seize the financial reins. By 1879 their grasp was almost complete. They had put America onto the gold standard alongside Europe, and largely tamed the 'wildcat' banking of the frontier epoch.

THE GOLD STANDARD AS A MONEY-CLASS COMPROMISE

By the time of Waterloo, it was accepted among England's mercantile intelligentsia that if the currency was redeemable into gold, an unfavourable balance of trade, by drawing gold out of the country, would contract the money supply, force down prices, and start an automatic trade-balancing mechanism.*

True, the deflation that accompanied Britain's resumption of gold payments had been painful and harmful to business, but with the march of Britain's steam-powered technology, other factors were entering the picture which altered the manufacturer's monetary attitude. First, technology was enabling him to expand his output without a comparable expansion in expenditure. A yard of cotton cloth could—thanks to steam-powered machinery—be produced more cheaply and quickly than ever before. Thus, even though slackening demand caused

---

* John Locke in his *Further Considerations* had first described this classical balancing mechanism in international trade, though the concept was widely absorbed from Adam Smith. Locke's balance worked as follows. England has a trade deficit with France and gold leaves London to balance the accounts. Locke pointed out that the outflow of English gold by decreasing the English money supply, would lower English prices. When English prices had fallen sufficiently for English goods to become attractively priced in France, the level of French imports from England would increase. Locke reasoned that if one side of the seesaw went up, the other side must go down. French exports to England would decline as the French gold supply expanded, and raised French prices. The shift in the money supply, and therefore in price levels, was the force that tipped the seesaw. But it was a self-equilibrating seesaw. The pendulum of trade would swing back as gold returned from France to England, when France in turn found she was importing more than she exported. Trade and payments would thus tend to balance, the economic behaviour of man producing—according to this delightfully simple model—perfect harmony in the commercial sphere.

by money scarcity might force the manufacturer to keep up sales by lowering his price per yard, constant new improvements in his machinery enabled him to reduce his production costs per unit, and thus to feel no 'profit squeeze'. In economic language, productivity tended to increase faster than prices tended to decline.

A second new consideration in an increasingly export-oriented economy was that though the market mechanism might send weaker brethren into bankruptcy, it helped the aggressive and competitive producer to keep his costs of materials and labour in line with competition abroad. Hence the gold standard was an integral part of a Free Trade system.

The arrival of the new steam-technology had brought the monetary interest of the producer into line with that of the City. London had emerged from the Napoleonic Wars both as the greatest banking centre and hub of the most productive economy. Total stability of the currency in terms of the most reliable monetary yardstick, gold, was a major inducement to foreigners to finance transactions where possible in pounds. Already in the 18th century, foreign exporters were regularly drawing bills not upon their importing counterpart but upon a British merchant who accepted the use of his name or credit to finance other people's trade. Through this 'acceptance' business Britain financed a growing volume of trade which never touched her shores. By removing the risk of loss on sterling's exchange, the gold standard greatly added to this 'acceptance' business.

Furthermore, the unity of monetary interest in a gold standard between borrowers and lenders included landed wealth and investors generally. A whole new economic class had emerged in England as a result of the Napoleonic Wars. These were the owners of Consols (the British Government's bonds or consolidated stock) sold to finance the war with Napoleon at a time of sky-high prices and interest rates. When prices tumbled after the war with the return to gold, the real value of the war loan rose, and with it the real burden of interest payments. In returning to gold Lord Liverpool thus handed a large bonus not only to the land-owning gentry but to a new monied middle class.

THE MIDDLE CLASS DREAM COME TRUE

And the bonus continued to accumulate. For during the seventy years after Waterloo, a downward trend of British prices continued, the lowest point being reached in 1896. Just as remarkable was the extreme price stability. If we call the price level of 1881, 100, the maximum fluctuation in either direction between 1826 and 1914 was 30 points.

Such a pattern of prices benefited owners of Consols in three ways. First, the stability of money's value made investment in them seem almost perfectly secure; secondly, the trend of decline in interest rates increased their capital value*—from 1826 to 1896 it rose steadily from 79 to 109 (in spite of two official conversions to lower interest rates to prevent public outcry); finally, the purchasing power of the dividends rose 50 per cent in value. No wonder that in those safe and palmy days a pension appeared more desirable than the lump of capital which would yield it.

By 1827, interest on the war debt absorbed over half of the British Government's total revenue. Indeed the burden of repayment had become so heavy that the great liberal economist David Ricardo proposed the surgical remedy of a once-and-for-all capital levy to remove the swelling growth. Fund holders became the object of angry denunciations and Marx, among others, was impressed by the spectacle of the nation's tax burden growing heavier year after year to provide an inactive group with continually increasing purchasing power.

The experience of Admiral Sir Provo Wallis illustrates the problems of financing a pension—and the delights of being a pensioner—in Victorian times. Wallis had entered the Royal Navy in 1795, and fought in the war of 1812. Towards the end of a long life (he died in 1892) he was invited to commute his pension for a capital sum, something that any pensioner would jump at today. But the wily old admiral declined. Bringing pressure to bear, their Lordships of the Admiralty reminded Wallis that under his current pension arrangements he could

---

*The steady fall in current interest rates increased Consols' capital value because a bond's market value is based partly on the number of years' purchase of the annual income. Hence, if the going rate of interest fell from $4\frac{1}{2}$ per cent to 3 per cent, Consols rose in value from 66 to 100.

still be returned to active service. Wallis, however, repulsed this
attempt to check the rising cost of servicing his 'fixed' income:
he in turn reminded their Lordships that, holding the rank of
Admiral of the Fleet, he would be entitled to command any
force to which he was assigned, and that he had last seen
active service in 1857.[7]

Why did prices reverse their historic jerky upward trend in
the century of Victoria? The root answer was the failure of the
world gold supply to keep pace with economic growth. It was
the gold standard's consequent ability to meet the requirements
of enterprise as well as the rentier that made it an ideal middle
class solution to the problem of money's control. For while new
industrial productivity counterbalanced the lagging gold supply, the long-term depression of prices spurred industry to
preserve profits with increased productivity. Britain would thus,
so the City of London believed, remain the world's workshop,
producing more for less than anyone else. The Bank Act of
1844's rigid link between the note issue and gold was the final
nail supposed to seal this automatic mechanism from any
meddling hand.

Among the factors that contributed to easing the transition
of political power in 19th century England from land to industry, the social dynamics of the gold standard have received
too little attention. Had the trend of monetary values continued
to decline, as they had throughout most of history, a far more
extensive transfer of wealth from its inheritors to men of enterprise would have occurred throughout Europe but especially in
Britain. Whether or not such a shift of power would have produced a social upheaval great enough to change the composition and outlook of the British ruling class is a matter for con-
jecture. But instead, the monetary standard onto which Britain
moved after Waterloo maintained an equipoise between the
propertied classes, allowing the productive to prosper while the
fruits of inherited wealth accumulated undisturbed.

3. GOLD GOES INTERNATIONAL

By mid-century Britain's gold standard system was the cynosure
of governments throughout the world. The rigid discipline of

gold, tempered by judicious oligarchic management, seemed the ideal solution to the vexing problem of controlling money's scarcity and, not unnaturally, other countries aspired to join the club.

By the 1860's, the franc was the base currency of most of Western Europe.* But the franc-based countries, like the rest of the world, continued on the bimetallic silver and gold system originated with the gold florin of 1272. Only Britain had developed the banking system and money-market mechanisms which permitted sufficient economy in the use of bullion for her to be able to rely on gold alone.

In 1849, however, a dramatic discovery in the tail race of a mill in Cripple Creek, California, intervened to help end the monetary standard of five centuries. In the 1860's, the new gold from California moved to Europe in a rush to pay for Civil War supplies. As it did so, full-value silver coins suddenly became more valuable in reality than the official 16/1 ratio allowed. In consequence they were driven out of monetary circulation into private hoards. A Latin Monetary Union, formed by France in 1865 to replace the disappearing silver 5 franc piece with a token-value silver coinage, struggled for almost ten years to insure future European price levels by protecting the bimetallic standard.

It was at this point of strain and confusion that the new German Empire burst upon the monetary scene determined to emulate the British, and back its newly begotten mark with gold alone. Then Scandinavia, Holland, Austria-Hungary and Russia, all followed Germany to gold monometallism in rapid succession, and the cause of silver became hopeless. France suspended silver coinage in 1878, followed, a year later, by the United States. Thus by the end of the 1870's the world (or all who mattered financially) was formally 'on gold'.

The international gold standard formally extended Britain's monetary practice onto a multinational basis. The basic

* Belgium readopted it when it was freed from the Dutch; it had legal status in the Rhineland until 1867; Italy adopted it as the lira after 1861; it had been the currency of Switzerland since the fall of Napoleon. Under other names it was also the basis of the currencies of Greece, Spain, Siberia, Rumania, Bulgaria and Finland.

currency unit of a participating country was defined as a certain number of grains of gold. Exchange rates between currencies were thus fixed, the holder of any currency being always able to obtain gold in exchange for that currency at a fixed price.*

Provided that gold standard countries obeyed the 'rules of the game', currencies could remain fixed to one another through gold, thus making payment across frontiers virtually as secure and certain as payment across the street. What were these rules? They really boiled down to one golden rule: allow the unimpeded movement of your gold reserves to be reflected in your money supply. A country in external deficit must therefore contract its money supply to reflect its loss of gold. The resulting deflation would lower prices sufficiently to bring the market mechanism into effect, reducing the country's imports and increasing its exports. Conversely, a payments surplus must also be reflected in an expansion of the money supply.

THE TYRANNY OF GOLD

International adoption of the gold standard meant therefore that the market was, in theory at least, victorious over state interference throughout the world. This was what made the international gold standard the crowning glory of 19th century economic liberalism. The morality of gold was called on to replace that of man. Gold was to act like a kind of censor which expressed, in Sir Robert Kindersley's phrase, 'the sins or virtues, as the case may be, of all the inhabitants of a country', its departure creating 'that anxiety which brings home to them that they are being extravagant'.[8]

But when a country was 'sinning', who was called upon to do penance? The trouble with the rule of gold was that its morality punished precisely those economic classes who benefited least from its government. The gold discoveries of mid-century had drawn the nations' money managers into fixing

* The actual rate of exchange could in fact vary by the amount of the cost of shipping the gold in settlement of a debt. This might be requested if there was a lack of confidence in the ability of the debtor's country to maintain the standard, but this was the limit of the permitted fluctuation. A German, for example, would therefore pay no more for dollars than their gold value, plus the cost of shipping the equivalent weight of gold instead.

their currencies to the metal, but the sudden growth in its supply was not sustained. Gold now had to bear alone the burden that silver had shared with it before, but in face of world economic expansion there was simply not enough of it to go round.

Between 1873 and 1896 the price level fell almost without interruption in all countries by about 40 per cent, and agitation for a return to silver (which, by an ironic stroke, was poured profusely from the mountain states of America in the late 1870's and 80's) became widespread. Inevitably, this agitation was strongest in the area where further gains in productivity were most problematic and thus where profits were most tightly squeezed.

Monetary shortage was, however, by no means the only cause of declining prices. Over-production had become widespread because social had not kept pace with material change. Steamships, railways, the telegraph and the myriad technological advances of more than half a century of intensive industrialization had all conspired to produce a general reduction of unit costs. But the bargaining power of labour had not developed sufficiently by the 1880's and 90's to provide the increased wage packets that permit mass consumption. Surging productive capacity had therefore begun to overflow a too-narrow consumption base. Today we face the same situation on a global scale: the capacity to produce plenty amid a sea of want.

THE SILVER REBELLION

In no area was this overproduction more serious than in the Great Plains of America and Russia. Squeezed between falling agricultural prices and the rising burden of mortgage payments on their land, both American prairie farmers and Russian landowners were driven to defy the deflating rule of gold.

The Populist Party, formed in 1891, was the chosen vehicle of American opposition to monometallism. American populism's panacea for the ills of both prairie farmer and mountain silver miner was the same: free coinage of silver at a ratio of 16/1 with gold. Russian populism, on the other hand, unbacked by any silver mining lobby, and debarred from the platform of democracy, concentrated upon secret proselytizing of its ideal of petty-bourgeois socialism, the rearguard action against gold being fought in Moscow by the landowners.

By 1897, when the State Bank formally declared gold convertibility of paper roubles, Russia, though 'on gold' for the purposes of international payments since the 1870's had clung to inconvertible paper at home: a practice which had done much to keep up domestic grain prices. Indeed the landowners' ability to resist full gold convertibility until the mid-90's had saved the steppes from the extremes of depression experienced in the American prairies. The Czarist government's determination to back industrialization, however, finally defeated the landed interest. A large gold reserve was vital to enable Russia to service the vast volume of foreign investment pouring into her nascent heavy industries. This reserve was built by a violently regressive system of indirect taxes, but most of all, by a ruthless drive for a payments surplus which involved restraint of domestic grain consumption even as famine conditions prevailed at home. "We may not eat enough," declared Finance Minister Vyshnegradsky, referring to the privation of the lower orders, "but we will export".[9]

Thus, thanks in part to the gold standard's operation, the social discontent of the final decade of the 19th century was strongest not, as Marx had prophesied, in industrial centres but in the farm belts of both the New and Old Worlds. In industry, meanwhile, cheap food's contribution to improving productivity helped employers to leave wages alone and still maintain their profits. Indeed the industrial worker was becoming better off than ever before. He was beginning to taste the fruits of middle-class saving passed on in the form of cheaper goods.

While the farmer protested his poverty, low food prices and industrial wages were piling up immense profits for industry and commerce. Never before in God's Country had the conditions of economic groups contrasted more sharply, and, for the first time in history, America felt the bite of widespread class-hatred. William Jennings Bryan emerged as the Populist champion. "If protection has slain its thousands," Bryan declared, "the gold standard has slain its tens of thousands." Swept by populism, the entire Democratic Convention of 1896

Trade follows the flag but Democrats follow the FOOL

was on its feet and roaring as the siege-gun voice of the great
fundamentalist demagogue railed against the financiers who
would 'press down upon the brow of labour this crown of
thorns', and 'crucify mankind upon a cross of gold'.

But though mountain state silver interests were lavish in their
support of the 'Prairie Avenger's' campaign, they could not
match the colossal Republican campaign contributions assessed
from metropolitan banks, insurance companies and railroad
corporations. Nevertheless Bryan, who carried the South and
Far West in 1896, might well have won the Presidency in 1900
had not the *deus ex machina* of South African gold moved into the
United States in the interim and eased the plight of the
prairies.[10]

American 'cornbelt' economists of the 90's had in fact
deceived themselves in assuming that somehow free coinage
of silver could improve overseas markets for American farm
produce. With the mints of Europe and, since 1893, India,
closed to silver, the result was much more likely to have been a
forlorn commercial and financial isolation for America. Closer
to the mark, however, was their denunciation of financial
dependence on London, the symbol and centre of the 'repres-
sive' gold-based system.

4. LONDON'S MONEY POWER: FINANCIAL OUTFLOW AND POLITICAL BACKWASH

Just why had London become so important to the operation of
the world monetary system by the end of the last century, and
what were the political implications of its monetary authority?

If the gold standard system as described above seems too
rigid and perfect for a changing and imperfect world, the
answer is that it was. In reality the standard was not an automatic and coercive mechanism, permitted to operate regardless
of the consequences. It was merely a rule of thumb principle
for the management of money. The 'rules of the game' were
constantly broken when they appeared to run counter to oligarchic interests. First of all the over-simple 'quantity theory' of
money which related a country's price level solely to its cash

supply, and on which the gold standard was based, did not meet the facts and was ignored in practice. Control of credit, in the shape of the lending policy of the central banks was the 'manual' mechanism that made the 'automatic' gold standard principles workable, bank rate acting as a shock absorber.

But beyond such fine adjustments there was a much more serious gap between theory and reality. The idea that any reduction in output and employment resulting from gold loss would be merely a temporary, transitory phase, and that the economy experiencing a foreign deficit would automatically return to full employment at a lower price level in a short time, rarely worked in practice. For developing countries the outflow of their money supply to pay for capital goods and other growth-producing imports would have stifled the economy at home. Without outside assistance, then, the gold standard cure for trade deficits was worse than the disease.

Fortunately the outside assistance was not lacking. Capital investment flowed across national borders and oceans throughout the 19th century balancing persistent trade deficits of the less mature economies. In the second half of the last century the United States, Canada, Argentina and Australia, among other countries, regularly financed their trade deficits with Western Europe's surplus. By the eve of World War I these investments had risen to an estimated total of no less than £16·9 billion. And of this colossal sum nearly half (about £7·6 billion or $18 billion) was provided by Britain alone.[11]

Between Waterloo and World War I, Britain invested abroad the equivalent of almost the entire surplus which her industrial headstart had earned for her in foreign trade. What produced this great and prolonged penchant toward foreign investment on the part of the City which enabled the international gold standard to operate? Was there truth in the claim of American 'cornbelt' economists and others that London consciously used the provision of capital and monetary services to extend its political power?

To see conscious plan behind the complex interlocking threads of London's monetary and financial control may have suited the silver polemicists. But they were seeing an effect and calling it a cause. The London-centred money power of the

19th century was real enough. But it was no more premeditated than the industrial revolution itself. British merchants and financiers had simply reaped the international advantages of their domestic monetary arrangement. To the extent that other countries were prepared to leave their liquid assets in British banks, these countries were making a continuous short-term loan to Britain, as these balances showed up on the plus side of Britain's balance of payments in any given period. The cosmopolitan outlook of the City was, however, greatly increased by this reserve role of sterling.

FINANCE CAPITALISM—THE ROAD BACK TO FEUDALISM?

Towards the end of the last century the advantage of the special role of sterling was one on which Britain had come to rely. By the 1880's Britain's industrial headstart had vanished. Germany, America and France had caught up and were forging ahead. This loss of industrial leadership was reflected in Britain's balance of payments, which, in the last two decades of the century, showed increasing deficits on trading account (the balance of goods and services imported and exported). The fact that at the same time Britain's *overall* balance of payments surplus went on growing right up until World War I was accounted for by a rising income from her swelling overseas investment portfolio. Indeed, this growing income was sufficient to provide continued investment abroad. Britain's importance as international banker was thus increasing while her position as industrial exporter declined.

Writing in the 1900's, Harold Mackinder, an Oxford economist, believed this shift of strength from production to investment would continue. Britain's future advantage, as Mackinder saw it, lay in the possession not of superior natural resources or industrial technology but in her great accumulation of wealth and the City's skill in using it. As the trend continued, British industry would progressively lag behind that of its competitors, while its foreign investment portfolio spread wider and deeper throughout the world.

What would be the eventual outcome? The logical conclusion of Mackinder's analysis was a post-industrial return to feudalism. While the investments and profits of the propertied classes grew, emigration or domestic service would be the alternatives for the rising number of unemployed among the industrial proletariat. It is hard to believe today that such a theory could be taken more seriously than a piece of whimsy to go round with the port in the Senior Common Room. But the prospect of an increasing shift to 'finance capitalism' was quite seriously considered by Mackinder's political economist contemporaries. Admiral Tirpitz had not yet breathed into the Kaiser's ear the outrage of a direct challenge to the British Navy, the brooding presence that guarded British overseas investment; and with the Royal Navy to guarantee the security of their overseas investments, and the gold standard to maintain the purchasing power of their investments' earnings, a gradual progression to 'finance capitalism' seemed a perfectly logical direction for the founding member of the international industrialists' club.

Only the unique strategic position which the City of London occupied in both British and international affairs could make such thinking possible. The carrying out of any British government policy which required money, required also the City's blessing. If the government wished to wage war, it would need the means of making payments in the war theatre. Meanwhile, though government support in the shape of gunboats was available in extreme instances, the timely pulling of a remote thread in Britain's international financial network by someone in the City was generally sufficient to keep debtor governments in line. Thus while the policies of smaller sovereign states were held in line by the need for a stable currency which would encourage further foreign investment, jingoistic impulses of the British government could also be checked. Conscious of this central role of the City, foreign governments increasingly came to London to raise loans. By the 1880's, floating such foreign public loans had become the most profitable activity of London's leading merchant banking houses.

The City of London, however, by no means acted alone as guardian of the investing climate. It was in intimate and continuous harmony with the other financial capitals in the Concert of Europe. Together they mingled finance with diplomacy so as to preserve a precarious armed peace among the rising national powers. Supra-national in outlook, independent of governments, but in close touch with them all, the great houses of an international aristocracy of finance with brothers, cousins and connections in every great financial centre—Barings, Lazards, Hambros, Schroders, Erlangers and, above all, the Rothschilds—held the ring, maintaining the subjugation of politics to the interests of oligarchic money.

A 100,000 rouble note of 1921 (in 1914 the rouble was worth $1.25).
Lenin's prescription for the destruction of capitalism, the debauch of
the currency, was to continue for years after the revolution

At the height of the German inflation of 1923 waiters changed the
prices of menus in restaurants as patrons wolfed down their meals

The highest denomination banknote ever printed.
The 100,000,000,000,000,000 pengo note was distributed by the Red
Army as part of the Soviet campaign to destroy the Hungarian
economy in 1945

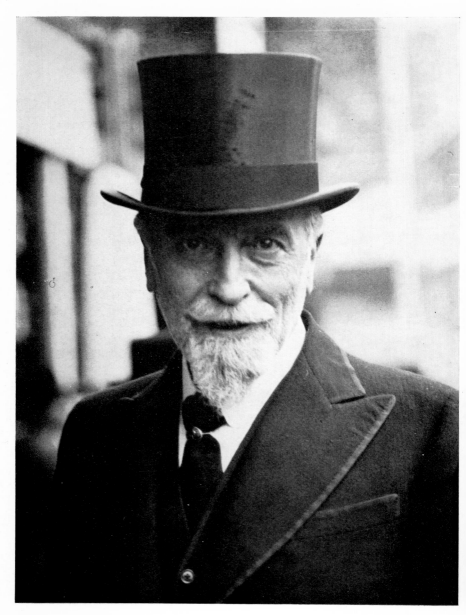

Montagu Norman, Governor of the Bank of England, 1920–44. His princely, Mephistophelian appearance was carefully contrived to enhance an air of aloofness and omniscience

WELFARE VERSUS GOLD

3

The Crisis of Oligarchic Money

Two fundamental conditions were necessary to oligarchic money's survival. The first was the link between currencies and gold. The second was the willingness of industrial nations generally, but especially Britain, the International Monetary Fund of the age, to invest much of the surplus earned in their overseas transactions in other nations' development. As early as the 1870's, however, just as this system was reaching full flower, the economic, social and political patterns which had produced it and were necessary for its survival, began to break down.

1. LENIN'S PRESCRIPTION FULFILLED

Despite rising pretensions and emotions of nationalism, and growing arms expenditures by the European powers, the gold standard mechanism worked smoothly right up to World War I. Paper inflation had even been avoided in the Franco-Prussian War's aftermath, although France was forced to pay a large indemnity by the Prussians. In fact the process of France's payment to Germany afforded a textbook example of the market mechanism at work. The French indemnity of 5,000 million francs, was the equivalent of well over a year's exports from France, or at least $10 billion in today's terms. But a sharp rise in French exports, which over a decade was sufficient to earn the gold to pay the Germans, was helped by the classic process of monetary expansion, thanks to the indemnity receipts, in Germany, and deflation resulting from higher taxes to raise the levy, in France. Meanwhile, France was cushioned by an inflow of private capital to take advantage of French cost-competitiveness.*

* See Fred Hirsch, *Money International*, London, Allen Lane, 1967. Hirsch also points out that it was France's unexpected success in paying this large indemnity which encouraged it in turn to demand the immense reparations which it sought from Germany after World War I.

But World War I, like the Napoleonic era, called for far more spending than could be paid for with gold, and nations were forced to inflate their currencies to finance the holocaust. The resulting price increases stole half of money's buying power in England; seven-eighths in France; eleven-twelfths in Italy; and virtually all in Germany and the successor states of Austria-Hungary and Russia. The relative modesty of Britain's war inflation resulted partly from her willingness to ship gold, to sell securities abroad and to borrow from American bankers rather than resort to the printing press, but much more from the fact that her naval strength had enabled her to maintain a considerable wartime export trade. London had, as a result, been able to 'peg' sterling's exchange rate at $4·76 throughout the war. But in 1919, the Bank of England, like all other monetary authorities excepting the gold-flooded Federal Reserve of the United States, was obliged to 'unpeg' the currency and let it 'float' down to the level determined by demand for it abroad as the alternative to seeing British goods priced out of world markets.

Lenin's prescription for capitalism's internal collapse was thus faithfully followed not only by the Bolshevik leaders in Moscow, but by the capitalist adversaries. The loss of savings involved was so overshadowed by other, more painful losses, that it was scarcely separately comprehended. Yet it produced a vast redistribution of wealth among classes. More important, it destroyed the basis of Europe's social psychology.

Inequality in the division of wealth had grown to unprecedented extremes in the world before the war. Conservatives saw this imbalance as the old order, which changeth not unless human nature can itself be altered. Liberal thinkers, on the other hand, excused society's dangerous top-heaviness as the dynamo for material progress. Great accumulation by those who did not need their incomes was the most efficient way of achieving high reinvestment, and hence the enlargement of wealth. Provided that the cake of national product was not consumed by war, or by Malthus' spectre of high prices for imported foodstuffs (which the growth of America's population was beginning to conjure up again for Europe in the 1900's), they believed that at some undefined future time a more equitable division would make economic as well as social sense. But, in the meantime, because the cake's size in relation to society's appetite was still very small, the current division of wealth seemed to be justified.

By consuming this cake in one vast gulp, World War I undermined this liberal optimism. Worse, it actually lowered national output relative to the continent's growing population. It therefore not only toppled the delicate equipoise of a top-heavy structure, but destroyed much of its base. In *A Tract on Monetary Reform*, John Maynard Keynes summed up the prospect.

> What was deemed most secure has proved least so. He who neither spent nor speculated, who made proper provision for his family, who sang hymns to security and observed most straitly the morals of the edified and the respected injunctions of the worldly wise— he indeed who gave fewest pledges to Fortune has yet received her heaviest visitation.[1]

If the fall in money values discouraged saving, it also discredited enterprise. To the out-of-pocket wage-earner, unable to fathom the social legerdemain of inflation, the large windfall profits that it brought to businessmen seemed the cause and not the consequence of the painful price rise. It was a confusion which the governments responsible for the inflation preferred not to dispel. Instead they intensified the atmosphere of recrimination, themselves witch-hunting for 'profiteers'. Such castigation of the businessman passed some of the opprobrium of inflation from government to enterprise. It did not, however, promote faith in the capitalist system.

Thus in the 1920's Europe's leaders set out to rebuild a promised prosperity in societies not only shaken by external conflict but torn by internal disappointment and discredit as well.

CITY AND INDUSTRY: THE MARRIAGE OF BRITAIN'S MONETARY INTERESTS

So much for the link of currencies to gold. But before that link was broken by war, even, indeed, as Free Trade and gold were winning their greatest victories, the second underpinning of the British-based world monetary system was also failing.

Since before Lord Liverpool fixed sterling's post-Napoleonic parity so favourably for landlords, the Tories, as the rentier party, had begun to form a natural monetary alliance with the money lenders and changers of the City. But it was during the 19th century that the magic circle of land and finance was formed in Britain which survives and flourishes to this day.[2] The alliance was not, of course, based solely on convergent monetary interest. With their aversion to 'trade', sons of the landowning aristocracy naturally gravitated toward the City's glamour, just as successful City merchants and bankers succumbed to the charms of broad acres.

But throughout the days of Britain's industrial leadership, her manufacturing interests had been Liberals and Whigs. Sluggish markets and growing competition in the 1880's and 90's, however, saw many manufacturers shift their political allegiance. Britain, by the late 1870's, could no longer count upon the export surplus that her leadership in mechanical ingenuity had earned her for a century. Partly this was because her industrial rivals had by then mastered and indeed often improved upon her traditional industrial skills: partly because industrialization had now entered a new science-based phase, where the electrical and chemical industries upon which expansion was increasingly based were ill-served by the classical and imperial bias in English education. Both of these developments helped cause the rate of expansion of British exports to slow in the 1880's and in the 1890's, actually to stop. At the same time the depressed prices and over-production of the 70's and 80's had strengthened protectionist pressures all over Europe. By 1879, in fact, Britain was the only country still pledged to the doctrine of Cobden.

Britain's Free Trade persistence did not, however, stem from any stoical acceptance of the hardship for millions, the depopulation of whole areas, the abandonment of traditional skills and ways of life which unprotected exposure to a changing world implied. Rather, imperial expansion in Asia and Africa suggested that the export of capital to finance traditional British exports to these undeveloped parts of the world might more than replace losses in Britain's traditional export markets. The foreign bond issues and investments of the City were to be called upon to finance purchase of British manufactures. Thus after half a century of monetary truce under the gold standard, a marriage of interest between City and industry began to occur.

2. CENTRAL BANKERS AS STATESMEN

Within Britain, this shift of manufacturers to financial conservatism served to strengthen the City's monetary authority and control. Elsewhere, too, gold's vice-regent, the central bank, had continued throughout World War I as oligarchic money's protector. But its orthodoxy and rentier-mindedness in raising war finance brought it into incipient conflict with the monarch's monetary interest, now represented by his Treasury.

Treasuries' paper inflation to finance the war was resisted energetically, and for long successfully, by the central banks of both England and France, which urged taxation and public borrowing as the only 'moral' solutions, and came down strongly in favour of the latter. In France, the political weight of the rentier class was such that war finance was raised by borrowing rather than taxation right through until 1917. In England, although income tax was raised to 6 shillings in the pound early in the war, the bulk of wartime revenue was also raised by government borrowing via the Bank of England. Moreover, the Bank's fiery Governor, Lord Cunliffe, tussled furiously with Chancellor Bonar Law over the distribution of the war's financial burdens.

In 1917, as the government prepared to raise a £600 million War Loan, Cunliffe stood out for the going market rate of 6 per cent. His advice was rejected, however, and £700 million was raised by the Bank at 5 per cent. But the Chancellor had to threaten the Governor in order to make him handle the loan at the lower figure: if the Bank of England would not handle the loan at 5 per cent he would raise it through the Joint Stock Banks.

A still more serious clash occurred between Governor and Chancellor over the Treasury's foreign borrowing. Cunliffe, fuming at the Treasury's 'financial fecklessness' in running up unsecured war debts with America, decided to remove the Bank's gold reserve from Treasury control. As a wartime precaution, much of the Bank's gold had been shipped to Canada for safe-keeping. Cunliffe therefore wired the Canadian Government an instruction that no more gold should be delivered on demand of Sir Hardman Lever, Financial Secretary to the Treasury. But here Cunliffe went too far. Indeed, so eccentric and tyrannical had his rule at the Bank become that even his subordinates there agreed that he was the victim of megalomania, his successor, Montagu Norman, describing him in his diary as 'dangerous and insane'.[3]

Cunliffe was forced into retirement in March 1918, despite desperate and shameful intriguing by him for extension. The successor who had questioned Cunliffe's sanity, however, was himself no stranger to psychiatric disorder. In 1913, Montagu Collet Norman, wealthy scion of a great City family, had visited Jung in Zürich for diagnosis of an acute nervous collapse. The great man apparently informed the future Governor that he was suffering from general paralysis of the insane, an incurable by-product of syphilis, of which 'delusions of grandeur', unmistakably betrayed by the patient, were a tell-tale sign.* Cunliffe, who had himself recently been ordered by his doctor 'to give his mind a complete rest', had brought Norman full-time into the Bank on learning that Norman was suffering the delayed effects of nervous breakdown, commenting that he 'felt that there was only one cure for this—hard work'.[4]

Such was the City's system of inheritance, personal loyalty and family friendship, that this unbalanced, yet clearly able, man was promoted from Deputy Governor's Assistant to the Governorship within eight years. Commanding control over the British economy in the inter-war years thus passed into the hands of an obsessional financial aristocrat through the therapeutic kindness of his unbalanced predecessor.

---

* This diagnosis, however, proved utterly erroneous. As Norman's biographer points out, Jung's published correspondence shows that in the spring of 1913 he himself was the victim of deep neurotic disturbances, and should himself have been under treatment rather than attempting to treat others (Andrew Boyle, *Montagu Norman*, p. 95).

Emile Moreau, his counterpart and, later, adversary at the Bank of France, was impressed at his first meeting with Norman. 'He seems to have walked out of a Van Dyck canvas; the long face, the pointed beard and the big hat lend him the look of a companion of the Stuarts', Moreau recorded in his diary.[5] It was a characterization of curious perception; for Norman proselytized his monetary beliefs with a passion and an idealism unfamiliar in England's leaders since Stuart times. Moreover, according to his biographer, his princely, Mephistophelean appearance, aided by the habitual black silk hat and cloak, was carefully contrived to enhance an air of aloofness and omniscience.

When Norman ascended to the seat of power as Governor in March 1920, the City of London was, as it largely remains today, a quasi-feudal hierarchy. A strong Bank Governor commanded absolute and unquestioning loyalty, from the heads of great banks, discount and insurance houses down to the humblest clerk. The City has always had its quiet way with rebels. Critics and dissenters from within the hierarchy may quickly find that vital channels of confidence and credit close if they choose to step too far out of line. Thus Norman ascended to an office already invested with vast autocratic power. But the reason why he so rapidly came to personify the City was that his mind was its archetype. He disdained reasoned economic argument. 'I have no reasons—only instincts,' he responded on one famous occasion before the Macmillan Committee on Finance and Industry in 1929.

With such background and powers, it was almost inevitable that if Norman had one over-riding obsession it would be not just for a return to the gold standard (which all vocal groups in Britain, including most liberals, then agreed was desirable after unpleasant post-war experience of inconvertible currencies' violent fluctuations) but a full revival of the *status quo ante*, with the restoration of Britain's financial supremacy that this implied. For this to be established, the pound had not merely to return to gold convertibility, but to 'look the dollar in the face' at the parity that had been maintained by Norman's forbears.*

* George Warde Norman, the Currency School champion, was Montagu Norman's grandfather.

The City was with Norman all the way. Few there paused to consider the effect of raising sterling from its depressed post-war 'floating' level on British export industries, whose share of world markets was dwindling even at sterling's depreciated level. There was almost no talk of return to gold at a lower price.

Yet Norman's desire to restore British leadership in international finance was not simply the offspring of narrow chauvinism. Norman was, in fact, an ardent internationalist: a United States of Europe being the prize at his rainbow's end. In the years between Versailles and Locarno (1919–25), his was the crucial support behind the League of Nations Finance Committee's remarkably successful work of stabilizing European currencies. He was to take a leading role, too, in establishing the Bank for International Settlements to deal with national payments problems arising from the settlement of international war debts. But his ambitions for unity and co-operation in Europe foundered, like those of other pro-European English statesmen since, on the rock of his relations with America.

Had Norman recognized the dangers of Atlantic ambivalence and pressed, through the League's Finance Committee (of which the United States was not a member), for a new and lower linking of all European currencies, led by the pound, to gold, what strides in economic and social co-operation the resulting assurance and stability in trade and capital payments might have brought! Europe had little gold left at this time. Most of its reserves had crossed the Atlantic to pay for war *matériel*. By substantially raising the price of gold in terms of their currencies, Europeans could have made their gold supply, sparse though it was, sufficient to settle intra-European debts, and to finance the needed revival of trade, thus enabling them sooner to repay their American debts. But amid the bitter and suspicious politics of the early 1920's, such enlightened co-operation was not even on Europe's political horizon. Besides, America, which Norman regarded with special warmth and respect after spending several happy years on Wall Street in the 1890's, would have regarded any mass devaluation of European currencies against gold as a hostile act, forcing it to choose between devaluation and non-competitiveness in international markets. So far was Norman from considering any such monetary severance from the United States, that it was he who was most insistent that Britain's £900 million war debt with America be promptly settled regardless of Britain's debt claims on other nations: a decision which, in absorbing precious gold reserves, would make return to sterling's pre-war parity all the more difficult and painful.

Norman's problem, which was the cause of his later branding as the financial villain of the age, arose from this Atlantic ambivalence. He saw restoration of British leadership as essential to reconstructing international monetary order, without which the prospects for prosperity, either in Britain or anywhere else, were exceedingly poor. But a restored pound meant to him equality with the dollar. This was the final, fatal link that no skill of Norman's could make hold.

GOVERNOR NORMAN, THE ARCHITECT OF CURRENCIES

Surveying the chaotic scene which Europe presented in 1920, Norman set himself the massive task of international reconstruction and stabilization. So delicate a task as rebuilding currencies and reopening the networks of trust and confidence between financial capitals was not, in his view, for politicians, who knew nothing of such matters. Their current posturing testified to the fact that they preferred instead to ride the tiger of postwar suspicion and hatred, assuring the electorate that they would squeeze war indemnities from the defeated enemy 'until the pips squeaked'.

Norman's view of politicians mirrored that of the City Fathers. His orthodox blinkers, of course, prevented him from seeing that his distrust of the electorate and his preference for gold was itself a 'political' view; for the deflation of economic activity necessary to return to the prewar gold parity meant the transfer of wealth on a massive scale to the rich while denying employment to the poor.

In the uncertain postwar atmosphere, confidence—or its lack—among investors was clearly reflected in relative exchange rates. Private French franc balances especially were shipped to England or America to avoid the inflation that continued unimpeded in France. European refugee capital that moved to London gave an invaluable leg-up to the sagging pound. Meanwhile, British banks could use this deposited gold to expand their credit. Thus, as the demand for sterling produced by these transfers from francs to pounds continued, the Continent's émigré wealth gave Britain increased room for manœuvre, and caused the pound to rise steadily on the exchanges. Little by little, therefore, the political uncertainties of the early 1920's, not only in France and Germany but in the successor states of the Austro-Hungarian Empire, were pushing sterling back toward its old parity.

As sterling rose, so did the spirits of the City. The benign circle of Victoria's day seemed, after all, to be re-established. A return of confidence in sterling meant a return of foreign clients for City banking, insurance and shipping services. The City seemed set to return again to its envied pre-war role as monetary metropole.

But the revival of the City's hegemony was by no means simply the result of political uncertainty elsewhere. Behind the scenes it was already being gently helped along by Norman's domestic monetary actions. Norman had come to the Governorship determined to put an end to the inflationary post-war boom. Inflation, he informed Chancellor Joseph Chamberlain, had to be curbed with the classic monetary weapon—a high rate of interest. With high interest rates forcing the government, the City, British industry and the man in the street to depend less on credit, the purchasing power of money could be stabilized. But the 7 per cent bank rate which he pressed onto a hesitant Chancellor appealed to Norman not merely as prudent housekeeping; it fitted into his grander design of re-restoring gold to its rightful throne. It encouraged more short-term depositors to leave their money in London, and this in turn helped boost sterling's exchange rate. Foreign demand for sterling could, Norman believed, substitute for the gold that had been shipped across the Atlantic and around the world to pay for the war.

GOVERNOR STRONG SPEAKS FOR AMERICA

Meanwhile, on the other side of the Atlantic, Congress showed little interest in the United States' role in the world economy. However, presiding over the New York Federal Reserve Bank (one of the twelve banks of the American central banking system delegated to act for the system in the international sphere) was a banker whose personal stature and knowledge of foreign monetary problems set him head and shoulders above any other American figure in international finance during this period.

Benjamin Strong had met Norman during the last two years of the war and the two had rapidly become intimate friends. They corresponded regularly in unusually affectionate terms and spent their holidays together at Bar Harbour, Long Island and in the South of France. They also travelled together to the major capitals of Europe in the early days of the peace to confer with other central bankers. Strong's and Norman's attitudes toward the management of money were identical. Both distrusted politicians and avoided theory. Like Norman, Strong felt the appeal of a return to the system which had proved effective in the past and was proof against political meddling.

As an internationalist, Strong persisted in efforts to aid European payments and recovery despite the bitter arguments and recriminations over war reparations which seemed to confirm, as one observer remarked, 'what most Americans had suspected—that Europe was a hopeless mess, incapable of sensible political agreements, unreliable in economic affairs and certainly unworthy of credit.'[6]

Strong had been aghast at the $33 billion in gold which the French-dominated Reparations Commission had fixed in April 1920 as Germany's liability. He warned politicians on both sides of the Atlantic repeatedly that attempts to meet the annual repayments would produce a collapse of the mark. Then, like Norman, Strong was forced to look on powerless as his gloomy prediction was proved correct. When French and Belgian troops occupied the Ruhr in January 1923, as a result of a German default in delivering a Reparations consignment

of telegraph poles, timber and coal, the economic collapse of
Germany became complete.

GOVERNOR SCHACHT—THE PHOENIX FIGURE

Although the German note issue had been expanded sixfold
during the war, the bulk of German war finance had been
raised by public borrowing. But lack of forced saving through
consumer rationing had withheld any check of the public's
spending on the few consumer goods available, so that between
1914–20 prices had risen by over 19 times. The post-war German government had made some attempt to balance the budget
with new and heavier taxes. But they could not extract from
a destitute public the massive sums necessary for war loan
interest payments to the middle classes and at the same time
meet the cost of caring for war victims and begin making
reparations payments to the Allies.

The printing of Reichsbank notes to meet government expenditures had at least the initial virtue of stimulating industrial activity. But as the inflation got out of hand, the economic situation deteriorated further, as a result of a general
flight from paper money. Government expenditures, which
had exceeded revenue by three to one in the years 1921–22,
rose to ten to one in January 1923 as the government printed
money to buy food for Ruhr workers who were passively resisting foreign occupation. By the autumn of 1923, this deliberate
'hyper-inflation' had run completely out of hand. The Reichsbank could no longer keep up with the sheer physical task of
printing sufficient currency. One hundred and thirty-three
additional printing firms using 1,783 machines were needed to
meet the demand, while more than thirty paper manufacturers
worked round the clock to provide the paper for banknotes.

Already by late summer, many employers had taken to paying their workers in kind, while firms needing investment or
working capital issued bonds repayable in potash, cement,
kilowatt hours, anthracite, etc., as money ceased either to store
or measure value. As the flight from money progressed, business
relations and morality were poisoned at every level. Naturally
the wealthy, educated classes then, as always, grasped the

situation much faster than the man in the street, and bought, as rapidly as possible, houses, landed property, manufactured goods and raw materials. The sharks who took over property from law-abiding civil servants and other salaried office workers for a few paper billions which they needed to buy bread grew richest of all.

The push of the intelligent and unscrupulous to exploit the ignorant majority produced a tidal wave of bitterness and mistrust, crested by demobilized soldiers, romantic adventurers and political schemers. One of these was ex-corporal Adolf Hitler, whose inflammatory oratory drew him to the leadership of the National Socialist Workers' Party *putsch* in November 1923 at the very nadir of the Reichsmark's debasement.

Here in most naked form was a government using its power to create legal tender to keep itself in being. Looking back on the hyper-inflation over a space of three years, Privy Councillor von Grimm, one of the Reichsbank's directors at the time, described the Bank's political dilemma:

> . . . To an ever growing extent, the Reich had to resort to the Reichsbank if it was to prolong its existence, and because the point at issue was the survival of the Reich, the Reichsbank did not regard itself justified in refusing [to print unlimited banknotes], even after the passing in 1922 of the law which gave it formal autonomy.[7]

Forced to abandon control of the currency, the Weimar parliament nevertheless kept the Army's loyalty. The Nazi *putsch* was dispersed with a volley, and Hitler entered the Landsberg Prison, where he was to dictate *Mein Kampf* to his cousin and fellow inmate, Rudolf Hess. Meanwhile Finance Minister Luther appointed, to the seemingly impossible task of currency reform a man whose willpower, imagination and boldness soon established him alongside the other central banking statesmen of inter-war Europe.

Dr. Hjalmar Schacht, Brooklyn-born of German parentage, had returned to Germany while still a child, and was a successful private banker before he was chosen as Commissioner of Currency in November 1923. A self-proclaimed financial genius whose flamboyant, daring and original approach to finance constantly confounded the sceptics, Schacht made his international reputation by rebuilding the hopeless German currency in incredibly short order. This he did by introducing a banknote, the *rentenmark*, equivalent to 1,000,000,000 debased Reichsmarks or one old gold mark, which was exchangeable on sight for a like sum in mortgage bonds on the whole of German landed property. The monetary principle behind this operation was simple. Because people continued to eat even though they had to spend a paper billion to buy a loaf of bread, land and agriculture prospered through the hyper-inflation. Farmers and landowners, who had paid off all their debts in debased marks, were able to adorn their homes with luxury furniture and grand pianos, exchanged in barter for their vital produce. An enforceable mortgage bill on land was thus an excellent security. Within two months of this drastic surgery—and with noughts dropped for the purpose of convenient book-keeping— the mark was improving on the exchanges.

Though Schacht was never Norman's creature, it seems most likely that he came to power as a result of Norman's opposition to the other candidates for the Commissionership.[8] Norman, whose admiration for Schacht anyway was growing all the time, realized that it was vital to the success of his plans for international reconstruction that he should work closely and intimately with the German and, although Norman's introvert secretiveness and Schacht's extrovert ebullience contrasted like night and day, an intimate working relationship between the two men evolved.*

Schacht's management of the mark set the stage for a German economic miracle no less spectacular than that which followed World War II. Hyper-inflation had wiped the slate of domestic financial relationships almost clean. Savings had disappeared; government compensation after currency stabilization restored less than a quarter of their interest-yielding documents' former value; debtors in general got off scot-free. But monetary stabilization released a frustrated nation's economic energies. The existence of millions of skilled, willing, unemployed hands,

* A highly controversial visit to Berlin by the Governor on the eve of World War II to attend the christening of Schacht's grandchild, named 'Norman' in his honour, testifies to the closeness of this association.

and wages at the very floor of subsistence, opened vistas of limitless opportunities to the foreign investor. Germany became almost overnight the new frontier for 'venture' capital. Between 1924 and 1928 foreigners, mostly Americans, invested no less than $6 billion in Germany, while Germany paid about $2·5 billion in reparations, and invested a further $2·5 billion abroad in her turn. Thus 'hardly a penny of Germany's payments came from her own resources'.[9] As under the gold standard in the previous century, foreign investment, this time from across the Atlantic rather than the Channel, had stepped in to restore balance in international payments.

CODE OF THE CENTRAL BANKERS

Long before Schacht's stabilization of the mark, Norman had been advancing his grand design to bring the world back onto gold. Through innumerable lines of communication and with the British Government's blessing and encouragement, he was swaying the policies of foreign financiers towards his objective. Norman at all times worked in intimate collaboration with Strong. Between them they made an impressive two-man team. Strong spoke for a subcontinent lately united as a nation—a land of unheard-of resources, productive power and income, but his direct participation was inhibited by Congress's isolationism. Norman therefore became Strong's *alter ego*. Knowledge of Strong's unqualified support enabled Norman to exert unrivalled influence in the Financial Committee of the League of Nations, from whose doors America's refusal to enter the League kept Strong debarred. So complete, in fact, was Norman's sway over this committee that his adversaries, especially the French, believed that it acted as his personal agent. As early as 1922, the Committee's Secretariat began to work out relief, stabilization and reconstruction programmes for a number of countries, starting with Austria. Norman, with Strong's backing, arranged the loans and central bank credits as they became needed.

At the same time Strong and Norman developed between them, a code of behaviour for central banking which their unchallenged leadership enabled them to impress upon their colleagues. The wild inflations of war and its aftermath had only heightened their orthodoxy and conservatism. Barriers, they believed, had to be built against such horrors in the future. To achieve this and to underwrite the active independent rôle of central banks, Norman insisted that stabilization credits be given to central banks which, like the Bank of England, were still private companies, on condition that they be kept independent of political control. Furthermore, Norman, with Strong's support, also insisted that central banks should deal *exclusively* with each other. To ensure these results, Norman and Strong extracted governmental assurances that international co-operation on monetary matters should be entrusted to central banks alone. Nor were Norman's prefectorial activities confined to Europe. He was instrumental in setting up several central banks in the British Empire during the 1920's, all of them founded upon his principles. Steadily and methodically, Norman was building the structure that would enable governments to make their currencies freely convertible into gold; preparing to return the levers of monetary control into the hands of the middle class's merchant princes and out of reach of the politicians.

THE GOLD STANDARD AGAIN

By 1924, the apparent imminence of the pound's return to convertibility had pushed its floating rate close to the magic pre-war parity of $4.87. But before the final declaration that the Bank was resuming gold payments could be made, certain steps had to be taken to protect Britain's low gold reserves.

The gradual shift of gold coin from circulation to bank vaults and its replacement with paper had been continuous since the 1870's. But world war had driven Europe's gold almost completely underground. After the armistice, gold was far too scarce for any possibility of a return to the full 'gold-coin' standard. The gold standard post-war style therefore was to be restricted to foreign payments, heavily circumscribing the national public's right to convert notes into gold. Within England, the Gold Standard Act of 1925 was to remove gold coins from circulation. In future the public was only to be

allowed to buy 400-ounce bullion bars worth more than
£1,500 each at Newton's £3 17s. 10½d. an ounce parity. And,
since Norman planned to close the mint to gold, these were
useless except for export purposes.

A second safeguard to Britain's scanty gold supplies was an
informal agreement between Norman and Strong regarding
interest rates in London and New York. If the rate was kept
higher in London, the pound, Norman believed, was safe,
because foreign deposits would stay in British banks. But, if
New York interest rates moved above London's, these deposits
would be attracted across the Atlantic, and would pull support
from under the pound. Thus in planning his triumphal return
to gold at the old parity, Norman won Strong's agreement that
interest rates in New York would be kept below those in London.

By the Spring of 1925, Norman had completed these arrangements. He had also educated the new Chancellor Winston
Churchill in his grand strategy. England, he assured his confused pupil, would soon return to her former glory as the stabilizing gyroscope of world finance. "I will make you the
Golden Chancellor," he intoned over him during one visit to
Chartwell.[10] Finally, on Budget Day, 28 April 1925, Svengali
watched from the Distinguished Strangers' Gallery as Churchill
announced Resumption. That evening, Norman noted the time
in his diary, 'about 4.05 p.m.'—then in block capitals, the
magic words: 'GOLD STANDARD'.

4

The Scissor Blades of Welfare and Nationalism

In November 1918, old economic beliefs confronted new social facts. The philosophy of Free Trade and the religion of gold met new demands for social welfare and a new sense of national community—both nurtured in the conflict.

The standardized welfare of army life—regulation rations, clothing, shelter and medical attention—had raised rather than lowered the average soldier's living standards. Meanwhile his wife had grown accustomed to the new security provided by a separation allowance and wartime opportunities to earn. The idea of a right to basic social security received official post-war sanction with 'homes fit for heroes to live in'. At the same time, shared hardships of war had brought a sense of national community in which the privileges of wealth were to be matched by more definite obligations. This was the new social climate in which Montagu Norman laboured to resurrect the old monetary order.

1. ENTERPRISE AGAINST ACCUMULATION

In Britain the Armistice had been followed by inflationary boom as businessmen and consumers rushed to replenish their stocks and to buy newly available goods. Adding to wartime inflation, a sudden post-war spurt of economic activity produced a trebling of wages and profits over the period 1914–20 and a parallel inflation of prices. Norman's 7 per cent bank rate tripped the sprinting economy and sent it sprawling. Unemployment, which in a hundred years of gold standard had averaged only 3 to 4 per cent and scarcely ever risen above 10, hit 19 per cent in 1921. No more homes were built for heroes. Over the course of a year the slump levelled out, but from 1921 to the end of the decade, unemployment in England never fell back below 10 per cent, 'the intractable million'.

Precipitated and aggravated by Norman's bank rate, the depression of British industry had basic structural causes. Between 1913 and 1920 both the size and the productivity of Britain's work force had grown significantly.* But in the traditional steam-age industries, especially coal, ship-building and cotton, on which British exporting had become dangerously dependent by 1914, productivity had not stayed sufficiently ahead of costs for Britain to regain the markets lost in four years of war to countries less involved in the holocaust. British exports in the 1920's, therefore, stood at only about two-thirds of their pre-war level.

What was to be done? Another great debate over monetary policy ensued. To a large extent it followed the classic division between those advocating monetary plenty and those who favoured its scarcity. Anxious to get the economy moving again, a section of the business community, entrepreneurs in the newer, more promising fields like electrical apparatus, automobiles and rayon, favoured cheap money. If this meant some inflation and a depreciation of the pound on the exchanges, at least the shrunken pound would lower the foreign price of British goods and stimulate exports. The spokesmen for this point of view were the Cambridge economics don, John Maynard Keynes, who emerged as its intellectual champion, and Reginald McKenna, the competent, bouncy, 'hideously conceited',[1] little Midland Bank Chairman who had been Chancellor of the Exchequer in Asquith's wartime Coalition Government. In a string of essays and articles Keynes sought to illuminate the issues at stake. The falling prices that attended the Bank of England's deflationary policies, he pointed out, led entrepreneurs to restrict production and increase unemployment while rewarding the non-productive class.

As it became increasingly apparent that the City of London and the Bank of England were preparing for a return to the gold standard at the old parity, a policy that would mean a continuing diet of deflation, Keynes' arguments moved from

* In the early 1920's Britain's productive potential was 10 to 15 per cent ahead of 1913.

protest to attack. He hurled barbed shafts at the gentlemen of the City who chose 'to provoke unemployment rather than disappoint the rentier', and attempted to shift discussion onto 'an allegedly moral plain, a realm of thought where vested interest can be triumphant over the common good without further debate'.[2]

But an influential, conservative group of industrialists took a more defensive line. These were the men who had under-written Chamberlain's Tariff Reform campaign. Unsure of their capacity to regain foreign markets, even with the help of a lowered sterling exchange rate, they preferred to shelter their high and inflexible production costs behind tariff walls. For them, monetary policy was not the real issue. Money borrowing rates were of comparatively little concern to large traditional industries that were not contemplating major expansion of their production. If anything, these industrialists had a de-flationary bias, being more concerned with maintaining a buyer's labour market so as to hold down labour costs. Mean-while, their proposal to exclude foreign competition from domestic and imperial markets would insulate Britain's price level and therefore the pound's exchange rate from the outside world.

But these 'Empire Free Traders' could not surmount one central difficulty. In return for granting protection in their home markets for British industrial goods, the Dominions would demand protection for their foodstuffs and raw materials in Britain. Throughout the 20's this problem tended to split the Tory Party. Protectionists, led by Press Lords Beaverbrook and Rothermere, felt that a few pence more on the working man's loaf was a small price to pay for guaranteed profits and employ-ment; those remaining loyal to Baldwin saw the shallowness of Empire Free Trade's electoral appeal. In the event the pro-tectionists, even with the formidable support of the Press Lords—the men who, as Baldwin put it, sought 'power without responsibility—the prerogative of the harlot throughout history'—could not overcome his *laissez-faire* alliance between liberal Free Traders and the City of London, a partnership of which Churchill in the 1920's was a leading spokesman.

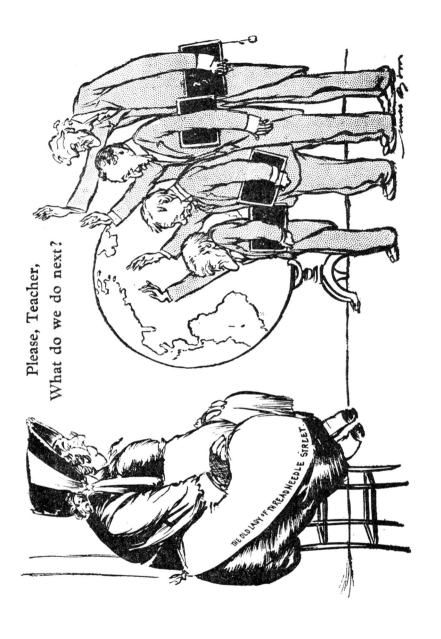

Please, Teacher,
What do we do next?

LABOUR JOINS THE CITY

This grouping of *laissez-faire* liberals with the City bankers formed the opposite monetary interest to expansionists like Keynes and McKenna. They formed also the political power behind Norman's attempt to put the monetary clock back. Ironically, this persuasion gained unexpected and unlooked-for support from the Labour Party, ushered into power in December 1933 by an unemployment figure of 1,200,000, a direct result of Norman's savage deflation. For, wonderful to relate, in socialist Chancellor of the Exchequer Philip Snowden the forces of monetary conservatism found their staunchest ally.

When he came to head the Treasury in 1923, Snowden astonished and delighted Norman by turning out a pillar of financial and monetary orthodoxy, a Chancellor who 'trod the path of deflation with ghoulish enthusiasm'.[3] In fact, Snowden bears political responsibility for the decision to press ahead with a return to gold. Himself a paradoxical figure 'to whom socialism was a luxury that had to be financed out of revenue—like roads and public utilities',[4] Snowden's monetary politics were, however, no private quirk: they were fully supported by the rest of the Cabinet. For the Labour Governments of 1923–24 and 1929–31, in both of which Snowden served as Chancellor, were prisoners of their own ideology. As they saw the situation, to accept the policies of Liberal radicals like Keynes would have been to betray their principles. They would be using their possession of power to patch up the capitalist system which they condemned.

Thus, with neither the competence nor the mandate to socialize the entire economy, the Labour government found themselves in an intellectual *cul de sac*. Socialist ideology offered no solution for the country's economic maladies short of complete socialization. So, with marvellous perversity but full Marxian logic, they stuck doggedly to 19th-century capitalist orthodoxy and the dictates of the City Fathers.

CONFRONTATION OVER COAL

The Socialists having paved the way, it was left to Churchill as Chancellor under Baldwin to do the deed. It was a deed that he soon decided was the worst mistake of his career. For Churchill never forgave Norman his advice to return to gold, the results of which followed in rapid and devastating succession.

In early 1925, Britain still had over a million unemployed and the exports of her basic industries were scarcely competitive at a sterling exchange rate of $4.20. Fixing sterling at $4.87 in order that the pound could look the dollar in the face was a policy akin to dosing a sick man with poison. The effects were felt first in the coal industry. The mine owners, whose coal was already too expensive in foreign markets, now faced the prospect of a still higher export price. Their difficulties were intensified within a few months by resurgent competition from the Ruhr as French and Belgian troops were evacuated in July. So the owners decided to meet the difference in costs with cuts in the miners' wages of between 10 and 25 per cent. Immediate confrontation was averted by a government subsidy, arranged while a Royal Commission looked into the problem of increasing efficiency in the pits. But the Commission's proposal that the mine owners rationalize their operations while the miners take a cut in pay met with flat refusal by both parties. On May Day 1926 the owners locked the miners out, and the General Strike was on.

What was the reaction of Strong and Norman to the 'unorthodox' refusal of the miners to accept the 'adjustment' process on which the gold standard depended? Norman thought of the strike as an 'essentially local display of senseless anarchy' while he 'blinded himself almost deliberately to its ill effects'.[5] The political danger of Communist agitation which so exercised the diligence of Churchill and Home Secretary Sir William Joynson-Hicks, left Norman quite unconcerned. Nor did Norman's *laissez-faire* principles desert him when Joynson-Hicks moved to embargo £100 million of strike funds received from the Bank of Moscow for payment to the Trades Union Congress. Intervention by the Home Secretary to embargo the money appeared to Norman simply as 'officious and clumsy State interference between bankers and their clients'.[6] Norman's unshakable orthodoxy was shared by his American colleague. For when Strong arrived in London during its second week to attend meetings on the economic condition of Europe, the General Strike was scarcely mentioned.[7]

In deciding to return sterling to gold at the old parity, Strong and Norman were perfectly well aware that sterling would, initially at any rate, be over-valued. They simply believed that, following the classic gold standard mechanism, the depressive effects of the over-valued pound on exports would rapidly push costs back into line. In other words they proposed to intensify unemployment so as to strengthen the employers' hands in reducing wages. The striking miners were, in Keynes's words, 'to be offered the choice between starvation and submission, the fruits of their submission to accrue to the benefit of other classes'.[8]

Norman knew what he was doing, but he deliberately blinded himself to the size of adjustment to be made. However, at least some of the blame for misreading the auguries under the hypnosis of a desire to return to former glories must be laid at the door of the British Treasury which actually made out the case that convinced Churchill. That the Treasury got its adjustment calculations so wrong is explained by their choice of indices for comparing British and American price behaviour. They based their judgement of the necessary British adjustment on the price behaviour of raw materials in international commerce (wheat or cotton, for example). But such commodities necessarily adjusted themselves rapidly to variations in exchange rates, and thus gave an entirely false picture of the flexibility of goods whose price included British labour costs. Had they compared the trends in British and American costs of living or in finished products such as clothing or machine tools, they would have seen that the real gap to be bridged by British wage-reductions was not two or three per cent, but in reality ten or twelve.

Raising the exchange value of sterling by 10 per cent meant, Keynes calculated, transferring about £1,000 million into the pocket of the rentier from the rest of the community, and increasing the real burden of the national debt by some £750 million. It was, in the words with which Keynes concluded his scorching *Economic Consequences of Mr. Churchill*, 'a policy which the country would never permit if it knew what was being done'.

With no alternative available but wage-cutting, the pit owners acted with the strength of desperation. The miners held out until December when cold, hungry and bitter, they crept back to work for less pay. But in other industries whose backs were not pressed to the wall, labour was more successful in resisting wage cuts. Instead wages stuck at the 1925 level for nearly a decade: the alternative to wage cuts being uncompetitive export industries and massive unemployment.

The attempt of the City of London to force the working man to bear the 'fundamental adjustments' in order that British banking and insurance could prosper thus failed. Battered and eroded by the Depression, the scissor blade of welfare had refused to budge to the extent demanded by *laissez-faire* economics. Its refusal drew down the blade of nationalism onto international economic ties.

2. THE BLADE OF NATIONALISM

As the world watched sterling's return to gold, the dangers of Norman's and Strong's make-shift monetary system rapidly became apparent. Because there simply was not enough gold outside the United States for a full-dress return to the gold standard, Norman, with Strong's support, had been prepared to stretch sound financial principle in order to avoid the meddling hand of the politicians. Employing, therefore, his considerable charm and finesse as a salesman, he persuaded other central bankers to agree to use sterling and (to a lesser extent) dollars, the currencies with which much of world trade was financed, instead of gold as the reserves behind their own currencies. The gold that backed sterling was thus to do duty several times over, which of course made nonsense of the logic of controlling money's value through the scarcity of gold. Thus in future, the key to money's stability was not to be provided by mother nature but by uncles London and New York.

As this system became generally adopted, reserves held in foreign exchange, which totalled under $500 million in 1913, increased to $3,250 million by 1928.[9] But this attempt to circumvent the shortage of gold made the new system inherently unstable. The 'gold-exchange standard' (as the new arrangement was called) hinged on the international convertibility of sterling, which accounted for an estimated 80 per cent of foreign exchange holdings in 1928. However, by that same year, foreign holdings of sterling had reached between three and four times Britain's total gold reserves. This meant that there were three or four claims on every gold brick in the vaults of Threadneedle Street. This was too many saucers for even the skilful jugglers of the City to keep in the air at once. Under pressure from this international commitment, sterling creaked alarmingly with every financial gust that blew. The reward for this thinly-disguised manœuvre of monetary nationalism was not long in coming. It came in the form of a monetary challenge from England's oldest rival.

POINCARÉ'S MONETARY STRATEGY

France had adopted almost exactly the opposite budgetary and monetary policies to Britain at the close of World War I. In 1919 the franc stood at about half of its pre-war exchange value. But the French, whose financial establishment commanded only a fraction of the relative prestige and power of the City of London, gave economic recovery clear priority over financial stability. Rather than balance their budget by heavy taxation as the British had done, they preferred to accept large deficits in the budget, new expenditures being met by continued borrowing from the rentier class. The result was that when the collapse in world prices hit both Britain and France in 1921, the more lightly taxed French industrialists suffered less than the British and their trade remained comparatively brisk.

But her occupation of the Ruhr in 1923 had backfired on France's monetary situation in a serious and humiliating fashion. British and American alarm over France's re-occupation of Germany was reflected in heavy selling of the franc. As a result, a hastily agreed 20 per cent increase in taxation was necessary in order to reinspire confidence in France's financial stability. This incident served to demonstrate France's dependence on the goodwill of many thousands of foreign investors. It also paralysed M. Poincaré's current efforts to stabilize his currency. In any case, this veteran patriot's rigid right-wing nationalism, which had led him into the Ruhr adventure, helped bring his downfall at the polls in May 1924 and ushered in a left-wing coalition. Under first Herriot, then Briand, this coalition tried to stabilize the currency without recourse to heavier taxation. Their failure to do so was blamed at least partly on continuing and unsettling speculation in the franc in the Anglo-Saxon money markets (speculation, incidentally, in which Keynes himself was heavily and lucratively involved).

The outflow of 'hot money' from France to Britain and the United States in the early 20's had meant that the floating franc was quoted on the exchanges at a rate a good deal lower than the French price-level would warrant. In other words, the franc became under-valued, and this under-valuation further cheapened French exports, providing a strong stimulus to French industry and commerce—precisely the opposite effect to that of Norman's over-valued pound upon British business.

Just as the franc showed great strength upon de Gaulle's return in 1958, so the underlying strength of the French position was revealed in 1926 by Poincaré's re-election. A surge of confidence in his National Union Government, which followed the collapsed left-wing coalition, brought French capital flooding back from abroad. The franc soared, moving from 260 to 125 to the pound within a few months, as Frenchmen fell over each other to get back into their own national currency at a favourable valuation. Now a ticklish dilemma faced Poincaré and his trusted financial adviser, Emile Moreau, Governor of the Bank of France. If he allowed the franc to continue to rise and then stabilized it at a high level, he would penalize French industry with a high exchange rate, as Norman had done in England. Alternatively he could benefit industry with a lower stabilization and take buying power away from the investing class and those living on fixed incomes.

Moreau had watched Norman's revaluation of sterling 'provoke unemployment without precedent in history' as he recorded in his diary.[10] In Moreau's view 'the level chosen ought to represent a balance of sacrifices demanded of the different social classes in the population—debtors and creditors, lenders and producers'. But for tactical reasons Poincaré preferred to postpone an official decision. Meanwhile he agreed with Moreau to hold the exchange rate *unofficially* at the still relatively low level of 125 to the pound. Charles Rist, Moreau's chief lieutenant, would have liked to see the franc's level fixed lower still, but at 125 francs to the pound the Bank of France already leaned clearly in favour of debtors and producers. How different this reasoning from the monetary politics which the high priest of the City had recently foisted upon Churchill!

But Moreau had a second motive for picking the lower 125 exchange rate. As most of the 'hot' French money had been in London, Moreau picked up mostly pounds in exchange for his francs, so that by May 1927 the Bank of France held a hundred million pounds with no countervailing flow of francs moving into foreign hands. In stabilizing the franc Moreau had achieved a potential stranglehold on the London money market. The stage was now set for the great attack upon Britain's financial citadel.

MOREAU'S FINANCIAL DIPLOMACY

French determination to put pressure on the pound was a part of her overall political strategy. Two German invasions in half a century had given France one overriding foreign policy objective: to hold Germany down. Reparations had been the principal weapon to ensure Germany's political subjection to this policy. Clemenceau had made sure that the sum was sufficiently astronomical that, even after successive scalings-down under Allied pressure, they would still be beyond Germany's financial capacity. In this way the French hoped to drain off Germany's surplus energies in the form of gold, and at the same time have a permanent excuse for military intervention in the event of default.

But the British and Americans had a totally different policy towards Germany. They believed that for Europe to be secure ⚡ and prosperous—particularly in face of Bolshevist Russia— a strong and prosperous Germany was essential. Thus, by the mid-1920's, the French had come to believe that their British and American allies were doing everything in their power to frustrate French policy and to build Germany up as a counterweight to France. Britain had objected to French and Belgian occupation of the Ruhr in 1923; together with the United States she had taken the initiative of the Dawes Plan, scaling down Germany's liabilities and arranging a large loan to set Germany on its feet again. Then, while American money had poured via London into Germany to finance her extraordinary economic come-back, the British had been playing their old game of using short-term loans (the balances of 'hot money' held by France and others in the City of London) to make longer-term—and more profitable—loans to the Germans and Austrians. Furthermore, it was widely believed in Paris that the foreign speculation in the franc which for years had kept its value out of French government control, represented Anglo-Saxon retaliation against France's intransigence over reparations.

Officials at the Bank of France, in particular, were deeply suspicious of Norman's intimate friendship with Strong and Schacht. They had watched the authority he wielded over the League of Nations not only in stabilization of the mark, but also the currencies of Austria, Hungary, Bulgaria, Poland and Greece. In the mind of Governor Moreau, suspicion blended with admiration and envy. To Moreau, Norman and his colleagues were the new diplomats *par excellence* wielding power in a game for which they wrote the rules and which they played over the heads of the politicians. Moreau had been impressed by the central banking philosophy expounded by Norman at their first meeting. Norman had been equally frank about his attitude toward France. 'I want very much to help the Bank of France', he told Moreau, 'but I detest your Government and your Treasury. For them I shall do nothing.'[11] Nevertheless, Norman's talk of separating finance from politics appeared the purest form of Anglo-Saxon hypocrisy. 'They talk about sound currency,' he recorded in his diary, 'but really they are in love with power.'

The French counter-offensive to Britain's support of Germany came at a time when Norman's power was already on the wane. By 1926 his secretive methods of working and his intimate relationship with Schacht had led Norman out on a limb. Other central bankers besides Moreau had come to suspect the bearded wizard of political machinations. Indeed, Norman's domination of the European monetary scene had even begun to worry Ben Strong. By the end of that year, Strong was writing to advise his emissary in Europe to cease dealing through Norman in any further currency stabilization operations.[12] As Strong wrote that letter, a prop was knocked from beneath the Bank of England in its dealings with Europe. From this time onward, European central bankers began to deal directly with the Americans.

Meanwhile, Norman remained convinced that in stabilizing the franc Moreau would need the Bank of England's help. This would be the moment to inform Moreau of the tariff for membership of the bankers' club. Accordingly, when the franc started its spectacular rise on the exchanges with the return of Poincaré, Norman travelled to Paris to lay down his terms for helping the franc. They were simple—a public manifestation of the political independence of the Bank of France.

Had Norman understood France's long history of defending her soil with her gold he would have saved his breath. To suggest to a Bank of France official that monetary policies should be separated from foreign policy was akin to suggesting that he should hand out blank cheques on his reserves. France had historically helped maintain her position in Europe by the skilful exercise of her purse strings. More than one English sovereign had been released from a painful bartering of royal power for parliamentary grants by subsidies from the French court. Now that France, no longer naturally pre-eminent on the continent, was struggling to regain ascendancy, it was inevitable that she should resort to her traditional blending of finance and diplomacy.

The failure of understanding between Norman and Moreau was mutual. Moreau was by now as suspicious as Norman was trusting of the Frenchman's willingness to play the game and enter the club on the usual 'non-political' terms. Shortly after Norman's return home, Pierre Quesnay, a trusted lieutenant, was sent to spy out 'the workings of the London money market as organized by the Bank of England'.[13] His report confirmed all Moreau's convictions that Norman, with his financial knights—Sir Otto Niemeyer, Sir Arthur Salter, Sir

Henry Strakosh, Sir Robert Kindersley—was working to make London once again the metropole of international finance, the pivot of 'the economic and financial organization of the world, which appears to the Governor of the Bank of England to be the major task of the 20th century'.[14] Quesnay also reported that Norman's opinion of France's financial health was as low as his view of Germany's was high. It was as well for Moreau's plans that Norman was so deceived. For with the Ruhr invasion's failure and the Dawes Plan in operation, France's monetary pressure upon Germany's Anglo-Saxon promoters and protectors was the only diplomatic weapon to hand.

The pounds that Moreau had bought to stabilize the euphoric franc were precisely the weapon he needed. As soon as the French currency was firmly on its feet, Moreau ordered the presentation of some of his £100 million for gold in London. The axe was laid to the root of the top-heavy tree. Norman at once protested, but Moreau had his answer ready: raise your bank rate so as to curb the gamblers of the City of London who continue in their attempts to unsettle the franc.* At this Norman blenched. A higher bank rate would mean a further squeeze on British employment. Churchill had been sent into a towering rage on an earlier occasion by Norman's raising of the bank rate without first consulting him. Moreover, as the politician responsible for the effects of the return to gold, he had taken the brunt of the deluge of contumely. Churchill's antipathy to Norman was therefore considerable. He felt his confidence in the City's omniscience, fair-mindedness and detachment had been betrayed. There were stormy scenes between the two men as Norman's proffered halo turned out to be a noose. Norman realized that Churchill would refuse a higher bank rate point blank. Quite truthfully, therefore, he explained to Moreau that raising the British bank rate was, under the circumstances, simply out of the question. But why, Norman asked, did Moreau not produce the same result by lowering

---

* The franc, though unofficially stabilized by this time, was not officially so until 1928, the interval of uncertainty having been skilfully protracted so as to draw additional capital back to France in the hope that the franc might be stabilized at a higher rate, a move which would increase the value of franc balances.

his? Moreau was equally adamant. A lower bank rate held absolutely no charms to a man who had just achieved the return of French wealth to France partly through Paris's attractive interest rates. Besides, he had not provoked this crisis so as to oblige Norman by coming up with a convenient solution.

NORMAN TRUMPS AN ACE

Norman was therefore forced to resort to the type of stratagem at which reputation had him so skilled. Churchill had recently infuriated the Governor by agreeing with Finance Minister Cailleux to easier repayment terms for the very large war debt that France still owed to Britain. He had intentionally refrained from consulting Norman on the subject, being well aware of Norman's objections to letting the French Treasury off lightly. Now Norman's mind found a means of discomfiting Churchill, while applying counterpressure on the Bank of France. The key figure in this stratagem was Sir Otto Niemeyer, Norman's intimate friend and the real power at the Treasury. As Moreau ordered the withdrawal of gold from London, Niemeyer, speaking ostensibly for Churchill, issued a grim warning. Further gold withdrawals would result in presentation for payment of the large number of French Treasury obligations held by the British Treasury. Meanwhile, Norman was telling Moreau that the Bank of England would do what it could to help out the French, but that he was having great difficulties with Churchill at the Treasury. His diaries suggest that the astute Moreau failed fully to grasp the subtlety of Norman's double game against the English Chancellor and the Governor of the Bank of France.

> The Bank of France incontestably dominates the Bank of England, but the British Treasury dominates the French Treasury, so that when we put pressure on the institution of Threadneedle Street, M. Churchill threatens M. Poincaré. However, M. Montagu Norman seems to have understood our situation: he has promised to support us even though he is said to have great difficulties with Winston Churchill, and it appears that the latter is blamed by Chamberlain and Baldwin for the situation . . .[15]

This teamwork between Norman and Niemeyer checked the French gold raids. But they added fuel to French suspicions of an elaborate British plot. Norman, they believed, was applying an ingenious pincer movement against them: British gambling with the franc and the British Treasury's claims on France were being used to counterpoise the Bank of France's grip on the Bank of England.

Deadlock was the result. The French continued to demand British gold, while Britain countered with proposals for French repayment of her outstanding i.o.u.'s. It was broken by intervention from the now detached Ben Strong. To satisfy both parties he agreed to absorb shipping charges so that American gold was available to the French at no greater cost than gold from the Bank of England, while the British could transfer their obligation to the Federal Reserve who would be satisfied with British paper.

Such an offer of co-operation Moreau could scarcely refuse. But monetary hostilities were resumed when Philip Snowden, returning to the Chancellorship again in May 1929, told the Hague conference on reparations that the French Finance Minister M. Cheron was 'talking nonsense'. Retaliatory withdrawals that same week cost the Bank of England an estimated £20 million worth of gold. The following summer further Anglo-French disagreements over a reparations bond issue led to new gold reprisals.

A more public demonstration of French hostility to London was provided during the foundation of the Bank of International Settlements in 1930. Thanks to Schacht's driving energy, the Dawes Plan had worked sufficiently well for all German payments to be met promptly and in full. Now it was time to set up a more permanent arrangement for the long remaining period of German payments. A new reparations schedule, the Young Plan, had come into effect that January. One of its provisions was for an international bank to smooth balance of payments disruptions caused by the large cash transfers involved in making the reparations payments.

From the first, Norman took an active interest in the establishment and operations of the new bank. For him it represented the possibility of embodying in an institution the

ideas of 'non-political' central banking co-operation so close to
his heart. At one point he asked Lord Layton, publisher of *The
Economist,* if he would draft a constitution for the new bank
that would place it beyond the reach of governments. When
Layton objected that, 'It's the right of every democratic
government to reserve its freedom of action', Norman's
response was characteristic: 'Was it not Cardinal Newman
who said that the will of God is perfect freedom?' [16]

The French, however, from their position of new-found
strength, were grimly determined to preserve this new organ of
co-operation from British domination. If necessary they were
quite prepared to jeopardize the bank scheme and even the
whole Young Plan rather than agree to the establishment of the
new bank in London. Norman, now under the shadow of the
massively re-founded franc, could do little but agree to their
proposed arrangements. Moreau's successor, Gustave Moret,
insisted on heavy French representation on the board: three
Bank of France directors and only two from the Bank of
England, and the first General Manager was to be French.
Moreover, operation of the bank was to be restricted exclusively
to Europe where French financial hegemony, based on the
franc's new strength, was already becoming a reality.

3. THE BLADE DESCENDS

From the moment of *de facto* stabilization of the franc, the Bank
of France had worked steadily to use France's competitive export prices, and hence large balance of payments surpluses, to
build up its gold reserves. Until 1928 most of the gold came from
the United States which was glad to be disembarrassed of some
of its huge hoard. But as the Wall Street boom of 1928–29 began
its ascent, the attractions of home profits to American investors meant that American gold ceased to flow to Europe.
By 1929 France's continued policy of hoarding the payments
received for her exports in gold was beginning to hurt other
countries. That January, with French gold reserves at £420
million (compared with £800 million for the United States and
£150–160 million for Britain), chronic gold shortage in the rest
of the world was causing serious weakening in world prices.

Loud objections were voiced that France was causing monetary famine and economic depression. But such complaints were soon forgotten in the ensuing economic deluge.

In October 1929 the great American boom, the result of wild speculation on credit, broke. In January 1930 the slump reached Europe. By March 1931 the 'economic blizzard' had raised unemployment in Britain above 2½ million. The plunge in business earnings caused an electric atmosphere of financial foreboding. The credit position of many banks was obviously dangerously exposed. Then, on 11 May 1931, the dominant bank of Central Europe, the Rothschild-controlled Creditanstalt of Vienna, failed, its collapse triggering an unprecedented chain reaction. Headlong runs on first Austria's and then Germany's currency ensued.

Paris was the one financial centre strong enough to undertake a massive supporting action. But Paris withheld its hand. Then France offered Austria a small loan conditional upon guarantees that the projected customs union between Austria and Germany be forsworn. German-Austrian refusal to bow to this open economic coercion brought Norman, whose slim gold backing of his overworked currency put him in a desperately weak position, into the field. Wiping the Frenchman's eye to applause from the entire non-French financial world, Norman came forward with the full amount required by Austria.

French revenge was not long delayed. Under French promptings, panic withdrawals that had occurred first in Vienna and then in Berlin began to occur in London.[17] Now the tottering gold-exchange standard edifice erected upon the pound's small gold base had to face the full force of a monetary hurricane. Wanting the security of gold instead of their paper pounds, and knowing that there was not enough to go round, people dived to be first in the line. It was an international run on the Old Lady of Threadneedle Street. As the run gained momentum in June and July, the Bank of England withheld the classic defence of high interest rate to bring money back to London. Partly this was because of implacable opposition in the country to further credit restriction at a time of slump and record unemployment; partly because of Norman's realization that the 'hot' money that it would bring in would only leave again at the first opportunity; partly because a record-level bank rate could well suggest that the crisis was even worse than it seemed, and hence scare off still more depositors. So Norman kept bank rate as low as 4½ per cent. Meanwhile, the Bank raised three separate loans in Paris and New York to buy time. But in August, as successive waves of sterling selling for gold became clearly overwhelming, a fourth loan was refused in New York on the sensible grounds that the pound was now beyond recall.

Norman, whose delicate health had been overcome by nervous strain in July, was in mid-Atlantic on his way back from Canada, when he received a puzzling cable signed by his two deputies at the Bank, Harvey and Peacock. 'Old Lady goes off on Monday', it read. Completely out of touch with the situation, Norman was incapable of believing that his Bank of England was about to go off gold. His mind sought another interpreta-ation of the message. His overbearing mother must be off on a holiday.[18] Norman learned the truth, on disembarkation, from the newsvendors' tattered placards in the Liverpool streets.

The blade of nationalism had descended on Norman's paper edifice. Having lost £200 million in gold in three months, the Bank of England suspended gold payments on 1 September 1931, and allowed a now unbacked pound to find its own level on the stormy sea of the international exchanges. The fall of sterling from the standard which he regarded as 'a mystic symbol of all that was finest in the struggle of mankind to better its lot on earth'[19] altered Norman's character. He sensed that he was living in a different world. Never again would he wear a top hat, 'except on the most solemn occasions'. Shunning banquets and other public functions, he increasingly withdrew from the world.

The change in Britain's domestic power structure was equally immediate. A new simile for assurance had to be found to replace 'as safe as the Bank of England'. Six years later, addressing a gathering of Commonwealth bank governors, Norman himself summed up the political change succinctly:

When the gold standard was abandoned, there took place an immediate redistribution of authority and responsibility which deprived the Bank of its essential functions. Foreign Exchange became a Treasury matter . . .[20]

This transfer of power was the institutional consequence of a political victory. The immediate victor, the catalyst, was France. But out of this triumph of nationalism was to emerge a more permanent victory. A victory of democracy over oligarchy; of both business and organized labour over the deadening hand of the rentier.

4. NATIONALISM TO THE RESCUE OF WELFARE

In September, 1931 France stood at the zenith of her financial power. Her fears of Germany had been largely removed by the new crisis of the mark; in Hungary, financial pressure had produced a change of government to suit French interests; in Austria, the Foreign Minister and central bank chief had been replaced by men more favourable to Paris; London was in no position to help anyone. Paris was the sole source of financial support throughout Central and Southern Europe.

France had leaned her political and economic weight against the pillars of co-operation. Her leaders had been prepared to bring down the international house, convinced that France's economic self-sufficiency and her thick cocoon of gold would protect her from the falling masonry.

Surveying the surrounding chaos that accompanied sterling's collapse in October 1931, the French Financial General Staff* believed that having shattered the sorry scheme of things to bits they could re-mould it nearer to their heart's desire at leisure.

But there was one nut—perhaps the toughest—left to crack. Only America could now offer the Germans succour, and thus keep them from France's financial grasp. But as they turned their eyes across the Atlantic, France's Financial General Staff now had good reasons to believe that even the transatlantic giant lay within their magic circle.

America in 1931 possessed more than twice the gold reserves of France, but France's financial leaders were well aware that

---

* The phrase, significantly, was current at the time in financial journalism. (See Paul Einzig, *The Fight for Financial Supremacy* (London: Macmillan 1934.)

the American monetary position was far from secure. In fact, a deeply shaken Wall Street was now in a position analogous to, though far less precarious than, the City of London. For the felony of the pound's return to gold at the pre-war parity had been compounded by Ben Strong's complicity. Strong's 'easy money' policies on the New York money market from 1925–28 were the fulfilment of his agreement with Norman to keep New York interest rates below those of London.[21] For the sake of international co-operation Strong had withheld the steadying hand of high interest rates from New York until it was too late. Easy money in New York had encouraged the surging American boom of the late 20's with its fantastic stock market speculation.

Here was the central irony of the rule of the central banker statesmen: not only had they helped deepen economic depression in Britain, but paved the way for catastrophe in America as well.

Like the Wall Street boom which halted the dollar crisis in 1968, America's stock exchange boom of 1928–29 had reversed the flow of funds across the Atlantic. Then, exactly as forty years later in 1968, soaring share values on the New York market not only attracted European investors looking for a large killing, but produced large-scale short-term American borrowing in Europe. As a result, in 1931, foreign lenders and depositors could lay claim to $3 billion of America's $5 billion gold reserve.[22] This foreign indebtedness made American authorities uneasy. Heavy foreign withdrawals could, they realized, remove enough gold to start a domestic run on the banks.

In October 1931 such withdrawals suddenly began. In a a short space, $600 million, representing withdrawals of French dollar balances in gold, was shipped to Europe. At the same time, M. Lacour-Gayet arrived in New York, the advance guard for an official visit by Prime Minister Pierre Laval. Lacour-Gayet did not beat about the bush. France was contemplating the withdrawal of the whole of her large official dollar deposits, a move which he well knew could produce a complete collapse of banking confidence. Then Laval arrived to reveal his hand to an astonished President Hoover. Paris was prepared to refrain from withdrawing her deposits provided that the

President undertook no new initiative over the revision of Germany's war debts. America must agree not to come to Germany's aid.

But this time France's financial leadership had overplayed its hand. Hoover, temporizing while he sounded out the opinion of participants in the Lausanne Conference (called in mid-1932 to re-examine once again the reparations question), refused to give Laval any categorical assurances. At the same time he gently raised the question of France's own war debts. American opinion, meanwhile, was deeply aroused. If France could afford to keep dollar and gold deposits in New York sufficient for 10 years of annuity payments on her war debt, she had been let off far too lightly at the recent Beranger–Mellon war debt re-funding agreements. Outrage at this financial blackmail was not soothed by another French tactic. Rumours, apparently officially sponsored, spread from Paris that British and American speculators were borrowing in Paris at 3 per cent to lend to Germany at 8. (At the time, Germans were borrowing limited sums in London at between 2⅝ per cent and 3⅝ per cent.) This was the French justification for the morality of her own financial arm-twisting.

Nor was France's heavy-handed use of her monetary advantage reserved only for Germany's creditors. Elsewhere in the world, too, the springs of goodwill toward France were systematically polluted by her Financial General Staff in the belief that resistance to their pressures simply meant that France was not squeezing hard enough.

INTO THE MAELSTROM

Tragically for France she had exhausted most of her goodwill just when she was about to need it all. In 1932 the monetary seesaw on which she had risen so high reached its limit. With British foreign exchange policy now in the hands of the Treasury, the pound had been allowed to fall unsupported and at one point it sank to $3.20. Countries that did most of their trade with Britain let their exchanges fall to keep level with the pound. By the end of 1931, ten European countries and most of the rest of the world had followed Britain off gold.

France, meanwhile, remained on the gold standard. But like a lucky card player intent on holding onto his winnings, she steadfastly refused to 'play bank'. Instead of taking over the coveted role of London and pouring forth her surplus gold in loans that might help restore international monetary equilibrium, the French government stepped up its public hoarding policy while stopping the issue of gold coin. Disillusion with Paris's financial pretensions rapidly became complete. As one authority wrote at the time, 'It has now been realized that Paris had nothing to gain financially through the elimination of London as a rival centre, as she is neither able nor willing to take her place.' 23

Meanwhile, partly as a result of France's contribution to the general deflation, controls were clamped onto foreign commerce throughout the world. They were needed to prevent the indefinite lowering of the international value of a country's money which would occur under floating exchange rates if its imports continued to exceed exports: for if the international supply of a currency exceeds international demand, its exchange value, unless 'supported' by its central bank purchase of the excess supply of its own currency with its gold and Foreign exchange reserves, will continue to decline.

The United States, although still on gold, had been the first to resort to protection as slump hit its economy in 1930. The Smoot–Hawley tariff raised duties on imports into the United States by an average of 40 per cent. In Britain the National Government, formed to deal with the worsening economic crisis, faced a 1931 foreign payments deficit of over £200 million, a deficit which, without protective measures, was beyond the power of a devalued pound alone to cure. For while the devalued pound initially made British goods and services cheaper abroad, and imports more expensive, distressed foreign producers who could sell nowhere else 'dumped' their goods at cut prices through Britain's open ports so that her import volume scarcely had decreased. Seeing no respite from this predicament the government broke with the trade philosophy of a century. A flat 10 per cent duty (up to 20 per cent and more in the case of manufactured articles) was placed on all imports except a few foodstuffs and raw materials.

"Phew! That's a nasty leak. Thank goodness it's not at our end of the boat."

By protecting her domestic market from foreign industrial goods while allowing the pound to find its 'natural' supply-and-demand level on the exchanges, Britain aimed to keep out imports while expanding exports. But the aim of going one higher than one's neighbour with one's protective trade barriers, and one lower with one's currency, simply turned into a self-defeating free-for-all with everyone in this way hoping to export his unemployment and save himself by ruining his neighbour.

THE NEW FEUDALISM

Just as tribal anarchy that followed the fall of Rome led to the feudal system of protection in exchange for service, so the commercial anarchy that followed the fall of the pound began to produce fortress communities: blocs of nations between which monetary arrangements were made for defence against a hostile world.

France, Belgium, the Netherlands, Italy and Switzerland—the 'gold bloc'—held their exchange rates at the values fixed in the 1920's. Suffering heavily from their currencies' extreme over-valuation, they tried to check the progressive worsening of their balances with the outside world by rigid restrictions on trade. Both Americas became a natural dollar bloc under the sway of the United States. The sterling-using countries and those that did the bulk of their international business with Britain lashed their exchange rates to the pound. Meanwhile, the 'imperial preference' system, outlined as Conservative policy in November 1930 by Neville Chamberlain, son of the founder of Empire Free Trade, came into effect at the Ottawa Conference in 1932.

Britain's objective at Ottawa was to return in a limited area to her 19th-century trade pattern in which she exchanged her manufactured goods for primary products. This had been the basis of Sir Oswald Mosley's ideas that had produced his split with Labour in 1930. Now, with the Free Trade voices of the City smothered in the avalanche of falling currencies, protectionist sentiment dominated the Conservative Party and, through it, the new coalition National Government.*

* In the heat of emergency, the government managed to sidestep the

Imperial preference did much to reduce British unemployment. But as an attempt to regroup Britain's trade into a sheltered Free Trade area it met with only limited success. For the brutal fact was that while the Empire was becoming less and less dependent on Britain, Britain was getting more and more dependent on Imperial markets.

But it was the indefatigable Dr. Schacht who (after resigning from the Reichsbank in 1930 in opposition to German concessions over the Young Plan), returned in 1933 as Hitler's finance minister, and carried this economic feudal system to its logical conclusion. In other monetary blocs the arrangements for service and protection were more or less voluntary agreements. But Schacht put Germany's relations with her weaker neighbours on the clear basis of the warlord and his serfs. Within the Reichsmark's sphere of influence (the Danube states and the Balkans particularly) Germany offered to buy whatever her weaker neighbours had to sell at prices well above the world level; but she paid them in heavily over-valued 'blocked' marks which could only be spent for the purchase of German goods. Meanwhile, with the outside world, she protected her trade balance by restricting her commerce to barter.

By the mid-1930's bloc protection was helping to raise world trade from the depths of 1931–32. But ironically France was the greatest sufferer under the new economics of siege. The franc's descent was made the more catastrophic by French fondness for gold. French hoarding had forced Britain and a host of other nations to step off their end of the seesaw when it hit bottom in September 1931. But their act of stepping off made it inevitable that the French currency would descend to join them in their confusion. With her gold-fixed franc now desperately over-valued as a result of the skelter of surrounding devaluations, her balance of payments, despite high trade barricades, swung deep into deficit. At the same time, political paralysis returned to Paris. Leon Blum's Popular Front government, formed to arrest the progress of depression-born Fascist Leagues, failed, giving way, by uneasy stages, to the radical regime of Daladier in 1938.

---

electoral suicide of taxing non-Empire wheat, through an elaborate face-saving series of 'quotas' with the Dominion governments.

Having bound herself, financial hand and political foot, France was now powerless to hinder Schacht's economic juggernaut. She was forced to devalue the franc by one third in 1936 and to lower it again two years later. Meanwhile French capital once again quit French shores, this time in search of the political safety of America.

ROOSEVELT—DEBONAIR EXPERIMENTALIST

The crisis which closed all United States banks in March 1933 had forced President Roosevelt to take America formally 'off gold' by calling in all gold coin and bullion owned by the public in exchange for Federal Reserve notes. But while the dollar dived on the exchanges in reflection of the fact that it was no longer convertible, the President still leaned towards some agreement that might pave the way for a return to gold. In fact, hovering between the choice of international stability and national freedom of action, Roosevelt remained sceptical of the usefulness of *any* monetary action.

In his inimitable administrative style, therefore, the President sent, as his representatives to the World Economic and Monetary Conference, called in London in June–July 1933 to arrange a monetary ceasefire, an array of senators, congressmen, bankers and economists from both political parties. This United States delegation was, of course, unable to agree among themselves, arguing fiercely and publicly with one another. Inevitably gold–silver arguments flared up again. The squabbling became scandalous when a 'free silver' senator from Nevada was seen chasing a 'gold bug' down the hall with a drawn bowie knife.[24] Meanwhile, back home, 100 congressmen signed a petition for Roosevelt to send Father Coughlin, the (wildly inflationary) quasi-fascist radio priest, to the Conference as an 'adviser'.

In the conference hall itself, the 'gold bloc' states immediately became locked in conflict with the currency floaters over the question of whether to return to gold, and at what price. Roosevelt was cruising off the New England coast on his yacht when his lawyer-emissary, Raymond Moley, pressed him to accept an innocuous resolution extracted from the Conference which called for some currency stabilization and an eventual return by all to gold. But with the banking crisis of the previous winter and a renewed plunge of the stock market fresh in his mind, the President was determined not to be bound internationally to any deflationary measures. Urged on by yachting mates, Henry Morgenthau and Louis Howe, he instead sent a defiant message to the assembled nations, on his arrival at Campobello, torpedoing the Conference's attempts at monetary co-operation. In future, the President announced, America's currency would be managed to suit domestic needs rather than the preferences of those concerned with international trade.

The Campobello message scandalized conservative monetary opinion throughout the world. In effect, it was an announcement that the United States would progressively inflate its currency hoping to get the economy going again by raising domestic prices. Nevertheless the Campobello message was endorsed by the arch-establishment bank of J. P. Morgan; Bernard Baruch was for it; and in England Winston Churchill, having long rued his own misleading of 1925, called America's international severance from gold 'noble and heroic sanity'. Keynes too unhesitatingly approved. The President's message, in Keynes's words was,

> . . . a challenge to us to decide whether we propose to tread the old unfortunate ways, or to explore new paths; paths new to statesmen and to bankers but not new to thought. For they lead to the managed currency of the future . . .[25]

THE DOLLAR DEVALUED—IN SLOW MOTION

The halting of foreign gold payments in April 1933 had forced the exchange value of the dollar down 15 per cent and a boost was at once felt in American export performance. But within the United States, prices did not rise; for, although the dollar had become inconvertible into gold, the United States government had not significantly expanded the money supply. The dollar was thus, from April onwards, backed by the same quantity of gold as before, only the gold was no longer obtainable.

Economic depression in the United States contrasted with high intellectual excitement as proposals for bold monetary experiment filled the air. Outstanding among these was that of the great American economist, Irving Fisher of Yale. Fisher had anticipated other economists of the day, including Keynes himself, by proposing a 'commodity dollar'.This was to be a domestic money standard, tied to no specific commodity like silver or gold, but one that measured the composite of domestic commodity price movements, and therefore of business activity and of liquidity requirements.

Such a standard was (and is) the ultimate logical one for money's value. It implies, of course, monetary management as a tool for controlling the domestic economy as a whole: a practice that, with the failure of the gold standard, was just beginning to gain acceptance with government. But who outside the United States would accept her commodity dollar in place of gold? International acceptance of Fisher's dollar would have meant foreign submission to American economic management, which was scarcely in high international repute at the bottom of an American-originated depression. Besides, no nation would begin to consider the sacrifice of their political sovereignty which accepting the 'managed' dollar would involve. Thus, Fisher's idea, so excellent in theory, would almost certainly have reduced America to international barter in practice. Instead, Henry Morgenthau, a Hudson River Valley farming neighbour of Roosevelt and now his Secretary of the Treasury, introduced the President to an obscure economist from New York State Agricultural College, named George Warren. It was on Warren's much disputed advice that Roosevelt set out to raise prices and relieve the acute farm distress through a steady process of devaluing the currency.

Starting at the end of October 1933, the United States government began to raise prices by buying gold in the domestic market; in other words, by paying American gold producers progressively more paper dollars for every new ounce of gold. Every morning, beginning on 25 October, Morgenthau, Warren and Jesse Jones, Chief of the Reconstruction Finance Corporation, met in the President's bedroom to set the price of gold for the day on a schedule calculated to raise the prices of wheat, corn and cotton to pre-fixed targets. The gold buying was purposely erratic so as to confuse speculators. One day

Top left: Hjalmar Horace Greeley Schacht, President of the Reichsbank, 1924–30, and Hitler's Finance Minister, 1933–37. A self-proclaimed financial genius, his flamboyant, original approach constantly confounded the sceptics

Top right: Emile Moreau, Governor of the Bank of France, 1922–28. His attitude to Norman combined suspicion, admiration and envy

Left: Benjamin Strong, Governor of the Federal Reserve Bank of New York, 1920–28. Unshakably orthodox, he felt the appeal of a system which was proof against political meddling

Harry Dexter White (*left*) with Keynes at the inaugural meeting of the IMF and World Bank, Savannah, Georgia, shortly before Keynes's death. In one negotiator's opinion, the happiest moment in Harry White's life was when he could call Keynes 'Maynard'

Roosevelt suggested a rise of 21 cents in the government's offering gold price. 'It's a lucky number,' he laughed, 'three times seven.' Morgenthau was deeply shocked at such frivolity. 'If anybody ever knew how we really set the gold price, through lucky numbers, etc.' he recorded in his diary, 'I think they would be frightened.'[26]

At first the London and Paris price of gold followed Roosevelt's new prices upwards. But as it became apparent that all United States government buying was restricted to domestic gold, the United States gold price became higher than that abroad: the dollar was becoming more devalued at home than it was abroad. If this continued, domestic trade might start to recover, but the balance of payments would be worse than before. So in November 1933 the government began reluctantly to buy gold on foreign markets as well as at home. By January 1934 the United States government had pushed the world gold price up to $35 an ounce. Here, having reached Warren's pre-fixed commodity price targets and devaluing the dollar by almost 40 per cent in the process, they stopped. The official monetary price of gold has stayed there ever since.

THE LIMITS OF MONETARY MANAGEMENT

But like Newton's gold parity of 1717, the new gold parity of the dollar proved a failure in terms of its initial objectives. Monetary measures were insufficient to restart the stalled American economic machine. For, as Keynes was busy explaining to the world in the mid-1930's, instead of having reached the bottom of another trade cycle from which the enlivening nudge of cheap money, or even inflation of the currency, could help budge it into a new upswing, the American economy—like the British economy in the 1920's—had found a new level which left a large part of the economy's over-expanded productive capacity unused. In such a situation 'easy money' did little harm; but it did precious little good, either. It proved quite incapable of getting things going again.

This new economic malady, which Keynes had recently diagnosed in his *General Theory of Employment, Interest and Money*, and the cure of which he had been preaching since well before he fully understood the disease, required *fiscal* medicine—government spending so as to create a resurgence of demand.* Tinkering with the abundance or scarcity of the money supply by itself was useless under such circumstances, as was demonstrated by the fact that the new American undertaking to buy gold at $35 an ounce failed utterly to give a kick-start to the economy. All it achieved was to make gold dearer to gold buyers everywhere, handing large windfall profits to gloomy hoarders, and creating boom conditions in the gold mining areas of the world.

Nowhere did these boom conditions benefit national policy more than in the Soviet Union which, under Stalin's rule, had recently begun to encourage private enterprise gold prospecting in Siberia, in an effort to stimulate a pattern of development similar to that which followed California's gold rush in the 1850's. For Stalin, curiously, was an avid reader of Bret Harte. Realizing from Harte's writings that the secret of California's success had been the opportunity for the ordinary man to achieve riches, Stalin believed that he could use the lure of gold to counter Japan's threat to Russia's Far Eastern territories, tempting people and industry into development of the Siberian wastes. True the Bolsheviks believed that, as Lenin had predicted, gold would be relegated to the decoration of public lavatories under international communism. But until that day dawned, the metal clearly had its uses in helping balance Soviet trade with the capitalist world.

During the 1930's, therefore, the Soviet government offered up to 30,000 roubles in lump-sum rewards to discoverers of new goldfields. Moreover, still following the trail of Harte's forty-niners, Stalin established special stores in the goldfields, supplied with food, clothes and luxury goods unavailable in other parts of the Soviet Union, but accepting only gold, or gold-backed certificates, in payment. For Stalin, therefore, the new

---

* The fiscal remedies applied successfully in the form of deficit financing by Sweden, Germany and, to a limited extent, the United States during the 1930's are beyond the scope of this book. Many excellent books are available which deal with Keynesian fiscal policies in theory and practice, a recent and most readable one being Michael Stewart's *Keynes and After*, (London, Pelican), 1967.

American gold price of 1934, coupled with the abundant cheap labour resulting from the purges, provided a crucial stimulus to the success of his strategy. Indeed by the mid-30's Soviet gold production had more than doubled to 5 million ounces a year.[27]

By 1939, the new gold price, having the effect of a major gold strike, had increased world gold production by two thirds of the 1933 level, but it had done nothing to bring back prosperity. During the 30's, Britain, with her imperially protected balance of payments, built up a vastly larger gold reserve than she had ever had before in return for investments in South Africa. France, however, continued to lose gold, her deficits enlarging yearly as Frenchmen moved their money out of Paris, away from the reach of the neighbouring Fascist dictators whose rise to power they had done so much to foster. Thus, the bulk of new gold production went to America which, while the safest haven for capital, had ceased lending abroad. By the outbreak of World War II, America's monetary gold stock stood at close to $17 billion, of which $10 billion was foreign-owned.

The American government was forced to protect the dollar from an embarrassment of gold. Much of this vast influx was transferred from the Federal Reserve to the Treasury for 'sterilization' (*i.e.* severance from influence on the money supply) deep in the earth of the Kentucky countryside in the vaults of the specially built Fort Knox.

By sterilizing gold in Fort Knox, the United States had removed the world one step further away from gold as the basic standard of value. After the miseries and sufferings which a return to its rule had caused, this metallic symbol of economic insecurity—of greed, apprehension and fear—was ostracized and hidden underground by the nation which only recently had been its staunchest ally. But the aftermath of its rule—national barriers erected against the free flow of goods, services, savings and ideas—remained everywhere, a legacy of the fetishistic symbol that had gone to earth.

During the 19th century the middle class's political preponderance had assured support for the gold standard. But between the wars the domestic political balance throughout the Western World had changed. Labour, organized to resist the gold standard's 'adjustment process' of wage cuts and unemployment, was tilting the political scales against gold.

Gold's failure as a money standard had brought nationalism to the aid of welfare. 1931 saw the catharsis of the political drama—an attempt to return to the monetary system suited to the balanced Victorian world of free international movement of goods and money foiled by the facts of post-war life. For the post-war world was not in balance. Wide disparities in national price levels and a hopelessly lopsided pattern of debt and of the distribution of gold necessary for its settlement had replaced Victorian equilibrium with chronic imbalance.

Montagu Norman's limitation had been that he failed to understand that such lopsidedness was quite beyond the power of the gold standard mechanism to correct. In Victoria's time the burden of unemployment or wage reductions, which the 'corrective' mechanism of deflation called upon the working class to bear, was always temporary and never excessive. The free flow of savings across national borders had lightened the yoke of gold. But the Great War's aftermath, the one-way street of indebtedness and the pile-up of gold in America, introduced a totally new degree of economic strain. Expectations of welfare had increased just as the gold standard adjustment mechanism was to call for a hitherto unheard-of working class sacrifice.

The alternative to lower standards of living in the debtor nations was to borrow abroad. This was the underlying motivation behind the scramble for foreign capital after the war. It put power into the hands of the country in a position to lend. It was what encouraged France to use her golden bullets against political targets. Meanwhile, in circular fashion, the banner of full employment, symbol of working class refusal to bear the brunt of 'fundamental adjustments' with a lower living standard, was the stimulus behind economic nationalism. The worker's spanner had jammed the golden works.

5

Tales from Bretton Woods

1. THE POLITICS OF WARTIME HOUSEKEEPING

Before Keynes, war redistributed wealth to the rich. Governments borrowed at the sky-high prices of wartime inflation: taxpayers repaid the lenders during post-war deflation in money worth more than when it was lent. Keynesian ideas enabled the profits of World War II to be more democratically spread.

The World War II belligerents faced the familiar problem of how to prevent runaway inflation while financing war production. In *How to Pay for the War* Keynes proposed the answer. He did this by applying his antidote for inadequate demand to the opposite situation. During the war there was bound to be an excess of demand over the supply of consumption goods. Full employment increased the *number* of wage packets, so that even with the wartime wage freeze spending power was bound to get ahead of the supply of consumption goods, and was bound therefore to produce steep inflation.

How could such inflation be averted? Heavier taxation was an obvious answer, but this had low limits of political tolerability for wage earners whose pay was already frozen. Another way must be found to 'mop up' consumer demand. Keynes's mop was 'deferred pay'. He proposed to persuade the labour unions to accept in the form of compulsory savings what they would baulk at in the form of taxation. The bait to the unions, and the great advantage of the scheme as far as Keynes was concerned, was that it would gently introduce a major redistribution of wealth. The wage-earning classes, and not the capitalists, would emerge from the war as the main holders of the national debt. Furthermore, if spending power were mopped up by compulsory savings, the need for high wartime interest rates to check inflation would also be removed.

Official absorption of the rudiments of Keynes's thinking

during the 1930's paved the way for wartime acceptance of his
'new economics'. Both British and American governments,
blenching as much at Draconian wartime taxation as they did
at the inequities of major inflation, turned to Keynesian solutions. Keynes's contribution to distributing the burden of
Britain's World War II sacrifices is impressive: in 1945 Britain's
National Debt was three times that of 1919, but because the
need to check inflation with high interest rates had been removed, the total interest burden was only about 50 per cent
higher. Had Keynes's 'deferred payment' proposals (adopted in
Britain under the name 'Post-war Credits') been more exten-
sively used, the diffusion of wealth in the post-war years would
have been far greater. In the event, however, the British
Government relied much more upon full-scale control of consumption by rationing, a more orthodox alternative, than on
Keynes's proposals.

Americans rightly question the extent of Keynes's influence
on the New Deal policies of the 1930's; but they adopted
Keynes's views on war financing, wholesale. However, the
abundance of America's resources enabled Secretary Morgenthau to persuade President Roosevelt to keep war saving voluntary; as he put it, ' . . . the hard way . . . the democratic way'.[1]
Nevertheless, the funnelling of potentially inflationary spending
power by 'voluntary' subscription straight from the payroll into
$2\frac{1}{2}$ per cent War Bonds enabled the American people to finance
their own and their allies' war efforts with an unprecedentedly
low burden of interest charges.

On the continent of Europe the Axis Powers also went to
great lengths to curb wartime inflation in the Third Reich's
newly won Empire. Driven by a desire to build a stable foundation for Germany's thousand-year rule, Hitler was determined
to hold back the immense inflationary pressures of the Axis war
effort. The *Führer*'s dread of wartime inflation and the dangers
of another money-inspired upheaval sprang from vivid personal
experience. His demagogery during the *putsch* of 1923 had relied
heavily upon the disastrous social consequences of the hyper-
inflation, then at its height. The rigour with which currency
inflation was opposed by the Nazis is illustrated by Economics
Minister Funk's reaction to Himmler's plan for counterfeiting

Bank of England notes, so as to cause chaos in the British economy. After the initial scheme had been abandoned—largely through fear of retaliation in kind—Funk refused to allow Himmler's Secret Service even to use the counterfeit notes in Paris, Athens and elsewhere to pay for intelligence operations for fear that the fake money would upset the currencies he was trying to stabilize.[2]

Until the Nazi march of conquest was halted in 1943, Hitler's minions succeeded remarkably well in their efforts at currency stability in the conquered nations, considering the pressures and difficulties which they faced. Had the Allies been prepared to apply German experience with occupation currencies and controls (Allied intelligence had laid all the necessary information before the wartime planners) some of the chaotic and ruinous inflation arising from the Allies' use of occupation currencies in the war theatre might have been prevented. But study of enemy monetary practices was unthinkable at the time. It would have required a recognition that the Allies and the Germans had at last some objectives in common—an outlook utterly alien to the mood of the hour. Instead, in the euphoria of Allied advance all enemy experience was utterly ignored. Not till they faced the task of reconstructing Europe in 1947 did the Allies come to recognize that 'the viciousness of Allied wartime financial practices in Europe left the Germans far behind'.[3]

KEYNES GOES TO WAR

While the outcome of the Battle of Britain hung in the balance in the autumn skies of Southern England, the British Treasury was 'scraping the barrel' to finance desperately needed supplies from overseas. British gold and dollar reserves had all but run out. Fighting alone, and in desperate need of reinforcements, the British had no means of payment in sight. Britain's portfolio of investments in America was of considerable value, as Americans were well aware; but their sale *en bloc* on the New York market would have toppled their price and reduced this vital reserve to a fraction of its potential. Careful selling of these British securities therefore yielded only a monthly trickle of dollars, while encouraging many Americans to believe that the

British were unwilling to liquidate their assets, preferring to
make a poor mouth in the hope of direct American aid. In fact,
though, by the end of 1940 with no financial relief in sight and
even the scrapings removed from the barrel, the British were
ordering tanks and aeroplanes for which they could not pay,
hiding the bareness of the cupboard from British eyes and
relying on the United States War Department and Treasury
to do the same with Congress. Responding to the British predicament with vision and daring, War Department officials
ordered supplies far above their immediate needs so that the
British could buy the excess output and thus save the time and
capital expenditure needed for the construction of new factories. At the same time, Morgenthau at the Treasury was
assuring the American press that he was not concerned at the
colossal British munitions orders because 'the British have
plenty of money'.[4]

Meanwhile, in Whitehall, senior Treasury mandarin Sir
Richard Hopkins, a hard-line fiscal and monetary conservative
who had duelled with Keynes in hearings of the Macmillan
Committee on Finance and Industry in the dark days of 1929,*
had succumbed before the fertile flow of ideas and proposals
that poured from the Bursar of King's College, Cambridge. He
offered Keynes, who remained an unpaid outsider throughout
the war, a room in the Treasury close to Lord Catto. (The two,
whose monetary philosophies were poles apart, inevitably became known as Catto and Doggo.[5]) A year later Keynes was
elected to the Court of Directors of the Bank of England.
Orthodoxy, as he remarked at his inauguration, kept catching
up with him.

Almost at once Keynes's influence was felt on every major
question of financial policy. Inevitably it also extended into the
more strictly political realm. In a full-scale propaganda campaign, Hitler was offering the peoples of Europe a future of un-
dreamed prosperity and security under Funk's New Economic
Order. This the British Ministry of Information proposed to
discredit by contrasting the New Order's authoritarian implications with the solid advantages of private enterprise and the
gold standard. Keynes was not slow to point out that such a

* A 'drawn battle' according to the referee, Lord Macmillan.

riposte invited disaster. Reminders of the heavy unemployment and hardship of the regime of gold might well encourage soldiers and civilians to give Funk's New Order a try. Searching, therefore, for a more positive line, Keynes began drafting ideas for a broadcast which would expose the fraudulence of Funk's promises, and show how his New Order, based on the dominance of the mark and the exploitation of slave economies, would simply extend the Schachtian feudal system to continent-wide dimensions. At the same time Keynes proposed to offer Europe an alternative order: like Sir William Beveridge, who was busy drawing up the blueprint of a post-war welfare state, he realized that British soldiers would not beat the Germans fighting for a return to the dole and the breadline.*

Ironically, however, Keynes's preoccupation with full employment after the war led him to propose an economic order similar in principle to Funk's. Britain's and Germany's economic policies in the 1930's had, after all, much in common. The Schachtian system had produced full employment under Hitler: Britain had Chamberlain's Imperial Preference. Now, therefore, in response to Funk's mark-dominated offering, Keynes proposed a system based upon sterling and on the wide resources of the British Commonwealth and Empire which, he stressed, would in future be opened to Europe.

Keynes showed his war aims draft to Roosevelt on a visit in May 1941. But though Roosevelt was enthusiastic over the principle of a war objective, he was guarded over Keynes's suggestions. The President felt that economic war aims ought to be world-wide in scope and their promulgation should be given the force of a joint Anglo-American declaration.

Three months later, from Placentia Bay, Newfoundland, the historic Atlantic Charter communiqué was issued. But in framing this first great testament to Allied solidarity, a deep-rooted

* There was widespread fear in British official circles as the Germans moved from victory to victory in North Africa, and the British sustained staggering reverses in the Far East, that the British soldier's traditional will to fight had vanished. It was a fear that Churchill himself seems to have harboured, and which caused him to attach crucial significance to the publication of the Beveridge Report as stimulus to working class morale, both military and civilian. (See Harold Nicolson, *Diaries*, Vol. 2, pp. 210–211.)

clash between American and British economic interests became
apparent, a discordant counterpoint in the otherwise har-
monious fugue of wartime co-operation. In Washington, Keynes
had remarked to his American colleagues that after the war,
unless a great Anglo-American effort was made to restore
balance in international trade and payments, Britain would be
forced to 'employ all the weapons of Dr. Schacht' in order to
prevent cataclysmic lowering of her standard of living. State
Department officials had recoiled in horror. Secretary of State
Cordell Hull in particular believed that just such measures of
economic nationalism had been the principal cause of both
world wars. Firmly convinced that 'if goods can't cross borders,
soldiers will', Hull at once insisted that a clause making American aid supplies dependent upon Britain's post-war elimination
of 'discrimination' (Imperial Preference) be written into the
Lend–Lease Agreement then being negotiated. This was the
famous 'consideration': the price that Britain must pay for
wartime help.

Preoccupied with the basic issue of survival, and desperate
for the succour that Lend–Lease would bring, the British
attached little significance at the time to a generalized undertaking regarding the post-war settlement. But Keynes was outraged at 'the lunatic proposals of Mr. Hull'.[6] He knew that if
Britain was to put her house in order and make good the staggering losses of war without the benefit of her protective Empire
trading system, either her living standards must be drastically
reduced, perhaps by a politically intolerable amount, or open
access must be available to large and generous sources of outside help. It was, therefore, toward arrangements for some such
support, not only for Britain, but for much of the rest of the
world as well, that Keynes turned his mind on his return to
England in the summer of 1941.

2. THE UNTAKEN TIDE

Long before their entry into World War II, Americans had
made up their minds not to repeat the mistakes of World War
I. American planners for the post-war period were determined
this time to help create and participate in a universal organ-

ization.* Inter-war experience had grimly underlined the economic basis of political troubles. American planning for the post-war period, therefore, placed overwhelming emphasis on economic, financial and monetary solutions. If these could be made to work, it was believed, political difficulties would wither away.

It was against this background that United States Treasury specialists set out to prepare plans for post-war prosperity. Secretary Morgenthau, who had presided over the Treasury since 1934, and his New Deal subordinates, approached this task with particular enthusiasm. They shared the belief common among New Dealers, though still, however, foreign to most quarters of American business, that governments had an important responsibility for promoting economic prosperity. In the 1930's their efforts had been confined to the domestic scene. Now they were prepared to apply the principles of the Keynesian 'New Economics' to promoting international prosperity. To these liberal Treasury planners, the wild currency fluctuations, speculative capital movements and bank failures of the 20's and 30's had discredited private finance as the balance wheel of the international monetary system. They believed that government control of financial policy was essential if high employment and economic welfare were to be maintained. Morgenthau was explicit about what this would mean in practice:

> His overriding objective was, in his own words, 'to move the financial centre of the world from London and Wall Street to the United States Treasury, and to create a new concept between nations in international finance'. He wanted 'new institutions which would be instrumentalities of sovereign governments, and not of private financial interests', in short, 'To drive . . . the usurious money lenders from the temples of international finance'.[7]

Such international financial control was to be only part of the broader economic picture. American planners believed that after the war peace would be best assured by freeing trade.

---

* A corps of United States experts under Dr. Leo Pasvolsky began drawing up blueprints for the post-war world in the autumn of 1939.

They were convinced that the monetary chaos of the 20's had not only discredited private finance, but had caused the depression. Worse than that, the resulting strict exchange controls and discrimination of the 30's had become weapons of military aggression in the hands of the Nazis.

Secretary of State Hull's planners, preoccupied more with trade regulations than money and realizing that America's industrial advantage might be progressively offset if American products were debarred from foreign markets, were insistent that *all* discrimination be abolished. This was not a difficult proposition to promote in the United States. The wicked colonial exploitation of the British was taught in every American class room—a cornerstone of national folklore. The Ottawa Agreements of 1932, coming at the bottom of the Great Depression when American producers were desperate for foreign markets, had particularly incensed American exporters. It was not surprising, therefore, that the State Department campaign against trade discrimination focused with particular intensity on the preferential practices of the British Empire.

From early on in the war, State Department spokesmen began to insist that the only possible basis for a lasting peace was 'the natural right of all peoples to equal economic enjoyment', and the ending of national monopolies over generally needed natural resources and raw materials. Britain's wartime predicament provided the ideal opportunity to strike a bargain. The bargain had been the 'consideration'. But in negotiating the final version of the Lend–Lease Treaty late in 1941, the British had gained an important American concession. In the 1930's Europe had suffered immense economic hardships, and indeed been forced into discriminatory and protective measures partly as a result of the American slump. Britain's undertakings to end discrimination, her negotiators insisted, must be matched by American undertakings to promote 'the expansion . . . of production, employment and the exchange and consumption of goods'.[8]

To 'interventionist' New Dealers who had spent the 1930's trying to overcome the 'sit tight and ride out the storm' philosophy of the Republicans, such an undertaking presented no great difficulty. Nor did this international undertaking stick in the throat of a predominantly Democratic Congress. Indeed it would have appeared intolerably negative to refuse to give general assurances of international co-operation toward world economic expansion when so much was at stake.

KEYNES PROPOSES HIS SUPERBANK

Britain was going to face appalling balance of payments problems if she emerged victorious. She would have little gold, a greatly reduced income from foreign investments, and her industry's foreign earning power would be terribly reduced by the damage and distortion of war. If 'protective bloc' policies were now to be abandoned, it was absolutely essential that a substantial source of outside help be arranged. Keynes had already laid great stress on Britain's anticipated post-war readjustment difficulties. In June 1942 he produced his solution. A plan for a post-war monetary arrangement which would stimulate international economic expansion, while enabling the war-damaged economies to end discrimination, and embrace the open 'multilateral' system on which the Americans were so insistent.

The Keynes Plan was not simply a modification of previous practices. It was a wholesale alternative to previous monetary systems; a means to 'obtain the advantages without the disadvantages of an international gold currency'.

Keynes proposed to do this through creation of an international organization which he called a Clearing Union. It would operate between nations very much as a cheque clearing house operates among banks, a place where cheques and bills drawn on various banks are swapped, the balances only being paid in cash. Surpluses and deficits in the balance of payments of member countries would be reflected as credits or debits on the books of the Union, expressed as bancor ('bank gold'), an international money with a fixed gold value. Each national currency would be stabilized (but alterable) in price relative to bancor. Under Keynes's scheme, member nations of the Clearing Union would agree to accept bancor instead of pounds or dollars or gold in settlement of international imbalances with one another. But when deficit countries had used up their bancor balances, an overdraft at the Clearing Union, which could if necessary grow to the full extent of the credit balances of the creditor countries, would be *automatically* available. Thus bancor would be *created* by the Clearing Union, to match the gold and foreign exchange surpluses deposited with the Union by creditor countries. At the inauguration of the Union, member countries would receive a quota based upon their share of world trade immediately prior to the war.

But the most ingenious and controversial aspect of the scheme was the mechanism that Keynes proposed for discouraging nations from allowing their international trade from getting into imbalance. Variations in a nation's balance from its original quota (increases as well as decreases) would be subject to a penalty (an interest charge) payable to the Clearing Union. In the case of a creditor, the interest charge would increase with the size of his credit balance: in the case of a debtor, when his negative balance passed a certain point, pledges of collateral, that is, gold, national currencies or bonds, would be required.

Keynes's plan represented the logical culmination of his monetary thinking. Boldly internationalist and designed to cope with long-term future expansion of the world economy, it was nevertheless aimed at coping with the tremendous imbalances and need for basic adjustment that would afflict all war theatre countries immediately after the war. The gold standard system which Keynes had spilt so much ink attacking in the 1920's had deprived governments of control over their domestic price level. Gold shortage (caused by the lopsided distribution that resulted from World War I) had caused all countries to protect what reserves they had by maintaining a surplus in their balance of payments. The result had been a spread of deflationary forces for the purpose of creating an external surplus: high interest rates, falling prices and incomes, business slump and mass unemployment. The Clearing Union was designed to reverse this monetary tendency, to apply an expansionist rather than a contractionist pressure to world trade.

As Keynes had envisaged the scheme, the total overdraft available to the United Nations and their dependencies was about $26 billion, a sum large enough, he believed, to ensure that countries would not have to abandon policies of domestic expansion for the sake of correcting temporary payments deficits. The stability of currency values, so necessary to a flourishing international trade, would thus be preserved without the uncertainties over the production and distribution of international reserves which were the drawback of a return to gold.

WHITE PROPOSES HIS FUND

While British government departments and the Cabinet were working on the Keynes scheme, United States Treasury officials were also developing a plan. Back in 1934 the distinguished Chicago economist, Jacob Viner, had picked from the academic world several young economists to work for the United States government. One of these, Harry Dexter White, had exhibited such outstanding ability in applying the complex nuances of monetary theory to everyday practice that by the mid-1930's he had achieved an influence on United States Treasury policy no less pervasive than that of Keynes's in wartime Whitehall. While Keynes's plan was gradually emerging as the British negotiating position, White was developing a plan which, on a more modest scale, and with a more limited and conventional set of objectives, had many similarities to the Keynes proposal. With the same objective of enabling exchange rates to be kept fixed without throwing all the burdens of price level adjustment directly onto national economies, White proposed a Stabilization Fund, which would hold $5 billion in gold and national currencies paid in by members on a quota basis. White's Fund would, he believed, enable all nations to abandon restrictive controls on foreign exchange transactions,* and would thus satisfy the American determination to put postwar economic relationships on a 'universal' and 'multilateral' basis. As he originally conceived it, White's Fund would also have created an international unit of account, the unitas. But the unitas was to have a very limited role; it would not in any way be used as actual money; furthermore, it was not really international. The unitas simply represented the gold equivalent of $10 at the current United States price of $35 an ounce.

* Some having to do with capital transfers were exempted.

It could not, like Keynes's bancor, be used as a medium of exchange between nations, but was really a counting house convenience, a piece of international window dressing thinly disguising the American Treasury's determination that the basic world currency should be the United States dollar.

White's Fund would make short-term credits to national members who were in balance of payments difficulties, giving them time to adjust their out-of-line price levels without having to protect their reserves with deflation or devaluation. But the $5 billion with which White proposed to do this was a sufficiently small sum to ensure that in practice the major part of price level adjustments would have to be made by the traditional method of deflation. White's brain-child did, however, provide machinery whereby countries with a surplus could lend to those in deficit (the Fund was empowered to buy and sell gold and its own bonds so as to acquire national currencies for the purposes of lending), but there was nothing automatic about these arrangements. And as the control of the Fund was to be based by weighted voting upon subscriptions to the Fund, this in effect meant that the United States (clearly the only important surplus country in the post-war period) could control Fund lending at its discretion. If the United States chose to restrict this lending—this would clearly be at least partly a political decision—the pre-war deflationary pressure on the world economy could continue, with the creditor nation(s) able to hold back debtors by making it difficult for them to pay their debts.

This first version of White's plan did, however, contain a provision which might have gone some way toward liberalizing international debt settlement. An international bank with a member-subscribed capital of $10 billion would lend to countries both for reconstruction and development after the war, and also help finance member countries' payments deficits in time of depression.

The White Plan thus covered most of the ground of the Keynes Plan using two institutions instead of one, and leaving a great deal more power in the hands of the national governments of creditor countries—in practice, the United States. But the crucial difference between the two plans was not so much

The Federal Reserve Bank of New York which handles foreign exchange dealings on behalf of the United States government

The New York Federal Reserve Bank's gold vaults are the world's largest store of monetary gold. Here about $14 billion in gold bars is kept, most of it 'under earmark' for foreign central banks, the BIS and the IMF

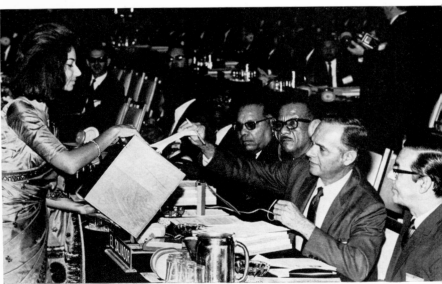

The dollar's defenders of the '60s: William McChesney Martin (*left*), Chairman of the Federal Reserve Board, 1953–70, and President Johnson's Secretary of the Treasury, Henry Fowler

The dollar's defenders of the '70s? National governors of the IMF voting on 29 September 1969 to approve the creation of Special Drawing Rights or 'paper gold' one of method as of scale. White's political judgement made him believe that the financing for anything more than minor international adjustments must be provided bilaterally; that the United States must allow only its own hands on its purse strings. Keynes, whose longer range vision foresaw the dangers of a repetition of the inter-war era under bilateral financing arrangements, argued for a more magnanimous settlement, one that would minimize any one nation's monetary hegemony.

3. THE WARTIME FINANCIAL SUMMIT

In September 1943 British Minister of State Richard Law led a mission, that included Keynes, to Washington to negotiate an Anglo-American monetary agreement, a blueprint that could be offered to the victorious United Nations and the world at large. Here was a unique opportunity for bold solutions to age-old problems. The barriers of prejudice and interest were down. The blast of war had swept away old suspicions among Allies, making common sacrifice to the furthest extent of their capacity for a common cause. If this tide of co-operation were taken at the flood it could, in Keynes's mind, and the minds of many who thought like him, lead on to undreamed-of fortune. But if it were allowed to run out, who knew what terrible future circumstances would be necessary to compel its return?

Armed with the bold vision of Keynes's plan, the hopes of the British negotiators were high when they reached Washington. But the mood of the capital had changed radically since the days of Placentia Bay and the signing of Lend–Lease. A Congressional election had occurred; the Democrats had lost many seats to conservative Republicans who at once formed a powerful coalition with reactionary Southern Democrats. New Dealers in the government were acutely aware of the shift to the right in legislative power. Some of the more unrepentant liberals were being ousted from the administration by leaders from the ranks of finance and industry. The liberals of the Treasury were losing ground to the diehards of Wall Street.

The Keynes scheme made the United States potentially liable for about $23 billion of the possible total $26 billion of international overdraft. But on arrival the British were told that any plan that would commit America to a contribution of more than $2–3 billion was, in the present atmosphere, politically impossible. Furthermore, it was explained that Congress, jealous of its exclusive constitutional authority to authorize Federal expenditures, would never agree to Keynes's concept of automatic overdrafts. Keynes's whole 'Clearing Union' concept was thus killed at one blow. But that was not all. For as the British and American negotiators settled down to hammering out a joint position, successive drafts of the White Plan, which became the basis for negotiation, were constantly trimmed, not to meet British and European needs for liberal treatment in the post-war period, but to gain acceptance in Congress.

The negotiations were not devoid of drama. The topics were technical and complex, but those taking part were well aware of what was at stake. The future lives and opportunity for fulfilment of much of the world's population would be greatly affected by the outcome of these talks. Indeed if the inter-war experience was anything to go by, and the United States State Department firmly believed that it was, the issue of future war and peace might very well depend on the grasping of this opportunity. This sense of drama was heightened by the fact that the two principal individuals negotiating the settlement were not professional diplomats representing familiar political interests, but academic economists whose life's thought and philosophy were bound up in the plans that each had conceived.

KEYNES AND WHITE: JOUST OF THE CHAMPIONS

Though both were sensitive, even arrogant, men, in manner and appearance, the contrast between Keynes and White was complete. White was small, of Russian Jewish parentage, an ambitious middle-class boy who had made good. Prodigiously energetic, hard driving to the point of ruthlessness, he could be rude and truculent in debate, caring little or nothing for the form and appearance of things. His intimates have confirmed that White had long secretly worshipped Keynes. The wielder of a pen which turned with equal elegance and facility to devastating polemic or close-knit logical argument had fired

White's mind and emotions from his student days. In one negotiator's opinion, the happiest moment in the life of Harry
White came when he could call Keynes 'Maynard'. But White's
satisfaction at sitting down to negotiate with his hero was tempered with wariness manifested at times in hostility and defen-
siveness. Sometimes when Keynes would draw him to the edge
of his intellectual depth, White would flash back with bitter
sarcasm—once referring to Keynes with mock obeisance as
'Your Royal Highness'—or would sharply remind the Master
which of them mustered the bigger battalions. Yet the two
worked well together. For Keynes, whose utterly individual
negotiating style blended biting sallies with disarming in-
timacies, knew well that White was a valuable ally, a staunch
internationalist and a Keynesian to boot.

No thumbnail sketch could hope to indicate the extraordinarily diverse talents, or the subtle, complex personality of
Keynes. The product of an assured upper middle-class academic background, Keynes's soft-spoken gentle manner con-
veyed the supreme self-assurance that must go with 'a theoretical training and practical experience unmatched by any other
living economist'.[9] He displayed extraordinary range and
balance both between his fields of interest and within them. He
had undertaken Treasury assignments at the highest level in
two world wars (deputizing for the Chancellor of the Exchequer on the Supreme Economic Council at Versailles in
1919). Between the wars, as Bursar of King's College, Cambridge, he had used his economic insight to increase the college
endowments ten times over, while, from his bedside telephone
each morning before rising, he had built a large personal fortune. The repeated fulfilment of his economic prophesies had
finally brought the establishment to his door: he had been made
Chairman of the National Mutual Life Insurance Company as
well as a Director of the Bank of England. His *General Theory of
Employment, Interest and Money*, which some had ranked in influence and originality along with Darwin's *Origin of Species* and
Marx's *Das Kapital*, had already gained widespread recognition
outside purely economic circles. An early collector of modern
art, Keynes had also built a notable book and manuscript collection which included the finest private collection of Newton's

writings in the world. Married to Diaghilev's leading ballerina, and a luminary of the Bloomsbury Set, his memory is recalled by colleagues and contemporaries most often for his *joi de vivre* and ebullient wit.

But this extraordinary mind was powerless against the conservatism of Congress. The 'compromise' which came out of the Anglo-American negotiations as *A Joint Statement by Experts on the Establishment of an International Monetary Fund* leant far to meet the suspicion and isolationism of the American legislature. A few important concessions were, however, won by the British. Keynes succeeded in insisting that, even though all drawings could not be automatic as under his own scheme, the Fund should be kept from being too 'grandmotherly', and that a substantial part of a country's quota should be available to it automatically, without 'policing or unforeseen obstacles'.[10]

Deprived of his scheme for liberal overdraft facilities, Keynes shifted ground on the question of the power to devalue rather than to deflate in order to correct a chronic imbalance in a country's payments. In his original scheme, as in White's, the consent of the Fund (a majority of the nations represented) would be necessary for exchange variations of 5 per cent or more. In the *Joint Statement*, however, the Fund could not object to *any* alteration in the exchange rate provided that it was shown by the country concerned as 'being necessary to correct a fundamental disequilibrium'. Nor could the Fund object to a change of exchange rate on the grounds of the 'domestic, social or political policies of the member proposing the change'. This was a victory of a sort for the British, but this retention of full national control over exchange rates, made essential as far as Keynes was concerned by the refusal of the Americans to allow the Fund more resources for the cushioning of national economies, went far toward putting the monetary order back to pre-war national autarchy.

When Keynes's Clearing Union was abandoned, all restraint on the action of creditor countries had been removed. However, the *Joint Statement* did include one clause which represented an important concession by America, the principal potential creditor to the post-war world. This was the so-called 'scarce currency' clause, which accepted the principle of at least *some* degree of responsibility of creditor countries for the maintenance of payments equilibrium. Under the 'scarce currency' provision it was possible that if, for example, the United States was running a large and steady balance of payments surplus after the war, paying out so few dollars that they became in short international supply, some discrimination would be permitted against dollars in exchange transactions. The clause was thus aimed at discouraging the Americans from continuing to pile up reserves and encouraging them instead to help other countries to get back into balance.

Throughout the negotiations in Washington, Keynes was acutely aware that Britain had already undertaken to abandon all trade discrimination after the war, and he had emphasized all along that such an undertaking could only be carried out if large-scale outside financial help was forthcoming. But no such large-scale financial assistance was mentioned in the *Joint Proposal* placed before the representatives of 44 nations convened in the summer of 1944 at Bretton Woods, New Hampshire, to hammer out articles of agreement for the Fund.

In the early stages of the Keynes–White negotiations, the British had expressed little or no interest in White's proposal for a World Bank. Under the Keynes Plan such an institution was unnecessary. Furthermore, the British feared that their share in a reconstruction and development bank's capital would make then a net *lender* rather than a borrower, and hence make the bank a burden rather than support to the British taxpayer. When, however, it became obvious that the American contribution to the Fund would be little more than $3 billion (in the end it came out at $3·175 billion), British interest in the bank as a potential source of post-war reconstruction financing was rapidly restored. But the United States Congress, suspicious of the international goings-on up in New Hampshire, put its foot down here too, with Congressmen intimating that they would not agree to an initial capitalization of more than $2 billion for the bank (a mere 20 per cent of the $10 billion authorized capital). So it turned out that the world entered the difficult and anxious period of post-war adjustment and transition with its brave new monetary order drastically cut down by the suspicions and doubts of American conservatism.

At the Bretton Woods Conference itself, apart from politicking over the size of national quotas for the World Bank and IMF, very little of importance was contributed. In mid-1944 the Allies still presented a solid front against the Axis, with the Russian delegation active participants at the Conference. The Soviets had wanted a large IMF quota ($1·2 billion) though they refused steadfastly to offer more than $900 million for the Bank. But at the final plenary meeting, amid wild cheering and applause, the Russians had upped their stake to the full $1·2 billion. A new day really seemed to be dawning: not only the Americans but the Russians as well seemed finally to be accepting the international view.

The achievement of getting 44 nations embracing the opposite poles of political ideology together to hammer out a new world monetary order was certainly impressive. The spirit of Bretton Woods seemed to give real grounds for hope; but the Fund had a pathetically small 'kitty' in relation to adjustment tasks at hand, while the Bank idea had also been hobbled by inadequate capital. Indeed, the yawning gap between these institutions' objectives and their substance was so curtailed by the forces of conservatism as to invite dangerous delusion.

6

Forging Fetters for the Future

Returning ill and exhausted to England after the Anglo-American negotiations, Keynes had a great deal of reassuring to do. Throughout the 1930's he had been an advocate of tariff protection; he had favoured the system of flexible exchange rates just as he had been a champion of cheap money and domestic expansion. Now he came home to a country apparently more in need of protection than ever before with a package designed to hasten free and unrestricted trade. In the House of Lords, in May 1944, he faced the protectionists head on. He asked them to trust him not to have turned his back on all that he had fought for. The new monetary blueprint, he declared, far from being a return to gold, was 'the exact opposite of it'.[1] The International Monetary Fund was not allowed to criticize British domestic policy; the British quota of its resources was available automatically for use as and when required. Britain would be surrendering nothing vital to the ordering of her domestic affairs; she need not be afraid of being prevented from meeting her international liabilities by causes outside her own control.

This Fund that Keynes was describing sounded very different from the one that the United States Treasury was busy selling to Congress. Between the first publication of the Keynes and White plans in April 1943 and Roosevelt's forwarding of the Bretton Woods Articles of Agreement to Congress two years later, American conservatives had plenty of time to muster their opposition to monetary internationalism. The opposition that emerged made strange bedfellows. Ignoring their monetary quarrels of more than half a century, Eastern bankers joined hands with mid-Western isolationists. From Ohio, Senator Taft caused acute embarrassment to White, who was testifying for the Treasury, when he recalled Keynes's remark to the House of Lords that the Fund in no way inhibited British

"It can't be ours! It's got golden hair!"

initiative to take what monetary steps she pleased. Participating in the Fund under such conditions, he objected, would be pouring money down a [nowadays familiar] rathole. Utah's Senator Thomas (the same worthy, it should be noted, who had proposed the amendment to the 1933 Agricultural Adjustment Act empowering Roosevelt to devalue the dollar and issue un-backed paper money) brandished a fistful of foreign banknotes during a Senate debate and challenged any fellow legislator to 'go down into Washington and get his shoes shined with this whole bunch of bills'.[2]

In a more sophisticated vein, the banking community objected to 'handing over to an international body the power to determine the destination, time and use of our money'. Randolph Burgess, as President of the American Bankers' Association, spoke for Wall Street against the Scarce Currency Clause calling it 'an abomination of the wicked' which put 'the whole burden of responsibility on the creditor'.[3]

1. CONGRESSIONAL POLITICS AND THE IMF

Ever since White had started to make radical concessions to protect his brain child, it was becoming increasingly clear that the United States Treasury was being caught in a pincer. For, by the Bretton Woods Conference, the Treasury's proposals had been so trimmed to get them through Congress as to render them incapable of the job for which they were designed.

Speaking as a representative of the opposition to the Treasury's monetary universalism, Professor John H. Williams of Harvard, a Vice-President of the New York Federal Reserve Bank, hammered this point home. He told Senators that after the war most countries would, under the Bretton Woods provisions, need to apply exchange controls to balance their payments anyway. These controls would remove the need for drawings on the Fund; indeed they would divert the Fund's resources from their intended use—currency stabilization—to use for national development and reconstruction; purposes for which they were neither intended nor adequate. Professor Williams and his supporters, who included among them the American Bankers' Association and most of Wall Street, were therefore in favour either of dropping the Fund or delaying setting it up until the major reconstruction problems were solved.

Wall Street's counter-proposal to the Treasury's universalism ran, predictably enough, along traditional nationalist lines. In counter-attack to Morgenthau's threat to move the centre of monetary power from London and Wall Street to Washington, Wall Street proposed to help the pound back onto its throne, but this time as junior partner to the dollar, to return, in fact, to a reshuffled version of the arrangement established by Norman and Strong. Accordingly they proposed that a large loan or grant should be made to meet the transitional needs of the British, so as to restore the pound to its key role as a reserve currency.

Morgenthau, however, stood firmly behind White, refusing to compromise the Treasury's insistence on universalism. In his planning, White, largely out of an antipathy for 'British imperialism', had completely ignored the special financial role of Britain in the world economy. Nor had Keynes, whose political sympathies were far closer to those of the liberal United States Treasury than to Wall Street or the City of London, and whose primary concern was to protect levels of welfare and conditions of economic expansion, been primarily concerned with sterling's return to gold convertibility. Thus the arguments of the bankers were met by continued Treasury insistence that establishment of the Fund was crucial to restoring balance and prosperity to the world economy. As one pro-Fund senator put it, ' . . . the time to stabilize economic conditions is when they need stabilizing . . . '[4]

In the event, however, passage through Congress of the Fund and Bank was won not by Treasury arguments, but by the overwhelming sentiment of the hour. Debate on the Fund coincided with victory in Europe. America's signature on the United Nations Charter was not yet dry. Riding this general atmosphere that a new age could be dawning, Administration witnesses reminded senators that history would be harsh on those who failed to learn the lesson of refusal to join the League of Nations. The feeling that Congress must 'take a chance', that it could not let pass this unique opportunity to institutionalize world monetary stability was widespread. It divided even diehard Republican conservatives against themselves. In the event the issue of the Fund's and Bank's passage was never in doubt.

THE RETURN OF REACTION

The passage of the International Monetary Fund and the World Bank through Congress lulled British opinion into a false belief that American monetary enlightenment augured well for post-war assistance. In this atmosphere of comfortable expectation, the American announcement, immediately following victory in the Pacific, that Lend–Lease aid was suspended and that all new supplies as well as what was in the pipeline would have to be paid for with cash, came like a thunderclap. Worse was to follow. For Keynes, hurrying back to Washington to negotiate a now desperately needed American loan, was met with formidable American conditions. Something had clearly happened to American sentiment since Congress set its seal of approval on the Bretton Woods agreements.

In fact, even as the terms of the Bretton Woods agreements were being thrashed out, a subtle change had been occurring in the power-balance among American policy-makers. With Fascist Germany facing defeat and Stalin beginning to reveal his intentions for Eastern Europe, disagreement arose over how to treat the defeated enemy. Morgenthau at the Treasury was suspicious that the British and many conservative Americans would press for a 'soft' peace and rapid German reconstruction as a buffer against the Soviets. Himself a Jew of German antecedents, Morgenthau was acutely alive to the dangers of resurgent German aggression. Reacting violently against the idea of German industrial reconstruction, Morgenthau went all out to press his plan for Germany's 'pastoralization'. His sentiments were echoed by many New Deal Treasury liberals. They appealed especially to Jews like White who felt more confidence in dealing with Russian socialism than with resurgent German industrial capitalism.

For a moment, at the Quebec Conference of 1944, Morgenthau appeared to have persuaded Roosevelt to accept his plan for Germany, while Churchill, until Lord Cherwell arrived on the scene and dissuaded him, was enthused over the idea. Indeed it appears to have been he who coined the word 'pastoralization' to describe the policy.[5] But the tide of feeling was turning. Apart from revulsion at the totality of the Morgenthau solution, sceptics already realized that such a plan would play directly into Russian hands. For by mid-1945 it was becoming apparent that the Russians were conducting their own 'pastoralization' in the sector of Germany which they occupied: stripping the country of any plant and equipment that they could dislodge under the excuse of reparations, and leaving a destitute population to turn in despair to communism.

By the end of 1946, after 18 months of devastating inaction by the veto-blocked Allied Control Council at Potsdam, Secretary of State Byrnes had abandoned all hope of 'Big Three' co-operation, whose net achievement had been, in his words, 'the needless aggravation of economic distress'. Meanwhile Churchill, borrowing, ironically, a phrase with which Joseph Goebbels had attacked the Russian sphere of influence to which the British leader had agreed at Yalta, was speaking of an iron curtain descending across Europe.

Already by the end of 1945 the chill of cold war was beginning to grip Washington. Morgenthau, on being refused leave by Truman to go to Potsdam, where he hoped he could exert a hard-line influence on arrangements for post-war Germany, had resigned from the government. His replacement by Fred Vinson, a monetary conservative, a trusty of Truman's and one of a group of Southern Democrats from the House of Representatives whose influence had been growing in Washington since the war, was a sign of the times. It was the end of the road for liberals like White who had recently been advocating a $10 billion Russian loan.

At once 'revelations' as to communist sympathies in the Treasury began to emerge from an empire-building FBI. The accusations of Whittaker Chambers and Elizabeth Bentley, a self-confessed communist courier, against many senior government officials brought a series of Congressional committee hearings that were precursors of the McCarthy era. Harry Dexter White was one among a number of Treasury officials accused. White had opposed unconditional gold shipments to Chiang Kai-shek's Nationalist Chinese during their struggle with the People's Army (though his opposition was shared by others such as the Allied Commander in China, General Stilwell, and the President's personal ambassador General Patrick Hurley).[6] He had worked on the Morgenthau Plan, though Morgenthau's diaries reveal that White had nothing to do with its authorship, and while agreeing with it in general was opposed to the closing down of the Ruhr coal and steel facilities.*

* For a collection of the supposedly incriminating evidence of White's role in American foreign policy decision-making, see material prepared for United States Senate's Judiciary Subcommittee To Investigate The Administration of the Internal Security Act and Other Internal Security Laws, entitled *Morgenthau Diaries (China)*, Vols. I and II, 5 February 1965,

Finally he had authored the Fund and Bank proposals. All these activities were linked with testimony of Elizabeth Bentley to suggest that White, during the entire war, was acting under Russian communist orders. White, who since 1946 had suffered from a severe heart condition, died during a great public scandal after hearings before the House Un-American Activities Committee in 1948. Some opponents have claimed that his death was due to an overdose of sleeping pills, but in fact he hastened his end by chopping wood in his garden, against his doctor's orders.

The full, tangled, story behind the branding of the author of the American plan for international monetary co-operation as a subversive foreign agent has not yet been told, and indeed may never be known. At any rate the details of this wholesale assault upon Treasury policy-makers still remains buried in bureaucratic hearts and files. It was a time of titanic battles between government agencies, including the Treasury, over security and intelligence empires, a time in which individuals became pawns in sweeping power plays.

But whatever the true origins of the accusations, this assault upon the Treasury won the heartiest commendation of Wall Street and conservatives in Congress. To them it symbolized the final rout of the 'pinko' New Dealers. To the rest of the financial world, however, it indicated something more—the triumph of monetary conservatism, just as liberal internationalism had at last seemed victorious. Despite Bretton Woods, financial power would not, as Morgenthau had planned, move to the United States Treasury. It would stay in the hallowed ground of Wall Street and the 'square mile' of the City of London.

As hot war gave way to cold, renewed emphasis on continuing Anglo-American co-operation was mirrored in the politics of the monetary settlement. Universalist solutions at once began to look uncertain, if not downright suspect. The Anglo-American alliance, on the other hand, tested in the fire of battle, had been found true. Surely this was a sounder basis for

---

and *Morgenthau Diaries (Germany)*, Vols. I and II, 20 November 1967, by Anthony Kebak, Chairman of the History Department, University of Dallas.

a post-war monetary order than the elusive, perhaps illusory, potentials of multilateralism?

Such American thinking met with an eager response from government and financial circles in London. Realizing the primacy of the need for continued American support, the Labour Party, still with no practical guidance from its ideology as to monetary policy, was glad to accept any support that could be raised to back the pound. From the City of London itself, the response was positively enthusiastic. It was no secret that the majority of Keynes's fellow directors at the Bank of England had always been extremely cool to his ideas, none more so than the ailing but unrepentant Norman who, with his orthodox teeth drawn, had soldiered on as Governor until the beginning of 1944. Indeed, since the time that it had become apparent that the Americans were not prepared to part with the massive sums called for in the Keynes Plan, official enthusiasm for the Keynes scheme back in London had evaporated with curious abruptness. At the same time, rumblings from among exponents of trade discrimination and bilateralism were becoming audible from off-stage both left and right.

2. COULD BEGGARS BE CHOOSERS?

When the terms on which America would lend to Britain became clear in the summer of 1946 these murmurs rose in deafening crescendo. Keynes had not been exaggerating when he warned that Britain's post-war financial position would be desperate. During the war, apart from vital supplies from America, Britain had relied heavily upon the Commonwealth and other countries which sold vast quantities of supplies and services to Britain against credit in pounds. Thus it was that the London sterling deposits of the Dominions, colonies and other sterling users which in 1941 had stood at £1·3 billion ($5·5 billion) had risen to almost £3·4 billion ($14 billion) by the end of the war.

Over the settlement of these debts, British honour and British interest became curiously entangled. British spending, especially in India and Egypt had taken place during, indeed had helped to cause, large-scale local inflation. At the end of the war,

Egypt, for example, whose prices had roughly quadrupled during British wartime occupation, held balances in London which represented approximately four times the purchasing power in British sterling than Britain had spent in Cairo. The enormous sterling debts, which have hung like a millstone round Britain's neck ever since World War II, were thus haphazardly and inequitably incurred as part of the effort to beat Hitler.

Shortly before he died, Roosevelt had laid down the principle of 'equality of sacrifice' in payment for the war: no nation was to grow rich through the war effort of its allies. Why, then, did Britain at the end of the war not simply scale down these balances to take account of equality of war effort, or at least offset the extra burden placed on London by wartime inflation so that Britain could move less critically encumbered into the post-war era?

The answer lies somewhere between the unavoidable encumbrance of imperial responsibilities and the structure of an economy that had developed as an integral part of that Empire. In the first place, Britain's stake in winning the war was incomparably greater than most of its creditors. Eire had remained neutral; the Egyptians were unsure which side they would have preferred to see as victors (many claimed they would have preferred Nazi domination); India had been brought into the war not by a popularly elected Parliament, but by the British Raj. Britain had therefore promised during the emergency to honour sterling debts in full, as any alternative would have risked defection by peoples whose support Britain could not afford to lose. After the war, with Britain involved in carrying through the ticklish business of a peaceful handover of power in India it was hard for the British Treasury to argue that on the basis of equality of sacrifice it should wipe out its sterling obligations to countries that were infinitely poorer than Britain. Furthermore, the Bank of England, against stiff opposition from Keynes, took the view that the war-built balances were solemn bankers' obligations on which future British credit depended. Finally the Board of Trade, anxious that Britain should lose no opportunity to encourage customers for industrial goods to buy in Britain rather than elsewhere, argued that the sterling balances would encourage the continuance of traditional patterns of trade.

During the loan negotiations the Americans proposed that Britain's sterling indebtedness be taken into account in deciding the scale and terms of assistance that Britain would need. In fact, they were only willing to proceed with the negotiations on the understanding that 'the bulk of the $14 billion frozen sterling assets be written off'.[7] Keynes, forbidden while negotiating to make any specific commitment on treatment of the sterling balances in the Financial Agreement and infuriated at the Bank of England's unreasoned long-range dictation of his actions, fired off one of his sharpest cables:

WE ARE NEGOTIATING IN WASHINGTON, REPEAT WASHINGTON. FIG LEAVES THAT PASS MUSTER WITH OLD LADIES IN THREAD-NEEDLE STREET WITHER IN A HARSHER CLIMATE.[8]

But to no avail. The loan agreement was signed by the Americans on the general understanding that the British war debt to the sterling area would be scaled down by about a third and the remainder funded over a long period (i.e., turned into fixed-term interest-bearing obligations, like the National Debt)—conditions which the British government was neither able nor willing to fulfil. The British government's decision to be chooser as well as beggar was dictated by what was believed to be political necessity. But it undercut Britain's capacity to fulfil the terms of the American Loan.

Since Morgenthau's departure from the Treasury the monetary views of the American banking community were back in the ascendant. Professor Williams's views on the need to return to the gold-exchange standard gradually became official American policy. Top monetary priority was therefore accorded to the earliest possible return of the pound to full convertibility, so that it could stand, twin pillar with the dollar, in support of an open world trading system. Britain had obtained the American loan ($3.75 billion, at 2 per cent*) on the understanding that sterling would become gold or dollar convertible within one

* The terms were more generous than this in fact, as there was an escape clause, waiving re-payment instalments in years of balance of payments difficulty.

year. This, together with a promise to end the preference system and to negotiate an open system for world trade, was the final settlement of the 'consideration' for American aid. It was the realization on the part of the Americans that total sterling debts vastly exceeded British gold and dollar reserves that prompted them to ease the purse strings for a substantial loan, which they believed would bolster British reserves sufficiently to enable the City to climb back onto the old stand of 'business as usual'.

THE PROPHET IS NOT WITHOUT HONOUR . . .

But was the loan adequate to do the job? Keynes had asked for $6 billion, and had been offered less than four. Britain as a result was forced to agree to a return to the gold-exchange standard without the reserves necessary to keep her there. On his return from Washington, weak from gruelling negotiations during which he had suffered a serious heart attack, Keynes faced a host of hostile critics of the final settlement. Feeling ran high in many quarters, and of enthusiasm for the agreement there was almost none.

The government supported the multilateral objectives of the settlement, believing that the major boost that it provided to Britain's reserves would serve to shield the working population when trade and exchange controls were ended. Meanwhile they relied upon the Bank of England to negotiate arrangements with members of the sterling family that would prevent a flight from the pound when it became convertible.

But the debate in Parliament prior to ratification of a package which included both Bretton Woods and the American Loan showed the general anger at what *The Economist* described as 'discovery that our reward for losing a quarter of our national wealth in the common cause is to pay tribute for half a century to those who have been enriched by the war'. It also demonstrated that the public and many politicians remained unaware of the seriousness of the country's financial position.

On the right, the heirs of the Empire Free Traders were outraged at the settlement. To Robert Boothby it was 'an economic Munich'. Meanwhile for the left, an equally incensed

Jenny Lee called the terms so 'niggardly, barbaric and ante-
diluvian' that they raised doubt that an administration capable
of offering them would be capable of solving the unemployment
problem in their own country, much less helping the world.
The right saw the settlement as a threat to domestic industry
and its imperial markets. In the eyes of the left it menaced full
employment and the welfare state. It was hardly surprising that
intellectual leaders of the left, like G. D. H. Cole and E. H.
Carr, should attack the Americans for using British economic
difficulties arising out of the war as an opportunity to prevent
the Labour government from putting its socialist principles
into practice.

In the face of this intense opposition, the government's case
was set forth in weak and negative fashion. Full employment
and domestic expansion would not be hampered by multilateralism, they assured their critics; and even if they were,
what was the alternative? Britain was in no position to refuse
the American terms. Not a word was mentioned about American offers to help negotiate a scaling down of the sterling
balances, or the dependence of convertibility's success on
Britain's getting agreement from the sterling family to do so.

Keynes alone in the debate was able to recapture the vision
of free-flowing multilateral trade on which Britain's prosperity
had been traditionally based. Summoning up his remaining
strength to defend the loan in the House of Lords, Keynes
spoke of a determination to make trade truly international as
'the world's best hope, an Anglo-American understanding
which brings us and others together in international institutions which may be in the long run steps to something more
comprehensive'. And he closed by begging 'those who look
askance at these plans to ponder deeply and responsibly where
they think they want to go'.[9]

DOLLARS DOWN THE DRAIN

Keynes had raised the crucial question: where did Britain want
to go? The British government, more realistic perhaps than the
American who believed that an orderly return to *laissez faire*
both at home and abroad was perfectly feasible, utterly lacked

the broad view of objectives necessary for a coherent policy. From their handling of sterling it was clear that the government's outlook was heavily influenced by the Bank of England which, since its nationalization in 1946, had, ironically, gained more real influence than at any time since the 1920's. Behind the Bank, the City, determined to return to its old splendour, still pressed for policies that would enable Britain to remain banker to the rest of the world, even though her financial grip was based not on trading strength or reserves, but on financial obligations to a disenchanted sterling area. Thus, despite the bold adventure of the Keynes Plan, the monetary thinking of both Whitehall and Threadneedle Street in 1946 showed a pre-1931, or even pre-1914, mentality.

Just how rocky were the foundations for such attitudes and just how little confidence the post-war world had in sterling was shown when the Labour government honoured its convertibility undertaking a year later in 1947. Following Parliament's ratification of the United States loan agreement in December 1946, the Bank of England had begun hurriedly to renegotiate the closed-circuit monetary arrangements that it had developed with the sterling area during the war.

Now for the first time since the war, earners of sterling were to be allowed (though only to the extent that they needed to for current purchase of non-sterling goods) to transfer their pounds into dollars. Agreements along these lines had been signed with 18 countries by 15 July 1947, when the fatal convertibility date came round.

The attempt at convertibility was doomed to ignominious failure. Britain was quite unable to provide the goods that the sterling area countries desperately needed, and could well afford if they could convert their sterling deposits. A fantastic hunger for dollars with which to buy freely available American products was waiting to be met. British industry was only just beginning to recover from the war, and it was far from clear whether British export capacity still justified the current $4.03 exchange rate.

The fixed date of convertibility loaded the dice still more heavily against the success of the experiment. The obvious weakness of the British position made sterling a target for speculators, and as if this was not enough, many of Britain's creditors, knowing the size of the American credit to Britain, decided to break their 'gentleman's agreement' not to convert into dollars more sterling than they currently needed and began to convert pounds so as to take what they considered their fair share of the American credit.

Inevitably then, as soon as convertibility was announced, a desperate run began out of sterling. Between 15 July and 20 August, when this limited convertibility was abruptly suspended, the Bank of England lost about $1 billion in gold and dollar reserves. In one year the entire American credit was gone, and Britain was forced to return to her complex cocoon of bilateral controls.

The trauma of that one month of convertibility made a deep impression not only upon the British who had lost so much of the American Loan by fulfilling the conditions on which it was made, but on other European countries. It was regarded as a lesson and a warning. In the coming years it did much to stiffen resistance to American pleas for the abandonment of exchange controls and the launching of national currencies unprotected onto the uncertain waves of the monetary ocean.

FACING THE MORTGAGED FUTURE

With their backs to the wall in 1941, the British had agreed to abandon the protectionist policies of the 1930's in the *hope* of a world monetary order. Amid the adrenalin of conflict, Britain's leaders had ignored the hard political realities of money, swallowing whole the lucid, idealistic logic of the Keynes Plan. The seductive notes of the Pied Piper brought them out in search of an internationalist fairyland. The Piper had persuaded them that they could achieve an international monetary system which would provide sufficient liquidity to help nations who, like themselves, faced appalling balance of payments difficulties in the future. The Piper's flute sang sweetly of a monetary order remote from the old problems of the gold standard, with its alternatives of grinding deflation or disruptive devaluations and controls.

Then, suddenly, the Piper was gone. Worn out by his wartime exertions, Keynes had died on Easter Day 1946. The dream had vanished inside the mountain. The advantages of bilateral co-operation with the United States now seemed overwhelming, the alternatives bleak. Besides, the requirement that sterling should play a special role together with the dollar in the post-war monetary settlement seemed to many appropriate and natural. Few stopped at the time to consider the wisdom of committing Britain, already bowed with debts, to a monetary role which would gravely restrict her freedom of economic manœuvre. Leadership in world finance was considered in the nature of a British duty—a responsibility from which she would not shrink. Britain had fought to preserve her greatness and together with America she had won. It was hard to understand that Britain's capacity to wield world power had been a casualty of the war.

Stemming from this error was another which for long went unrecognized. By refusing to shrug off her imperial war debts Britain had voluntarily shouldered world responsibility. But the conditions on which she held this responsibility were in fact dictated to her. They were dictated by the United States on the basis of the quite reasonable and unsentimental American interest in opening up Europe, the Commonwealth and the world to American goods and capital.

All that the Americans demanded of sterling and of British trade policy could not be met on time. In the event, Britain refused to be forced into measures which might jeopardize her economic viability for the sake of American free trading aspirations. Sterling did not return to convertibility until eleven years after the abortive attempt of 1947. Protectionist measures, though modified, continued despite the existence of the 'consideration'.

Nevertheless, Britain had allowed her hands to be tied. The demands of a welfare economy and the drain of overseas defence spending were to prove heavy burdens on her post-war economy. To sustain them, what was necessary above all was freedom of economic manœuvre, but the international commitments of sterling put Britain in a vice.

ATLANTIC POLITICS AND GOLD

7

Onto the Dollar Standard

1. TO THE BRINK AND BACK

In the Spring of 1944 British and American planners were still nursing the illusion of Allied solidarity that lingered after the Big Three's Teheran Conference of the previous November. Unity was above all essential while enemy resistance continued. But as the Allies faced the prospect of occupying a conquered Germany, political divisions over post-war objectives rapidly surfaced. Perhaps the first real issue of cold war politics was over currency.

MORGENTHAU'S REVENGE

As political authority collapsed before the advancing armies, so the authority behind the German currency broke down and, to Americans at least, the idea of paying troops in banknotes bearing the insignia of the Third Reich was politically repugnant. On Germany's division into four occupied zones, the military governments had seized control of all banks, sequestering currency, gold and balances against Allied occupation expenses. Yet the victorious armies needed a locally acceptable currency with which to procure provisions and pay the troops. The easiest and most effective way to achieve this, while ensuring that all occupation costs be borne by the Germans, was to enforce the acceptance of an Allied currency.

The Soviets were prepared to accept a single Allied military currency for Germany provided that they had complete control of its supply in the Eastern sector, a condition which sparked furious argument among American officials who, by April 1944, had prepared engraved plates for the printing of Allied Military (AM) marks. Should the Russians be given a duplicate set of plates, as they demanded? The alternative, threatened by Molotov, was that they would produce their own currency, thus breaking the appearance of political solidarity considered so vital in the West. Morgenthau's Treasury, filled with men like Harry Dexter White, who in their implacable hatred of Nazism tended both emotionally and rationally to be pro-Soviet, proposed to hand over the duplicate currency plates. More conservative and cautious souls in the State Department and elsewhere were strongly of the opinion that the Russians should only be offered 'unlimited' currency to be provided by the United States, so that an eventual check could be placed upon their monetary activities.

Morgenthau, on his own initiative and without consulting either American colleagues* or the British, sent off the duplicate plates. They arrived in Moscow, together with formulae, inks and other materials, in April 1944, so that by the time that the Red Army entered Czechoslovakia and Germany they were spreading AM marks 'like falling leaves, all over the country. Their troops were paid salary accumulations of up to six years in these marks and Russian purchasing missions with satchels of these bills, roamed the country buying anything saleable'.[1] A month later, Eisenhower was reporting to the War Department that 'the Russians distribute AM marks to their troops in any quantities they request . . . by handful with [their] rations'.[2] Soon the tide of American-supplied, Soviet-printed currency, indistinguishable from the other allies' AM marks,† was flowing westwards to the American Zone and Western Sector of Berlin, buying great quantities of black market American PX supplies, and being converted on a substantial scale into dollars through the medium of United States finance offices.[3]

As part of the Russians' systematic campaign to destroy the socio-economic structure of Eastern Europe‡ and reduce their

* It is not known whether or not he obtained verbal permission from the President for this move, but it seems likely that he did not. (See Vladimir Petrov, *Money and Conquest*, pp. 129–30, especially footnotes.)

† At first the Russian marks *were* distinguishable (by a dash before their serial numbers) but when worried American officials pressed for greater identification of the different zones' currencies (all the Western allies' currencies were printed in the United States), the Treasury responded by putting a dash in front of *all* serial numbers.

‡ Soviet-induced inflation in Eastern Europe, prior to absorbing it into the rouble bloc and sealing it from the West, was particularly drastic in

standard of living to something below that of the Soviet Union, the Soviet-induced inflation in East Germany was far less successful than elsewhere because the Westward flow of the notes to buy plentiful American black market supplies preserved a much higher value for the AM mark than would otherwise have been the case.

That the Soviet policy of economic prostration should be checked through Russian access to American supplies and even dollars, was not the intention of the United States Treasury which, by dint of the Morgenthau team's vengeful determination, dominated United States foreign policy toward Germany between the war's end and mid-1947. Morgenthau and White had one aim—to reduce Germany, if not to a pastoral state, then at least to economic desolation and chaos. Inflation was to be their chief weapon. The strategy was set forth in a directive of the Joint Chiefs of Staff[4] which was basically a Treasury-prepared document. By forbidding the American Army to maintain price, wage or market controls, this directive literally, as one State Department official put it, decreed economic chaos, forbidding any steps 'designed to maintain, strengthen or operate the German financial structure' except in the interests of the occupying power.

But by the autumn of 1946, in a mood of revulsion from the disastrous results of the 'Morgenthau Boys' '* policy, the Western Allies were planning a monetary reform for Germany. Europe's plight had deteriorated to the point where post-war hopes were drowning in despair. Desperate for the goods and materials needed to begin reconstructing its ruined economies, Europe was so short of the means of payment that her imports were declining to a trickle. Private capital estimated at $600 million left the continent and a similar sum left London in 1947

Albania and Bulgaria, but reached its peak in Hungary in punishment for remaining loyal to the Axis until the end. Here the inflation even exceeded the extremes of Germany's hyper-inflation of 1923, with hundred quintillion (100,000,000,000,000,000,000) *pengo* notes issued.

* This was the term given to the network of Treasury officials working within the United States occupation forces, who, under the leadership of Bernard Bernstein, supervised the execution of the Treasury's nihilistic policies.

alone. Apart from this flight of capital, \$7·8 billion for debt repayments and gold subscriptions required to found the IMF and to finance a vast trade deficit had raised the regions' payments deficit to a staggering \$9 billions for the year. A vicious circle of despair was developing. Communist cells thrived on the destitution of a starving continent, and declining capitalist confidence in Europe's future moved communist takeover from the realm of possibility to that of potentially self-fulfilling prophecy. Besides, the need to feed starving Germans, helpless beneath the deliberate economic dislocations of the Cominform and the United States Treasury, was costing the Western Allies almost \$600 million of the \$1 billion a year distributed by UNRRA, the Relief and Rehabilitation Agency of whose resources America contributed almost 70 per cent.

But Anglo-American plans for a re-founded Deutschmark, mooted in early 1947, met with implacable opposition from the Soviets, who saw the reform as undermining their planned chaos and laying the basis for German capitalism's *revanche*. In fact, it was the currency issue that catalysed a showdown on the question of joint Allied control. Finally Western determination to press ahead with a German currency reform, 'Operation Bird-Dog', as it was known, triggered the split over Germany and precipitated the Berlin Blockade.

MARSHALL AID AND MONETARY FRUSTRATION

Such was the situation of sudden cold war confrontation when Secretary of State George Marshall addressed the American Congress in July 1947. Congress had grown cold to the language of international brotherhood in the face of Soviet hostility. Now it had to be galvanized into yet another turnabout of sentiment. But this time the legislators were asked to embrace a much more limited international objective: co-operation with European capitalism against the chaos on which communism fed. For the second time in two years Congress was reminded of the lessons of the World War I financial settlement. But this time it was asked to agree to peacetime aid on a totally unprecedented scale—and not as a loan, but as a free gift.

The response was immediate and positive. A strong pragmatic sense of necessity became manifest with a remarkable upsurge of that uniquely American blend of optimism and generosity. Congressional conservatives who had curbed the objectives of the White Plan now responded dramatically to the danger that threatened Europe.

It was ironic that after all the hard-nosed attitudes that had greeted Keynes and White, Congress should feel itself obliged to come to the aid of America's allies on so vast a financial scale: doubly ironic that Americans should feel it necessary to bail out free enterprise capitalism not just with loans, but with the much-despised 'handout'. Had the Keynes Plan been adopted at Bretton Woods, the value of the $13 billion of goods and services that were given free to Europe under the Marshall Plan would have been credited to the United States 'bancor' account in the Clearing Union. No doubt at the time Americans would have attached little significance to this high pile of paper promises-to-repay. But the $13 billion of 'bancor' credits would have come in extremely handy for the United States in later years. In fact they would have gone far towards preventing the crisis in which the dollar found itself in the 1960's. But in the urgency of the moment, as Senator Vandenburg, the ex-isolationist, was wooing fellow conservatives into the international fold, no one paused to reflect that the Keynes Plan would have solved this ideological paradox. The vision of Keynes was history. Europe was now immersed once again in the darkest depths of pre-war bilateralism in defence of its almost non-existent monetary reserves.

In 1947 the arguments for giving rather than lending the enormous sum of dollars needed seemed weighty. First, such a free gift avoided the specific dangers of restarting the tragic train of consequences which followed insistence on post-World War I reparations and debt repayments. Also, the fact that aid was given rather than lent would safeguard future American exporting to Europe from being inhibited by the Europeans' need to out-export the United States in order to earn the dollars and gold necessary to repay their outstanding debt. Looked at this way, the American taxpayer was being asked to make a $13 billion down-payment so as to protect American exporters, hence taxpayers' jobs, later.

For all the Marshall Plan's boldness of conception and generosity, lack of co-ordination between aid-giving and monetary planning retarded the pace of European recovery. For the monetary system which had emerged from the murk of Bretton Woods had neither the scope nor the resources to ease the painful adjustment period in post-war payments. White's testimony to the contrary notwithstanding, the World Bank and IMF were simply not endowed or equipped to help Europe out of the mire.

In the immediate post-war years, the 'Free World' economies, faced with an acute scarcity of internationally acceptable money for trade and debt settlement, were forced to revert to the monetary stone age. Under strictly enforced controls, an importer was forced to pay the price of his imports to his central bank in his national currency. The importer's central bank would then make the payment to the central bank of the corresponding exporter. But the two banks would only allow the deal to go through if they estimated that they could balance their payments in trade over a given period. This was, of course, a return to barter at the national level. Generally, however, governments did not go quite this far, instead allowing each other narrow 'mutual credit' margins. But after these margins were used up, payments either had to be made in gold (or dollars), or trade had to stop.

By 1948, the shortage of acceptable international cash or 'liquidity' in relation to potential trade had become so serious, and barter, as a result, so widespread, that ludicrously wasteful situations commonly arose. A country in overall trade equilibrium was often unable to pay its creditors because it could not collect from its debtors. It might therefore be compelled to follow the logic of extreme liquidity shortage—to discriminate *against* the suppliers of the goods it most needed and in favour of the purveyors who had the least to offer.

The Benelux countries with their highly interdependent economies were clearly the hardest hit by the liquidity shortage, and were the first to tackle the problem. They formed an agreement between themselves whereby each of them could offset its debts to another with credits from a third. In this they were fully backed by the Americans; for one of the prime targets of Marshall Aid was to end as soon as possible the waste and divisiveness of exchange controls. In fact, Marshall Aid was made conditional upon the recipient granting drawing rights to other aid receivers in his own currency equal to his own Marshall dollar entitlement. This was the way in which Marshall Planners hoped to finance anticipated intra-European deficits. Unfortunately this device of 'conditional' aid dollars backfired in practice in a way which only encouraged further bilateralism.

The problem sprang from the urgency of the European situation which was such that the chief concern of the Marshall administrators was to get their dollars to work as fast as possible. Under such circumstances, recipients knew perfectly well that they would get their dollars even if they deliberately dragged their feet over fulfilling the conditions on which they were given. So a country in surplus with another found little incentive to give a drawing right to its deficit neighbour. If it did so on paper it was not difficult to stymie the drawing right's use by any one of a dozen stratagems such as raising export prices, or slipping in new export controls not covered in the Marshall conditions. The net result of all this was that while the United States could sometimes force a creditor country to give credit to its deficit neighbour, the creditor was then in a strong position to use such credit rights as a powerful bargaining weapon against countries in their debt.

Ironically, the outstanding exponent of this drawing right arm-twisting was Britain, the country that Americans had hoped would, together with the United States, be leading the world back to currency convertibility and open trading. Britain's calculated use of this dollar-fed economic bargaining power was a direct result of her monetary difficulties that followed the Anglo-American settlement. In stripping away such a large slice of Britain's dollar reserves, the convertibility undertaking into which Britain had been forced by that agreement, was now coming home to roost: it was to deny the goal of economic liberalization which remained the cornerstone of American policy. The fiasco of the attempted sterling convertibility in the summer of 1947 had lent new strength to the intransigents of both the left and right in British politics. Right-wingers, pre-occupied with the protection of traditional

markets, and left-wingers, afraid of the dangers of slump and unemployment, now stood shoulder to shoulder against American
pleas for a greater relaxation of trade and monetary controls.

Eventually, however, Marshall dollars, coursing through the
arteries of European commerce, financed the work of reconstruction in sufficient volume to wash away the Anglo-American
financial settlement's legacy of bitterness and mistrust. Between
1947 and 1951 the gross national product (GNP) of the OEEC
countries* increased by better than 25 per cent; gross fixed investment grew by the same amount; industrial output rose by
well over half and exports more than doubled. The clarion call
to workers' revolution was being drowned by the hum of industrial reconstruction. Meanwhile the return of American
GI's to counterpoise the continuing menace of the Red Army
across the border added to the inflow of Marshall dollars, and
helped stoke the fires of returning prosperity.

THE POLITICS OF THE EUROPEAN PAYMENTS UNION

By 1950, the inflow of dollars from America had sufficiently
expanded European monetary reserves to open the door to
region-wide co-operation over international payments. At the
initiative of the Marshall Plan administration, a European
Payments Union (EPU) was established in September of that
year between members of OEEC. The Union was basically a
means of providing incentives, in the form of cushioning
credits, to encourage nations to accept the risks of more liberal
trading arrangements. But it went further than this. Formed in
a genuine spirit of co-operation it provided for a greater
amount of supra-national control and supervision than had
either the Keynes or White plans. It was, in the words of one of
its intellectual parents, 'a remarkably clear and simple document, embodying sweeping and precise commitments of a

* OEEC standing for Organization for European Economic Co-operation
was the membership group (significantly the same group as formed NATO
with the addition of Sweden) of beneficiaries of the Marshall Plan. In 1961,
OEEC, which had expanded and lost its purely European focus, became
transformed into OECD (Organization for Economic Co-operation and
Development). Its headquarters remained however at the Chateau de la
Muette near Paris.

revolutionary nature, which drastically shifted overnight the whole structure of intra-European settlements from a bilateral to a multilateral basis'.[5]

The spirit of EPU was one of 'If we don't hang together, we'll hang separately.' As such it was in marked contrast to the Bretton Woods agreements, cooked up by the two leading financial powers and served as a *fait accompli* to a mass of nations who had no realistic alternative but to swallow them. Another contrast was in content. Bretton Woods had attempted a blueprint for all circumstances and seasons. EPU was designed to bring limited but immediate improvements to a system whose defects were painfully obvious to all concerned. Furthermore, the Union was regarded simply as a temporary mechanism, an interim device to speed countries on the road from total bilateralism to full gold convertibility.

Within the Payments Union, credit margins were made transferable from one country to another: in other words they were multilateralized, so as to avoid the cramping constrictions of bilateral settlements. At first it was suggested that Marshall Aid dollars should be used to settle balances in excess of the previous bilateral credit margins. But with the help of the staff of the IMF, an alternative formula, less totally dependent on the flow of foreign aid, became accepted. Under this system, the new multilateralized intra-European credits would be supplemented with either Marshall Aid dollars, gold, or IMF drawings of nations' currencies in monthly settlements. Multilateralization of payments thus encouraged nations once again to allow their precious gold to flow in international transactions.

Politically this progress towards the assumed objective of full convertibility of currencies into gold, towards, in fact, restoration of the gold-exchange standard, well suited the catholic–capitalist alliance, in the shape of the Christian Democrat parties which were by now in power all over Western Europe. But it was strongly resisted by Britain's Labour government. The Labour government was still licking its wounds from the 1947 convertibility debacle, and the trauma of the inevitable post-war devaluation which came two years later.* It was

* To improve Britain's dollar earning power, Labour devalued the pound from $4.03 to $2.80 in 1949.

determined not to participate in a plan which might, by draining British gold to meet a trade deficit with Europe, upset the fragile monetary structure of the sterling area, a structure upon which, they believed, British full employment and welfare depended. No arrangements, Labour Chancellor Sir Stafford Cripps informed the OEEC Council in February 1950, would be joined by Britain in which countries in surplus could force their deficit trade partners to part with their precious gold and dollar reserves.[6] For was this not the road back to the bad old system under which economically buoyant countries could force their weaker trading partners into deflationary measures by sucking out their monetary reserves?

Curiously enough, Labour were supported in their initial opposition to EPU by a majority opinion in the City of London. To the City, the idea of claims being automatically wiped out in monthly settlements, the balance becoming a claim on (or reduction of debt to) the Union, was a threat to the international role of sterling. They feared that the Payments Union might discourage Britain's creditors who would otherwise have been willing to hold newly acquired sterling balances as an integral part of their monetary reserves from doing so. In other words, the EPU arrangements might have discouraged countries from lending the City the short-term funds which finance Britain's role as world banker.

In the event, concessions were won by the British which made them feel able to join. Surplus countries were to be permitted to switch their EPU claims into sterling. This went far towards mollifying the City. Meanwhile the government's fears for the sterling area reserves were allayed by the concession that European holders of sterling prior to the formation of the Union were to be prevented from cashing in any more of their sterling balances than they needed to in order to cover their net deficits to the Union. But even with these concessions, British agreement to join EPU was only clinched by the implied threat of isolation for Britain if she stayed outside. For the United States agreed to underwrite the Union with or without Britain—with $600 million of European aid funds.

Once British co-operation had been achieved, however, negotiations went forward with speed and smoothness.

Establishment of this Europe-wide agreement at once became a symbol of hope, a symbol of the return from the brink. It also boded well for further Europe-wide co-operation beyond the purely monetary sphere. Such hopes were to be rudely shattered at the political cross-roads of the Treaty of Rome in 1957, which demonstrated Britain's continuing determination to play a wider, extra-European role. But with Marshall Aid dollars flowing in, and exports rising, Europe was at least firmly on the road to physical recovery.

2. SIDLING BACK TO GOLD: THE SACRIFICE AND THE PRIZE

As a venture in international co-operation, the European Payments Union was blessed with extraordinary success. Its automatic provision that, when a nation got into balance of payments trouble, it would get credit to cover at least part of the deficit, added the vital oil of confidence to the rusty wheels of international trade. Five years after having set it up, however, the Union's members were looking forward eagerly to the day when it could be disbanded. Why?

The automatic settlement mechanism, which was the crux of EPU, held, as we saw, little appeal to the City; for it threatened the power and profitability of London as a monetary centre. It also made the central bankers of the continent generally uneasy. This business of automatic credits was all very well while people were getting back on their feet. But it did not accord with the live-within-your-means requirements of sound banking principles and monetary orthodoxy. Even before the Payments Union was established in the autumn of 1950, there was an assumption among central bankers on both sides of the Atlantic that their ultimate monetary objective must be the free convertibility of currencies into gold for the purposes of international transactions. The custodians of money's purchasing power shared the deep conviction that, despite experience in the inter-war period under the gold-exchange standard, the arbitrary and dispassionate rule of gold was always preferable to any situation in which the limitless demands of electorates for public spending could sway the management of money.

Furthermore, apart from encouraging Free Trade, free convertibility of currencies was the only way of engendering sufficient monetary confidence to get private wealth moving internationally in search of the highest rewards—the goal which bankers saw as fundamental to the freeing of markets generally.

Those who, remembering pre-war experience, were alarmed lest capital movements might once again act like a bull in a china shop, toppling the currencies of nations whose governments made owners of capital in some way uncomfortable, were reassured along orthodox lines: if governments manage their money properly, balance their budget, check their public expenditures, 'live within their means', then capital movements, flowing from surplus to deficit countries, will once again, as under the gold standard of the nineteenth century, become the balance-wheel of the payments system.

With conservative administrations now firmly installed not only in Europe, but also in Britain and the United States,* 1953 saw the first real move towards freeing international capital. Authorized banks were permitted once again to conduct arbitrage operations, that is, were allowed to move money between currencies in order to make a profit out of interest-rate differences. This was the first step in a long, gradual progress back to convertibility. As bankers' buying and selling of currencies, at first 'spot', *i.e.* for immediate delivery, then 'forward' for delivery in three months (later extended to six months) became general, the service gradually came to replace the hydraulic compensations previously performed through the official channels of EPU by the central banks. Central banks thus retreated from total control of supply and demand for currencies, to the more limited role of 'support' operations, *i.e.* to entering the market to buy and sell currencies only to the extent necessary to prevent excessive variations in supply and demand.

---

* Christian Democrat governments had come to power first in Belgium, Austria and Italy, later in France and West Germany; meanwhile the Conservatives came to power in England in 1951; the US political drift to the right brought in Eisenhower, surrounded by *laissez-faire* advisers, in 1952.

Such support operations were far from new to central bankers. They had become widespread in the 1930's as a means of stabilizing floating currencies. After coming off gold in 1931, the Bank of England set up a special Exchange Equalization Account into which it deposited its gold and foreign currency reserves. The purpose of the account was to buy and sell foreign currencies so as to keep the pound at the exchange level desired by the government. The Bank achieved considerable success in warding off speculative attacks on sterling by this method: speculators of the early 30's soon learnt to develop a healthy respect for the technical skill and perception of the Old Lady of Threadneedle Street, and, from then to the war, tended to leave her alone.

Gradually, between 1953–58, other parts of the exchange system reverted from automatic EPU procedures to traditional mechanisms. Settlement of monthly EPU accounts, originally 40 per cent in gold and the rest in credit, were progressively stiffened until by July 1955 they were payable 75 per cent in gold, and only 25 per cent in credit.

These moves back to the traditional method of balance of payments adjustment were made possible by one vital factor. Despite the ending of Marshall Aid in 1952, American military spending and civilian investment caused the United States to remain year after year heavily in deficit in its overall balance of payments with Europe. But such was the European thirst for liquidity to finance its growing trade that despite this heavy net outflow of dollars, economists were producing a string of theories to explain why Europe must suffer a permanent dollar shortage—the famous 'dollar gap'.

AMERICA—THE MONETARY AUNT SALLY

Just as generals prefer to fight the previous war, economists tend to solve the last crisis, or even the crisis before that. It must be admitted, however, that the historic persistence of the tendency for America's exports to exceed her imports made the temptation unusually great. In the ten years following World War II, the United States' balance of payments surplus with the rest of the world on merchandise (as opposed to capital) account had reached the astounding total of about $38 billion, an amount considerably larger than the value of the entire world's monetary gold. Contemplating this surplus and looking back to the experience of the inter-war period, when the United States had totted up total current account surpluses of over $17 billion, and scooped in almost $12 billion of the world's gold, European economists (and bankers) found reason to believe that the trend of the inter-war years connected with the post-war experience. So they set out to prove that the United States for some reason always tended to run a massive trade surplus with the rest of the world, thus always tended to starve the rest of the world of dollars and gold.

Theories as to why this should be so differed widely, in fact were sometimes in diametrical conflict. One sought to show that because the United States had more natural wealth in relation to human needs it would always naturally run a surplus in trade with countries where this vital relationship was less favourable. Another tried to demonstrate that American productivity must always grow faster than that of other nations, and that this put the Americans at a permanent trading advantage. A third theory, more political than economic, and based solely on the experience of the 1930's, saw American isolationism and *laissez faire* conservatism as forces that perpetually led it towards deflationary policies accompanied by trade restrictions and protectionism, which in turn led to the contraction of world trade and the spread of deflation.

The substance of these theories, which were all so rapidly proved irrelevant to the situation, is nowadays less important than the motivation behind them. For the tendency of European economists and monetary professionals to blame all monetary problems on America, the universal Aunt Sally, has outlived the arguments themselves.

Ironically, in more recent years, the United States has been blamed for provoking international crisis for the opposite set of reasons. Americans are nowadays blamed for running a perpetual inflation-causing deficit, as a result of their policing of the world and their export of capital supposedly destined for the 'take over' of Europe. Both these dollar outflow-producing factors were operating throughout the 1950's. But in the liquidity shortage of those days, European economists would have preferred the outflow of dollars to be very much larger.

However, just as these earlier complaints over dollar shortage were reaching their height, the monetary seesaw once again began to tip. In a trice, dollar gap had become dollar glut. What was the cause of this sudden transformation? The answer lay in the new trade relationship between Europe and the United States, the inevitable result of European recovery. The fulcrum of the seesaw was the triumphal achievement of gold convertibility by Western Europe.

3. BACK TO THE SEESAW

Over the long Christmas weekend 1958, the monetary wise men of Europe made their offer of gold to any of mankind who happened to own their currencies, provided that such persons did not reside in the offering wise man's country. In monetary language, they made their currencies freely convertible into gold (at parities fixed within a one per cent range either side of par) to all but persons resident in the country of the currency in question. This 'non-resident' convertibility marked the *official* return to a somewhat more restricted version of the gold-exchange standard, though the standard had in fact been increasingly in effect *de facto* throughout most of the 1950's.

What was it that made this long awaited return to official convertibility at last possible? In helping to finance the production of dollar-earning exports, and supplementing the credits of the EPU, America's dollar outflow had enabled European reserves to increase to the point where the last protective barriers could be knocked away from national currency exchanges. Thus, despite the alarms of cold war, flare-ups along ideological frontiers (United States involvement in Korea was a major additional source of dollars for the rest of the world), and a fluctuating East–West balance of nuclear terror, the 1950's were, on the whole, a period of international monetary quiet. True the pound ran into periodic trouble. But its relatively diminishing importance as a reserve currency outside the sterling area proper meant that the successive sterling crises were of a sufficiently modest scale relative to the monetary structure as a whole for the West to bail out the British where necessary, while continuing to reckon their international dealings more and more in dollars. The problems created by the international role of the pound did cause widespread anxiety at moments when sterling's useful function of providing supplementary liquidity seemed in jeopardy. But they were in reality more domestic headaches for Britain than full-scale international concerns. The Free World, with the exception of the slowly dwindling sterling area, was progressively moving onto a dollar standard.

Men were content to hold dollars rather than gold because they believed that the vast gold hoard of Fort Knox made the dollar impregnable. Indeed bankers preferred dollars to the yellow metal. For dollars, like sterling in the 19th century, but unlike any other national currency in the 1950's, were in fact the only vehicle, apart from gold, which could carry capital to any place where it felt sufficiently attracted to venture. And as deposit dollars also earned good rates of interest, who wanted to move their wealth around in the form of costly-to-insure gold?

Yet, the coming of European convertibility in 1958 spelt the doom of unchallenged dollar dominion; the beginning of the end for the post-war monetary Pax Americana. The change in attitude to the dollar began initially for technical rather than political reasons. European convertibility meant that the dollar lost some of its uniqueness, and therefore attractiveness as a reserve. European currencies now were as good as gold to non-residents of their parent country. And as demand for them increased, it naturally eased on dollars. There was another technical change connected with convertibility. The long post-war, and increasingly inflationary, boom in Europe was, by 1958, being checked by high interest rates. These interest rates were being raised just as the United States Federal Reserve Board was coaxing a slumbrous American economy out of the doldrums with cheap money. This interest-rate change, co-inciding with Europe's return to convertibility, reopened the continent to short-term American capital, because European securities were now backed by newly 'safe' (*i.e.* gold-convertible) currencies. Furthermore, these new inducements for short-term capital coincided with the launching (1 January 1959) of the

Common Market, whose promise at once began to lure a new wave of long-term investment from America. These accompaniments of convertibility—the competing attractions of newly convertible currencies, and new enticements to American short- and long-term capital—soon began to play havoc with the already sizeable deficit in the American balance of payments.

But the factor which tipped the scales of 1958, giving the Europeans an invaluable final leg-up onto gold, while causing the first faint tremors in dollar confidence, was a sudden temporary break in the previous pattern of trade. A post-Suez contraction of European demand for United States exports only became reflected in international payments in 1958. This falling away of export orders, the result of a short sharp industrial recession, hit the American balance of payments hard. The resulting American deficit was all the more dramatic because the previous year had been a splendid one for American exporters. At $8·5 billion the United States' 1957 surplus on merchandise account was sufficient, for the first year since the 1940's, to outweigh all American dollar outgoings, and chalk up an overall balance of payments *surplus*. But now, in the following year, with the new European inducements to American capital coming on top of new trade competition from rebuilt European industry, American payments dipped deep into the red, so much so that the American deficit for the last two years of the 1950's came to more than two thirds of the deficit for the rest of the decade.

The fading of the Suez backwash, and a new pickup in American productivity in the early 1960's saw a return to healthy surplus on America's trade account. But this surplus was consistently much more than offset by the new scale of dollar investment outflow. European central bankers now began to get worried. They were holding large quantities of dollars in lieu of gold. Just supposing—the spectre appeared first in 1958—that as a result of Europe's more competitive position and America's enormous fixed commitments to overseas spending the outflowing tide of dollars began to cause an inflationary rise in dollar prices—to cause, that is, an overvaluation of the dollar?

THE PARADOX OF THE DOLLAR STANDARD

Now the great dollar paradox began to emerge. For while the world was beginning to distrust the dollar as a standard of value, it was coming to depend upon it more and more as a convenient means of holding and exchanging wealth. From the end of the 1950's 'Eurodollars', the large dollar balances which had accumulated in the hands of foreign banks and firms, were beginning to be used as a European currency. These Eurodollars are not, as their name suggests, banknotes depicting George Washington disguised as Napoleon. They are simply bank credit of extra-national origin. Originally (that is, in the 50's) this bank credit was almost exclusively of American origin, but gradually, because of the restriction of convertibility to non-residents, foreign held balances have accumulated in other currencies, still out of habit called 'Euro' but actually freely used in Japan, Canada and other major non-European trading countries.

All these Eurocurrencies, but especially Eurodollars, whose total, incredibly, stood at between $33 and $37 billion in mid-1969, became more and more important as a source of liquidity to finance not only international, but also national trade. As such they created an 'unmanaged' money problem that tended to put central bankers somewhat on edge. One aspect of this problem was that re-lending, re-re-lending and sometimes re-re-re-lending of these Euro-deposits, vastly increased the number of dollar (or other currency unit) claims, and hence the total world money supply.

Strangely enough (although perhaps not so surprisingly, when we consider the historic timelag between banking innovations and comprehension of their social and political impact), very few of the operators of the Eurodollar market in the late 1960's seemed to understand its implications or even how Eurodollars came into existence. This after more than a decade of Eurodollars' growth from their accidental origins in the 1950's* to their role in 1970 as a factor of first-class importance

---

* The first Eurodollar deposits were of Communist-earned dollars which Eastern Europe refused to deposit in the United States for ideological reasons.

in the international monetary system. Bankers and financial writers almost always explained Eurodollars' existence as stemming solely from accumulated United States payments deficits resulting from Americans' excess of imports over exports, their foreign investment, or defence spending. Few people stopped to do the simple arithmetic that instantly proved the pool of Eurodollar credit to be vastly bigger than could be accounted for by any conventional definition of a United States payments deficit.

The reason for this was the old bankers' preference for Cloakroom Rule thinking, and their dislike of Banking School-type insistence that private bankers, by lending beyond their deposits, constantly create new money. When a dollar deposit is transferred from a London to a Paris bank, this loan to the Paris bank appears as an *asset* on the London bank's books. This increase in the London bank's total assets enables it (under the old 'fractional reserve' principle, whereby a bank used to issue more banknotes than it had gold) to increase its Eurodollar loans by, say, 90 per cent of the value of the Paris loan, keeping a 10 per cent 'fractional reserve'. Thus the more Eurodollars are lent or re-lent, the more can be created.

The problem of estimating the total size of this credit market readily becomes apparent. So does the concern of central bankers over the ability of this enormous volume of liquidity to splash around the international monetary system, uncontrolled by any international monetary regulation except ultimate drastic unilateral rule-making by the Federal Reserve System in Washington.

Unfortunately, the closer one examines the Eurocurrency phenomenon, the more cause appears for concern. For no-one really knows, in this opaque, not to say murky, jungle-frontier of international finance, what the rules really are or ought to be. The banks that supply the market try to lend their short-term funds on a short-term basis. But nobody knows who the ultimate recipient of re-re-re-lent funds will be or whether money initially lent at short term is not later lent at medium or long-term, as no maturity statistics for the whole market are available. Such a situation, if widespread as it almost certainly is, contains the classic ingredients for an international financial crack-up on a scale which could make 1931 pale in comparison. The Eurodollar credit system is, indeed, exactly analogous to the Americans' domestic financial structure in the 1900's which produced the panic of 1907 and the evolution of a central banking system between then and 1913.

Throughout the 1960's tension was developing between the foreign demand for dollars and concern over what they really represent. The story of that strain became our regular diet of financial headline news. The need for dollars with which to transfer investments and goods tugged insistently against dismay at having to store wealth in a constantly shrinking container. Various stratagems* were adopted to remove some of the strain from the overburdened dollar. Meanwhile within the United States, all-time record high interest rates, a savage tightening of credit, and a 10 per cent tax increase, were imposed to check inflationary erosion and support the dollar's overseas role.

Though slowing the drag on the world's monetary anchor, these economic measures have so far failed to check its drift. For three other factors—massive overseas spending on the Vietnam war, de Gaulle's challenge to American leadership in Europe, and the crumbling of the pound's capacity to continue as the alternative reserve currency—arose to endanger the dollar standard in the mid-1960's.

These are the political factors which have been the initial, if not the fundamental, causes of the dollar crisis of the present time. It is to the interplay of these factors on one another, and on the more fundamental forces that shape monetary attitudes, psychology, and therefore monetary politics, to which the rest of this section is devoted.

* Described below in Chapter 12.

8

The New Monetary Nationalism

1. TWO VIEWS OF ONE MONETARY SYSTEM

If a banker is revealed as a profligate spender, continually living beyond his income, it will not be long before his clients take fright. The proverbial sock or mattress will soon start to look more attractive as a repository for their savings than the vault of his bank. This is the reaction which has increasingly prevailed among foreign owners of sterling in recent years as they have watched the British balance of payments drift along in the red. Meanwhile clients of the senior Anglo-Saxon banker—holders of dollars, that is—have undergone an even more disquieting experience. They have watched the United States not merely stacking up theoretical promises to pay in gold far beyond the point where they could make them good, but they have witnessed the Americans increasing their international overdrafts to buy up their clients' factories and facilities. Both the world's banking nations have thus, under the gold-exchange standard, been accused by their more vehement critics of what, to the financially untutored ear, smacks of something approaching high-level confidence trickery. They seem to be exposed as financial operators who have run themselves colossally into debt, staving off total insolvency by financing their excess foreign spending with other nations' short term loans.*

What is more, their continental critics have claimed that an ugly corollary follows this Anglo-Saxon habit of perpetual profligacy. The constant expansion of foreign-held sterling and

---

* Actually, the constant expansion of foreign-held sterling and dollars has arisen from the willingness of foreigners to accept payment in these two currencies for their exports to the rich and large markets of the United States and Britain, and been permitted to continue by the willingness of these foreign governments to make credits available, particularly to Britain, when these are needed to enable Britain to go on buying more imports than she sells of exports.

dollars, which arises from British and American ability to print the money to settle their foreign debts, is supposed to have enabled the Anglo-Saxons to export the plague of inflation into the economies of their creditors. President de Gaulle was by no means alone in his concern about this automatic exporting of inflation. Many other continental officials, especially German and Dutch, found occasion to wag accusing fingers at the Anglo-Saxons for expecting others to endure the consequences of their over-indulgent domestic and foreign spending.

The Anglo-Saxons, of course, have another perspective. In many ways it is simply the mirror image of the above somewhat exaggerated version of what might be called the 'continental view'. They can claim that the capital markets and international banks of New York and London between them offer intermediary services which other nations have shown themselves either unable or unwilling to develop for themselves. Furthermore, any financial advantages that the Anglo-Saxons may have gleaned from their world banker role have been at least offset by parallel burdens and responsibilities. After all, they point out, a significant part of their overseas balance of payments deficit arises from overseas military spending, notably in Europe itself, which benefits and safeguards not only Anglo-Saxon interests but those of the continentals (inside or outside NATO) as well. Furthermore, some Anglo-Saxon protagonists argue that the responsibility of maintaining a high level of confidence in their currencies has forced the British and American governments to apply the brakes to their economies at extremely awkward moments politically, and often (see chapters 11 and 12) at great social and economic cost.

Much the most important of these services, whose value they never fail to hammer home, is the fact that the Anglo-Saxons' currencies provide the vital oil for the growing world trade machine. New gold production, they point out, is at best an uncertain, and at worst a thoroughly disruptive, source for new international liquidity. Anglo-Saxon deficits, on the other hand, provide a more governable supply of international money. Moreover, if international sterling and dollar obligations expand at the same rate as international trade, they provide an efficient means of international settlement which gets round gold's inevitable deflationary bias. Continentals, for their part, however, have remained sceptical of the value of this monetary arrangement in view of the inflation which they claim that it brings to their economies.

2. INFLATION—COMMUNICABLE DISEASE OR CONGENITAL CONDITION?

Tolerance of, and susceptibility to, inflation is a political preference which varies with the historical experience and structure of each nation. But, in order to decide how far the inflation-exporting criticism of the gold-exchange standard has been valid in itself, and how far it has been a useful means to other diplomatic ends, we must assess to what extent Europe's (and the world's) condition of creeping inflation really has been an Anglo-Saxon export, and to what extent a domestic product.

That all the rich industrial countries of the West have to a greater or less extent experienced a steady creeping inflation since World War II is beyond contention. It is equally clear that this inflation, like every other in history, is ultimately caused by a faster growth in the production of money than in the production of goods and services. At the same time it is true that the United States and Britain, in the course of financing their balances of payments, poured over $12 billion worth of new cash (liquidity) into the international money supply between 1950 and 1968. But here we must guard against that hoary old logical trap which, despite Aristotle's warning, has been catching people ever since. If sitting in a draught gives people colds, and I regularly catch colds, must it be assumed that I make a habit of sitting in a draught? Similarly, if all nations suffer from inflation, and the Anglo-Saxons steadily expand the supply of international money by increasing their foreign debts, are they *necessarily* responsible for the international inflation? Obviously not. In fact it is quite possible that Anglo-Saxon deficits have little or nothing to do with the international inflation.

If we compare the growth of international cash reserves with the growth in international transactions, we find that the expansion of the international money supply, far from being inflationary, has been quite the reverse. Total reserves between 1950 and 1964 grew at an average rate of under 3 per cent a year, while world trade expanded at more than double that rate, or about 7 per cent. This evidence of shortage cannot of itself be taken as conclusive, because it has no satisfactory reference point: it does not take account of the possibility that the reserve/trade ratio of the early 1950's might have been excessive. However, apart from the clear evidence that international liquidity has steadily lagged behind the growth of trade, the changing nature of the world economy has led to a general need for far more liquidity than ever before.*

Today's volume of international trade is far greater relative to domestic commerce than ever before in history. This means that normal year-to-year switches in trade patterns between nations have come to involve very large swings in national trade deficits and surpluses. The reason for today's greater reserve needs is thus not simply the political fact that today's electorates are not prepared to sit down under the Victorian medicine of sharp recession, bankruptcies and high unemployment; it is economic as well. The scale of industry—the capitalization of business—is today so much greater than in Victorian times that an industrialized economy cannot remain viable without a sufficiently sustained demand to pay the immense overhead cost of the capital equipment involved. The prospect of a really serious contraction of demand, and a sudden loss of markets that is anything more than momentary, is therefore intolerable to the entire fabric of modern capitalism. National reaction to this need to maintain demand as a first priority, and therefore to get deeper and stay longer in surplus or deficit, has been the perfectly logical one of aiming to keep larger reserves than formerly.

This factor itself has tended to sterilize a sizeable proportion of the world's monetary gold in national vaults and to create a demand for more. Victorian money managers at the Bank of England, who rarely operated with a gold reserve of more than £35 to £40 million (which represented about 5 per cent of Britain's annual imports in their day) would be scandalized by

* This case is set forth with great force and lucidity by Robert Triffin in *Our International Monetary System: Yesterday, Today and Tomorrow.*

modern statements that gold and dollar reserves of £1,000 million (roughly 12 per cent of annual imports in the 1960's) was grossly inadequate to tide Britain over adverse movements in trade.

At the same time, universal acceptance of high levels of demand and of employment has placed a 'floor' under both profits and employment. And in the absence of price and wage ceilings, this floor has become a spring-board: the sky, for want of any other barrier, being, generally, the wage/price limit. The effectiveness of this spring-board in speeding wages and prices on their upward trajectory has varied from country to country depending upon historical experience and institutional arrangements. The great range of difference that exists between national rates is another factor that increases the need for reserves by the less productive and/or more indulgent.

The argument about the export of inflation is thus one of degree. All nations experience the politico-economic factors that produce irrepressible inflationary pressure.* Some (like the Scandinavians with their relative success with wage and price controls, and the Germans with their inflationary psychosis) have managed to contain them better than others. It may also be asserted, however, that the existence of a widening international payments disequilibrium demonstrates a refusal by some nations to import inflation. If the Anglo-Saxons had really been successful in exporting their inflation, *i.e.* if their balance of payments deficits really passed freely into the money supply of their trade partners, then the classical mechanism would tend to resolve the problem—the deficits of the profligates speeding the general level of inflation of the world economy as a whole.

It is equally valid, therefore, to look at the export of inflation from the opposite point of view, and to identify the trouble as springing from the conservative nations which, for various

---

* The process of economic growth also involves some inter-sectoral shifts of manpower and investment that are inevitably inflationary. For example, the 'service' sector tends to grow much faster than the goods-producing sector after a certain point (hair cuts, medical services, governmental bureaucracy, etc.) and increases in productivity in this sector are difficult both to achieve and to measure.

reasons, have 'sterilized' their accumulating surpluses from their domestic money supply, and, by removing a considerable proportion of international liquidity from circulation, have to some extent sealed off their economies from the political and economic currents that surround them.

THE PROBLEM—TECHNICAL OR POLITICAL?

The arguments pro and con are endemic to the nature of the present monetary system. They have gone on since the end of the 1950's when 'fundamental disequilibrium' caused by different long-term national rates of inflation, productivity growth and spending abroad, began to strain the post-war structure of currency parities.

Prior to that time, the shortage of international liquidity restricted arguments over inflation to purely domestic quarrels. But the liquidity shortage of the continent was ended by the flood of American investment in search of new opportunities in Europe. The number of dollars held in national reserves, which had grown at an average annual rate of $600 million in the 1950's, jumped after 1958 to more than twice that rate as American business jostled to join the Common Market. The corollary of this American investment, as Jean-Jacques Servan-Schreiber pointed out in 1967, was not only stiffened American competition for European business, but the now familiar range of trans-Atlantic threats to European values, and the continent's way of life. The United States' dollar deficit, welcomed when it financed urgently needed American goods, was now attacked as the means of American acquisition. From a channel of aid the dollar had become a vehicle of imperialism, and America the beneficent was now America the beneficiary. It was at this moment that inflation graduated from a domestic embarrassment to an international accusation.

In the 1960's an additional political factor entered the picture. East–West *détente* bolstered European self-confidence and Atlantic strains developed sufficiently to give international monetary discussions a sudden political bite. The Anglo-Saxon 'confidence trick' became the continentals' obvious political pressure point. Such pressure on the system at least produced agreement that the system needed some degree of reform or overhaul. But the two diametrically opposed perspectives, outlined above, made discussion of any fundamental reform a dialogue of the deaf. Technical arguments over solutions to the monetary crisis inevitably became mingled with manœuvrings over the shape of the Atlantic Alliance and of Europe. European diplomatic pressures, seeking to link resistance to the 'American Challenge' with Vietnam, inevitably found expression in a probe for the American Achilles heel, the shortage of American gold in relation to the number of gold-backed dollars held abroad.

By 1967, rising American spending in Vietnam and investment in Europe permitted the diplomatic shoe really to pinch. America was, for the first time, having its hand forced from without. Rapidly the new atmosphere of monetary nationalism became strong. With it rose the spectre of a return to the monetary warfare of the 1920's.

During each of the ensuing monetary crises the public remained bemused by the alarms and diversions. Especially so as every interpretation of the problem, with its variant of built-in political bias, gave the story a new slant or look. Attention was naturally focused on de Gaulle's demands for a return to gold, and then to the Germans' monetary muscle-flexing as the symbol of their return to European primacy. What was often omitted in these explanations, however, was the deep-seated differences of psychology, public and private interest and above all of national financial institutions which tend to divide the continent from Britain and the United States.

9

Anglo-Saxon Profligates, Continental Conservatives

The Anglo-Saxon nations' position as the world's bankers stems from common political and commercial experience. Politically, Hitler completed for the dollar what Bonaparte's overthrow of the Dutch once did for the pound.* The attractions of security which in the last two centuries has drawn foreigners to the Anglo-Saxons' currencies has, of course, been based on their domestic political stability, which in turn was promoted by the safety-valve of frontier and empire. This attraction was increased by both 19th-century Britain's and 20th-century America's unusually favourable treatment of private enterprise.[1] But in neither case did use of an Anglo-Saxon currency for international payments come about by design. It spread as a result of the Anglo-Saxons' ability to inspire confidence, and their willingness to invest, abroad: ability and willingness, it must be added, in which the British Navy and the United States Strategic Air Command played a not inconsiderable part.

The commercial machinery which enabled Britain and the United States to operate as international bankers was likewise an offspring of parallel political fortunes. It consisted of the unique range of financial services which London and New York, as the world's two leading financial markets, were able to offer. In London's case, in fact, these services have outlasted political good fortune. For with Empire and sea power gone, London has maintained, and even increased, its importance as

---

* By the Congress of Vienna in 1815, as one economic historian has put it 'Twenty years of war had concentrated the world's trade in the British Empire, and had made Britain the only country in the world where capital might be invested with the maximum of contemporary safety.' (E. T. Powell, *Evolution of the Money Market, 1385–1915*, quoted in William Clarke, *The City in the World Economy*, p. 20.)

a world financial centre, dealing more and more in dollars instead of her own enfeebled currency and thus, as the leading Eurodollar dealer, dividing between itself and New York the role of capital provider and financial intermediary that once it was able to undertake on its own.

1. THE ORIGINS OF ANGLO-SAXON ATTITUDES

The key to Britain's early development of sophisticated financial institutions, as to so many of Britain's other peculiar characteristics, is her surrounding sea. As with the Dutch, Britain's great rivals as entrepôt and colonial traders until the Napoleonic Era, the reverse side of the coin of dependence on external maritime commerce was the provision of shipping, insurance and trade-financing services. Unlike Holland, however, Britain followed her pioneering commercial revolution of the 17th century with an industrial revolution that fed a new scale of capital accumulation into her already-formed financial channels.

Britain's earlier industrialization than her continental neighbours, and the consequently greater share of her national income paid out as wages and salaries, also encouraged the growth of new channels—pension funds, life insurance and, recently, unit trusts or mutual funds—for the transfer of small private savings in the capital market. But neither this creation of savings in liquid form, nor their efficient central channelling for use in other enterprises would have occurred without the elaborate structure of commercial organization that followed from the prior *commercial* revolution. The readiness of British companies to resort to the capital market to raise funds, like the willingness of the public to take up their obligations, indicates an acceptance by management of the implications of accountability to disinterested persons *i.e.* individual shareholders, and, increasingly today, to members of a financial technocracy who judge a company by the sole criterion of its potential as a producer of market value growth by expansion and merger. This pattern of capital-raising in turn has depended on the prior existence of other products of the commercial revolution—an independent auditing profession, widely accepted principles of accounting and generally full disclosure of profit and loss accounts and balance sheets.

The importance of this early commercial revolution in Britain can be seen if London's capital market is compared to those of the continent today. In 1965, both the value and turnover of domestic shares quoted on the London Stock Exchange easily exceeded that for all the Common Market stock exchanges put together. Moreover, more than one half of this massive British capitalization is today held by insurance companies, pension funds and investment and unit trusts which arbitrate the destinies of companies to an extent unknown on the continent.

The efficiency, breadth and absorptive capacity of the London capital market enabled it in the last century to handle foreign private and governmental demands for capital, as well as domestic needs. The outflow of such capital was also the essential mechanism which has so persistently upset Britain's and America's balance of payments (see Chapters 12 and 13) while providing the world with the great bulk of its new international money. However, the very efficiency of the British capital market may, ironically, have helped promote *in*efficiency in British industry. British companies, which can easily raise new capital by going to the market, may be encouraged not to distinguish sufficiently ruthlessly between new projects, whereas a comparable German or Japanese company, short of funds, but without such easy direct access to new money may feel greater pressure to employ every mark or yen available as efficiently as possible. However, Britain's experience of a commercial revolution prior to her industrial revolution, may yet stand her in good stead as she enters the highly industrialized, but in some ways still under-commercialized, Europe of today.

In America the democratization of capital ownership has proceeded much farther than in Britain. It was estimated in 1966 that 17 per cent of American adults were shareholders, compared to 7 per cent in Britain and 2–3 per cent on the continent as a whole. This American pattern of comparatively high capital democratization is obviously inherent in the American experience; the abundance of natural resources relative to scarce manpower, the fluidity of society and the absence of any traditionally dominant wealth-owning ruling class.* Unquestionably that ubiquitous moral motor, the Protestant Ethic, also had an important hand in diverting earnings from the bar-till into insurance policies and later, pension and mutual funds.

Another important stimulus behind the Anglo-Saxons' habit of market investment, and also behind the evolution of a reserve role for their currencies, was freedom from the experience of catastrophic inflation. Without freedom from inflation-neurosis, legal prohibition of private ownership of gold coin or bullion, which centralized both Britain's and America's bullion holdings in the interwar years, and provided the essential metallic base for their currencies' international banking function, would have been politically impossible. By contrast, the Popular Front French government of 1936, which attempted to limit private hoarding and formally required French citizens to turn in their gold at its pre-devaluation price, found such a regulation unenforceable, and promptly gave it up.

SWIMMING WITH THE INFLATIONARY TIDE

One consequence of the high development of the Anglo-Saxon capital markets is that the major Anglo-Saxon banks have less influence on the management of their domestic economies than do many of their counterparts on the continent. The great degree of autonomy given to many British, but more especially American corporations by the wide diffusion of their ownership (and their effective control by Galbraith's corporate technocracy) makes them, rather than the lenders of money, the focus of private sector economic decision-making. Under such a pattern of corporate ownership, the banking community tends to become the servant rather than the master of industry, hired

* Ownership of property in the United States was spread as an integral part of winning and developing the American continent. From the time of the War of Independence, when the wild inflation of 'Continental' currency made money payments worthless, the government resorted to the monetization of land, the revolutionary army being paid in grants of the land that was so plentifully available all around.

by it to store, transfer and manage its money. Meanwhile, content with their role as servant rather than master of their domestic economies, Anglo-Saxon—particularly American—bankers today increasingly see themselves as retail merchants of short-term high interest credit, and therefore not greatly more concerned over inflation than the expansion-minded managers whom they serve.

Good fortune in war and the restraint imposed by the gold standard responsibilities of the pound historically also produced a lack of violent inflation in Britain's monetary experience. But in recent years, memories of the inter-war deflation among labour, on the one hand, and the belief among management and the investing middle classes that equity investment in the stock market is, up to a point, an effective 'hedge' against the loss of money's buying power, have encouraged prolonged drift into inflationary indulgence.

Compared to the continental Europeans, Americans' inflationary fears have also generally been a comparatively mild and gentle force, though Americans have not shown themselves as ready to tolerate a 4–5 per cent annual price creep as have the British.* One reason why American apprehension at creeping inflation is greater than British may be, conversely, that they have had less 20th-century experience of it. In the 85 years between their adoption of the gold standard and the start of the Vietnam guns-and-butter spending boom, Americans have, except in war-time, generally chosen a high degree of conservatism in public finance, and thus until 1966–67, have only had spasmodic experience of the social strains of fast-creep inflation.

Yet compared with the continent of Europe, the differences of investing-class attitudes to inflation in the United States and Britain are insignificant. They share a common syndrome of monetary psychology. Furthermore, American organized labour, though far more productivity-conscious than its British counterpart, still retains a folk-memory dread of deflation from

---

* In 1967–68 the anti-inflationary centre of American politics took up the cry in earnest and, from housewives protesting the price of bacon to Republicans in Congress airing their views, 'inflation' became one of the dirtiest words in American housekeeping.

the breadlines of the 1930's to lay alongside the TUC's pre-occupation with the economic consequences of Montagu Norman.

FRIEDMEN OR SLAVES TO KEYNES? THE GREAT ANGLO-SAXON MONEY DEBATE

The strong parallelism in Anglo-Saxon monetary institutions and instincts has perhaps never been more vividly demonstrated than by the almost simultaneous monetary policy debate that emerged in the two countries in 1968–69. The year 1968 saw different sets of economic and political circumstances drive British and American monetary experts into the same dilemma. The upshot of this quandary was the almost simultaneous arrival by both Washington and London at the conclusion that Keynes might be dead.

Put another way, the discovery was dawning in both capitals that one of Keynes's most famous aphorisms was now, perhaps, applicable to himself. This was his remark in *The General Theory of Employment, Interest and Money* that 'Practical men who believe themselves to be quite exempt from any intellectual influence are usually the slaves of some defunct economist.' The slavery of the 'practical men' of Washington, London and New York was in this case to the Keynesian view, based on experience of the 1930's, that so long as governments maintain control over public and private spending (*i.e.* effective demand) by taxation, adjustments in public spending and interest rates, the actual *quantity* of money in circulation does not really matter. The trouble with this Keynesian viewpoint in the later 1960's, however, was that Keynes had (understandably) not envisioned the great changes in business behaviour that would result from universal acceptance of his ideas. But it was ironic that the anti-Keynesian revolution should break out first in the United States, the place where Keynesian disciples had done most to expand upon his monetary views.*

* In particular Professor Alvin Hansen of Harvard and his followers, who tended to dispatch all versions of the classic notion that the size of the money-supply was important by persistent ridicule rather than serious criticism.

In fact, however, the anti-Keynesian revolutionaries gained their foothold in public policy-making not so much because the Keynesian tools failed to work to control the American economy. Rather, in 1968, the Federal Reserve Board found itself confronted by the vast pressures of demand generated by the Vietnam war with the two chief Keynesian tools—tax increase and cuts in government spending—temporarily unavailable. Forced, therefore, to tackle the Hydra of inflation without supporting action either in the Executive or in Congress, the Board soon discovered that high interest rates alone were totally incapable of checking the nation's racing economic engines. Indeed, demand for money to finance further productive expansion remained undeterred by the highest interest rates since the American Civil War, and continued even when the interest-rate squeeze was backed, towards the end of the year, by a belated tax increase and major cuts in government spending.

As 1968 drew to a close, an over-heated economy drove on regardless of the fact that all the Keynesian brakes were hard on, smoking in vain. The reasons were not far to seek. As every financial newspaper and business magazine was busy assuring the businessman, long-term depression of demand was, in 1968, both politically intolerable and technically remediable. In other words it was nothing to worry about. The virtual certainty, so it seemed, of an early resumption of rapid growth-with-inflation made interest rates of 8 and even 9 per cent quite acceptable to the managers of growth areas in the private sector of the economy, especially as interest payments were fully deductible from corporate income tax. In fact, amid this deep-rooted inflationary psychology, the record-high price of money may actually have added to the upward pressure on other prices, thus increasing the force of the draught on which the economy roared.*

Faced with this alarming situation in the autumn of 1968, the Governors of the Federal Reserve System began to pay new heed to the voices of the 'Chicago School' of monetary economists, led and personified by the right-wing *enfant terrible* of

* A long-since ignored study made for Franklin Roosevelt in 1931 had conclusively demonstrated how high interest rates could have this effect.

American academic economists and Barry Goldwater's former economic adviser, the bald-pated, pixyish Dr. Milton Friedman. Perhaps, the governors conceded, the quantity of money in circulation was of real importance after all. At any rate, something had to be done to check the economy, so perhaps this was the moment to find out. Accordingly, in December 1968, after much agonized internal debate, the Federal Reserve Board reversed its 'open market' policy.

Since World War II, the policy of the Board had generally been to protect the market value of government bonds by entering the vast and active market in them, buying (where necessary) from anyone who wished to sell, so as to support their price. Such 'open market' activities, however, by feeding credit into the banking system, effectively increased the nation's money supply.* Indeed, for all the credit squeezing of 1968, the United States money supply (narrowly defined here as currency plus demand deposits in banks) increased during the year by a full 7 per cent. From December on, however, by abstaining from the routine price-support of government bonds (their price at first dived sharply in consequence), the Board began to stabilize the total supply of money.

The time-lag between the start of this policy and first indications of its effect in biting into incomes and spending power was, as Dr. Friedman had predicted, about six months. Accordingly, in June 1969, the first hints of response to the good Doctor Friedman's prescription began to appear. However, it seems likely (though it is still far too early to tell for certain) that these first signals were misread. As the reduced money supply came to affect incomes and spending, there occurred a decline in demand for loans, which was reflected in a slight dip in interest rates. This, Federal Reserve officials (who still obviously doubted the good doctor's prognosis) took to be a sign that their monetary influence was weakening. So they reduced the money supply still further, restricting money growth to zero in the third quarter of 1969. The anguished Dr. Friedman was now warning that such continued over-squeezing would produce recession in the economy in 1970. Belatedly, then, the Federal Reserve Board's governors relented in the final quarter, and

* This mechanism is explained in the footnote to page 28.

announced that money supply was being permitted to increase
at a 4 to 5 per cent annual rate.

Another group of monetary officials in Washington, however,
was somewhat more responsive to Dr. Friedman's commentary
on the American monetary scene. Thus, when in June 1969,
Jacques Polak, the IMF's economic counsellor and his group
of experts descended on London to conduct a 'joint study' with
Treasury and Bank of England officials preliminary to agreement on conditions for a further $1 billion credit to Britain, a
principal area of interest to the visitors was the British money
supply. In effect, Mr. Polak called on Mr. Jenkins to acknowledge the age of Dr. Friedman and the defunction of Lord
Keynes. Non-recognition of the new era, would, it was politely
pointed out, prejudice Britain's chances of getting the second
$500 million of the latest loan.

The British Government's formal recognition of Keynes's
defunction came in Mr. Jenkins's 'letter of intent' to Pierre-
Paul Schweitzer, Managing Director of the IMF. The British
Government, the Chancellor assured Albert Schweitzer's
powerful nephew, would promise to keep its domestic credit
expansion down to $400 million through to March 1970. Now,
therefore, after two decades of squeezes and stops produced by
pennies more on beer or petrol, the slashing of road, hospital
and housing programmes and raisings of bank rate, a new
weapon was to be employed. In the summer of 1969, for the
first time since World War II, a British government was revert-
ing to the drastic expedient of a real old-fashioned monetary
shrinkage.

What had happened was that the British government's
efforts to damp its inflationary economy in 1968 had run into
exactly the same problem as had the Americans'. Labour's
economic half-nelson on the economy, the 8 per cent bank rate,
the £923 million tax increase and the slashed government
spending—the whole package of the 1968 budget's post-
devaluation squeeze-and-freeze, in fact—was all the time being
paralleled (and offset) by a 6½ per cent annual increase in the
money supply. This £1,225 million of new money was, throughout 1968, being quietly tapped into existence on a typewriter in
a remote office of the Bank of England. It took the form of in-

creases in the balances of the commercial banks, paid out by the Old Lady in support of the price of 'gilts'.* Its effect on the economy was to enable businessmen to borrow from their banks the money with which to pay out inflationary wage increases to their employees. This steady increase in the money supply, then, was what enabled consumer spending to stay buoyant, and imports to remain massive, throughout 1968. One Bank of England department was, in effect, solemnly playing its part in contributing to the country's £400 million balance of payments deficit which, in its turn, was blighting confidence in the newly devalued pound and forcing a neighbouring department of the Bank to sell precious reserves in an effort to keep sterling's exchange rate above its $2.38 floor.

By December 1969, however (again after Dr. Friedman's six month time-lag) the British Chancellor's new grip on money supply was having its effect. Previously indulgent commercial banks were being forced to deny private firms the extra overdrafts with which they had traditionally met higher wage bills. The consequent check on British cost-inflation (partially neutralized by the government's repeated surrenders to labour in the nationalized industries but externally rescued by the mark revaluation's cheapening of British exports in the German market and the unexpected buoyancy of world trade) was at last bringing the British their long-awaited surplus.

Nor was the effect on the gilt-edged market the disaster for gilt-edge investors that prophets of doom in the Treasury had predicted. For, as *The Economist* of 2 August 1969 succinctly explained,

> When you buy gilt-edged from the public with artificially created money, you do not simply support gilts. You also stoke up inflation, and this in turn soon causes people to come and sell more gilts to you, thus keeping the downward spiral of gilt-edged prices in being. If you shut your purse, gilts may fall initially, but they will soon ground—in the same way as a floating exchange rate would not be a perpetually sinking rate, but one that fairly quickly found its equilibrium level.

This view that a stop to support-buying of gilt-edged could

---

* Gilt-edged securities, the City's name for government bonds, or 'paper'.

soon lead to a firming up of the gilt-edged market was regarded
as crazily academic. But of course it is what actually happened.

THE POLITICS OF FRIEDMANISM

So far so good. But what are the political implications of this
newly adopted Friedmanism? Perhaps these may best be summed up by the statement that Friedmanism, if applied by itself,
would represent simply a managed domestic version of the gold
standard, the money supply in this case being increased each
year by a fixed and agreed per cent. Under Friedmanism, a
government would decide upon its rate of monetary growth for
the year (say Mr. Jenkins's £400 million—about 2½ per cent).
If, then, a balance of payments leads to a foreign exchange inflow of £300 million, the Bank would be instructed, as under
the classical gold standard, to let the total amount of the money
supply grow to £700 million (about 4½ per cent). Conversely, if
there is a balance of payments deficit of, say, £300 million, then
there should be no permitted increase in the money supply. In
other words, under Friedmanism, because domestic money
supply is kept at a constant and controlled increase, it will again
become linked directly to exchange flows, but this time, not
via gold, but via bank-managed credit.

The great advantage of such a system is that, as an under-
writing device, it is (as the gold standard was) direct and
effective. Furthermore, it is politically less susceptible to resistance than tax legislation, government spending, wage and
dividend freezes or exchange and export controls, because, as
Keynes once said of taxation by inflation, not one man in a
thousand understands what is being done. Friedmanism may
therefore prove extremely effective if used to back up the politically exposed, and therefore generally unwieldy, Keynesian
tools of taxation and spending. The disadvantages of Friedmanism are those of every supposedly fixed, but in fact man-
managed, mechanism. It requires foresight but also flexibility—
in short, judgement tempered with wisdom.

The fact that the Keynesian–Friedman debate has so far
been limited in practice to Britain and the United States, illustrates further the uniqueness of the financial mechanisms

operated by the Anglo-Saxons. Only in London and New York is the volume of liquid and short-term money sufficiently great, the sources of domestic supply and demand sufficiently varied and the impact of international flows sufficiently complex to give grounds for serious dispute over influences on everyday money-market conditions.

What the *international* effects of Friedmanism on the management of the Anglo-Saxon money markets may be, few people would try to predict. One effect, however, if such policies were really carried through, would be to force a much clearer choice to be made by the Anglo-Saxons between the priorities of domestic growth and international expansion. Partly for this very reason, and for the political implications that string along behind it, it is safe to say that the Keynesian–Friedman battle is very far from won. The longer-term monetary solution which Milton Friedman proposes is for central banks to abjure altogether their discretionary power in money creation in favour of reliance on a formula of increasing the money supply annually at a constant 4–5 per cent rate. This concept, which might be called the 'classic Friedman-standard system' has a growing number of adherents. However, non-believers continue to argue—with considerable effect—that if such a policy were followed religiously by the Federal Reserve and the Bank of England, it could lead to rigidities in economic management no less severe than those associated with the rule of gold.

The likelihood, in fact, seems to be that however preferable a fixed formula may seem over improvisation in the face of present perplexities and uncertain time-lags, it will not formally be adopted. Its rigid theoreticism rubs too much against the ingrained Anglo-Saxon preference for expediency and eclecticism. What seems more certain is that the common monetary psychology and parallel sophistication of the Anglo-Saxons will continue both to dominate and disturb the international monetary system: to dominate for the reasons discussed above: to disturb—produce periodic disequilibrium—because they contrast so completely with the bastions of monetary conservatism to be found on the European continent.

2. CONTINENTAL CAVEATS

Europe's monetary experience mirrors her heterogeneous political past. Yet, when compared as a group with the Anglo-Saxons, continentals show marks of a distinct common geopolitical predicament, which makes them warrant examination as a single group.

Different expectations as to the stability of money's value have greatly affected the ways in which Europeans save and invest their wealth. Political distrust on the part both of the individual and of his government has, on the continent, kept the channels that in the Anglo-Saxon countries pour individual savings into long-term investments, relatively few and small. Such caution has not, however, produced a lower level of saving on the continent. In fact, the savings rate of the fast-growing continental countries has on average been far ahead of the Anglo-Saxons' since World War II. But the European practice of holding a high proportion of savings in cash or 'near cash' (*i.e.* short-term time deposits or short-term loans) has helped to compound fears over paper money's value and to strengthen the forces that favour deflationary national policies and the rule of gold.

A FRENCHMAN'S GOLD

French suspicion of all paper currencies including (and perhaps especially) their own does not deter them from participation in this 'continental' pattern of monetary saving. On the contrary, it simply prompts them, individually, to store their wealth in the hardest cash of all. At the end of 1968 it was estimated that Frenchmen owned *privately*, at the official valuation of $35 an ounce, $7 billion worth, or about one sixth of the world's supply of monetary gold.[2]

What accounts for the Frenchman's perennial love-affair with gold? The nation's record of political instability cannot alone explain this degree of private monetary caution. In fact, France's political record in the last half-century compares not unfavourably with that of her chief continental partners whose citizens privately hoard comparatively insignificant amounts of the metal. Deeper historical roots must be sought to explain French attitudes to money. Most often cited is the religious factor. It was Louis XIV's persecution of the Huguenots, and the resulting removal of their wealth to Zürich and Geneva which began these cities' rise as world financial centres. Even today the banking habit, both domestic and foreign, is still far better established in the Protestant countries of northern Europe than in the southerly Latin countries, though the Italians, the pioneers of Western banking, offer notable exceptions to this geo-religious pattern.

An early traumatic French experience with paper money certainly did not help. Prostrated by insolvency, industrial stagnation and social unrest in the wake of Louis XIV's disastrous dynastic campaigns, the French government turned to that magnetic Scots immigrant, John Law, adventurer, gambler, monetary theorist and financial wizard extraordinary, who offered instant and painless prosperity. Within two years of the founding of his Banque Général in Paris, Law had built an empire of paper credit so large that by 1718 he had monopolized the tobacco trade, the African slave trade, the East India Company, and had obtained personal title to Louisiana. His take-over of French finances became complete as Paris abandoned itself wholly to his apparently infallible Midas touch. Having undertaken the collection of French taxes, control of the Mint and the country's finances, his bank offered to 'fund' (*i.e.* to convert) the colossal French public debt of 1·5 billion livres from short- to long-term. But the Scotsman's reputation, though based on financial shrewdness, was fed by his ever more flamboyant creation of credit. Through the long-since familiar device of the printing press, he lifted France on a bubble of credit that quickly produced a 100 per cent inflation of wholesale prices. The French bubble burst in the same year (1720) as did the 'South Sea Bubble' in England. The overissue of notes collapsed Law's bank and, with its failure, stock and commodity prices fell far and fast. In both England and France it was a long time before joint-stock enterprise recovered from the resulting ill-repute. Financial and banking development, too, was set back in both countries as a result of the experience. But in France particularly, which had gone so far in honouring the paper of this fast-talking foreigner, distrust of banknotes sank deep enough into the national consciousness to survive more than one generation.

Experience with Law's paper money only helped stimulate France's celebrated 'peasant psychology', the hardy physiocrat philosophy which sees commerce and industry as second-rate human activity, morally unsound and economically uncertain when compared to gathering God's bounty from the soil. Even today the physiocrat outlook continues to draw nourishment from the French farmer-proprietor, still the dominant national group psychologically and politically, if no longer numerically.

This 'peasant' monetary psychology was boosted by the break-up of the great estates following the Revolution of 1789, when the peasant acquired his equity in French real estate. Since that time the French small-holder, bristlingly independent in his own little kingdom, preferred to trust the management of his money to nature rather than to commerce-dominated government, and thus continued to keep his savings in gold.*

The French, then, have taken only slowly and cautiously to the habit of banking their assets. Their overwhelming and notorious individual mistrust of paper money has undoubtedly been reinforced by the performance of a currency that has followed the violent swings of French politics. Indeed French political and financial habits tend to form a vicious cycle of instability. Private gold owning tends to weaken the public will to resist currency inflation, and so the tradition of inflation

---

* At the height of the Anglo-French monetary crisis of 1930, a best-seller by André Seigfried entitled *England's Crisis* attempted to show how 'over-developed' industrial England was enchained with obsolete attitudes and practices, unable to adjust to the modern world, and that the future belonged to the 'purer agrarian spirit' of countries like France. Today Seigfried's prediction seems to have been thirty years premature. But the reason for its late fulfilment is ironic. France has come to overtake Britain economically in large measure because a reserve army of agricultural workers, unavailable in Britain, was in the 1950's and 1960's being siphoned from France's 'pure' countryside.

It remains to be seen whether, in the closing decades of this century, France, with a mechanized agriculture and an urbanized workforce, follows the pattern of Britain, becoming more ossified industrially as she becomes more liberal monetarily.

"Make the hole a bit bigger and you can bury me too."

followed by devaluation of the already distrusted paper currency rolls on. The franc has seen six devaluations between World War II and 1969, and since 1914 has sunk to less than $\frac{1}{250}$th of its value.

A similar vicious circle has occurred in the organization and investment of savings. Monetary uncertainties of this magnitude have helped deter Frenchmen from the habit of share investment. This in turn has tended to perpetuate the cautious, paternalistic and financially self-reliant outlook of much of French industry. Far more than other major industrial nations, where share investment became important after World War I, French industry tended to restrict itself to investment by ploughing back earnings. A major factor here, of course, is the Frenchman's proverbial aversion to paying taxes. French company accounts are presented in such a way as to hide much of the profit in depreciation and provision items. Also the phenomenon of issuing 'bearer shares' (securities that are not registered at all officially but which change hands just like cash) is common in France, while almost non-existent in Anglo-Saxony. French employee benefits and pension fund arrangements also are very often handled by companies internally. This *auto-financement* has had a stunting effect on Paris as a financial centre. For though easily the pre-eminent banking centre of France, and potentially of continental Europe, Paris has, compared to London, a shortage both of available funds and of opportunities for investment. Indeed, shortage of investment opportunities and hence of ready investment capital is a problem faced not only by Paris, but by all other continental centres, and is a serious impediment to the financial integration of Europe.

The principal obstruction to development of France's financial machinery was the Bank of France itself. Founded by Napoleon in 1801, and controlled by a small and almost exclusively Protestant, financial aristocracy of shareholders, known as *la haute banque Parisienne*, the Bank of France guarded its early note-issuing monopoly with extreme jealousy. This monopoly was at first restricted to Paris but, after the revolution of 1848, was actively extended to the entire country. Not until after mid-century were any other joint-stock banks permitted;

not until 1879 was payment by cheque given legal recognition. Frenchmen were thus compelled, under the restrictive domination of the *haute banque*, to 'hold a far higher proportion of their money supply in the form of coin than any other economically progressive nation, a restriction that put a heavy brake on France's economic expansion'.[3]

From the earliest years of the 19th century, the practical philosopher Saint Simon had preached the marriage of French banking and industry. But, although France's branch of the Rothschild family had made a notable contribution to financing her railways, it was not until after the *coup d'état* of 1851 that Saint Simon's proposed get-together began to occur on a significant scale. It began in 1852 when the Pereires family, arch-rivals of the Rothschilds, founded the first *Credit Mobilier*, the great financial network which channelled the small man's savings to fund the development and control of industry not only in France, but throughout Europe. But this bold departure was shortlived. The Bank of France, aided and abetted by the House of Rothschild, struck back, achieving the downfall of the Pereires' and setting back the mobilization of mass savings in France by a generation.

GEOPOLITICS—THE FORCE BEHIND THE FRANC

Beyond such domestic machinations for financial control, France has suffered from the sensitivities of a continental power surrounded by ambitious neighbours. This geographical situation has produced a French tradition of using the nation's treasure in support of her diplomatic objectives that dates back from long before the Sun King agreed to keep his spendthrift cousin Charles II of England on a pension of French gold in return for promises to return his kingdom to the Catholic faith. The fact that France's long experience with such foreign aid generally produced a great deal more in the way of promise than performance has done little to abate this strategic compulsion. Indeed, the blocking of French overseas ambitions at Waterloo served to encourage French preoccupation with European financial diplomacy.

Throughout the 19th century, French foreign investment was

necessarily concentrated almost exclusively in Europe.* More-over, a strong tradition of subordinating personal profit to national power developed among French investors. At no time between France's defeat by Prussia in 1870 and the outbreak of World War I was the tacit but completely effective ban on German securities lifted on the Paris Bourse. As one noted financial historian of the period has put it, 'France simply chose not to risk having the force of loaned capital turned against her'.[4] And when Parisian financial circles pleaded in the years immediately before the World War I to have Hungarian securities admitted to the Bourse, the nation's industrialists supported the government in its adamant refusal of any con-cession to a possible military antagonist.

French private finance responded with equal compliance to governmental encouragement to move onto the offensive. The most dramatic single episode in French financial diplomacy remains to this day the massive purchase, under strong official encouragement, of Imperial Russian Bonds by the small French rentier. It is impossible to estimate to what extent these bond purchases did in fact serve French interests. As a form of private-enterprise military aid, they may indeed have helped keep Russia at war with Germany until the tide was turned in the West. But the Bolshevik Revolution in 1917 wiped out almost two-thirds of France's pre-war foreign investment portfolio. Nevertheless, despite this bitter experience, the early 1920's found the major banks of Paris continuing to mingle finance with politics. This time, responding to domestic as well as foreign uncertainties, their practice was to leave enormous liquid balances on deposit with foreign, especially German, Austrian and British banks, whose transfer could be (and was —see Chapter 4) used to upset capital markets and bring pres-sure to bear on France's rivals.

The centre and symbol of France's strategic concern as a

* Between 1816–51 only about 4 per cent of French foreign investment left the shores of Europe and in the period 1852–81 under 10 per cent was devoted to the entire non-European world, including France's colonies, according to Rondo Cameron (*France and the Economic Development of Europe 1800–1914*, pp. 62–63). By contrast, in the year 1913, 95 per cent of Britain's foreign investment was in her overseas Empire or in North or South America (William Clarke, *The City in the World Economy*, p. 13).

continental power is the Bank of France's official gold reserve. The young Keynes, writing at the start of World War I, epitomized Anglo-Saxon contempt for this Gallic totem. A gold hoard was, in his words, ' . . . some sort of charm, the presence of which is valuable quite apart from there being any idea of dissipating it—the emblem, rather than the prop of respectability'.⁵ The logical conclusion of such hoarding was, according to Keynes, to melt the reserve into a great golden image of the chief cashier, and to put it upon a monument so high that it could never be got down. A glance up at the idol would remove any qualms over the nation's financial stability; and if its magic did not work to restore confidence it was only that the image was not quite big enough. But Keynes's ridicule here missed the point. Historically the French desire for a great pile of gold in the vaults of the Bank of France has had more to do with her concern over powerful and proximate neighbours than with domestic respectability.

The philosophy of independence through gold thus characterizes the French outlook both as a nation and as individual people: it is what lies behind the Bank of France's comparatively strict subordination to the Ministry of Finance; it is the fact which gives gold's use as a political weapon a peculiar appeal to the French politician. In calling for a return to gold's 'immutability, impartiality and universality', de Gaulle well understood the groundswell of French popular support that greets any call to put the 'l' back in God.⁶

BANKING THEORY: ANGLO-SAXON HYPOCRISY CONFRONTS GALLIC LUCIDITY

Frenchmen's natural distrust of Anglo-Saxon financial attitudes springs essentially from this geo-political concern. It also, however, penetrates back to basic banking theory. Precisely because of their backwardness in developing banking practices, there have been few major French contributions to the theory of money and banking. Frenchmen therefore tend to be taught their banking theory from Anglo-Saxon-based texts. One trouble here is that the greater precision of the French language has a way of imbuing generalized and fluid concepts, which

allow latitude for pragmatic interpretation, with an unin-
tendedly rigid meaning—that is, when the statements of
principle in those texts are not more or less blatantly hypo-
critical exercises in preaching which differ utterly from practice. Examples of this problem of the translation of principles
and ideas across cultural and linguistic frontiers are all too
familiar to anyone with experience of international organizations. But in the case of banking theory the unwillingness of
Anglo-Saxon theorists to come out into the open and admit
how much of credit creation is a matter of judgement rather
than of rules, makes this problem all the more extreme. Furthermore, as the divergence between Anglo-Saxon theory and
international practice is not likely to narrow in the course of
international financial integration, the theoretical dialogue
between Anglo-Saxons and continentals may well continue to
bog down in differing interpretation of fundamentals.*

Tardy and hesitant at home in their acceptance of banking
principles, the French have naturally been still more cagey
over the practice of holding other sovereign governments' paper
as reserves. In international monetary discussions, the French,
together with their monetary following elsewhere in Europe
(notably among the Belgians, Germans and Swiss) have ad-
hered to the old 'cloakroom' arguments of the Currency School
in England's classic 19th-century banking debate. They have
not believed it to be sound banking practice for the 'reserve'
currency central bankers to allow their international note supply
(in this case all the interest-bearing assets convertible into their
currency at any given time) to exceed their gold supply, except
by a small—and preferably fixed—fiduciary margin.

Britain, which backed international holdings of sterling with
only the slimmest of gold reserves in the 19th century and again

* French pedantry is, however, happily absent from the Articles of
Association of the International Monetary Fund, the framework of rules
within which, or by addition to which, international monetary reform can
come about. Drafted by the Anglo-Saxons, and with the managerial decisions based on the Articles taken in Washington, their flexibility has helped
speed progress towards reform, a point to which the Fund's Managing
Director, Mr. Pierre-Paul Schweitzer, drew special attention in paying
tribute to the drafters in September, 1966, during the early and very sticky
preliminary negotiations leading towards the creation of 'paper gold'.

in the 1920's, has always offended French Currency School preferences; but both Britain and the United States do so today on a truly horrendous scale. Total foreign held dollar assets exceeded total United States gold reserves by well over 300 per cent at the end of 1968, while Britain, along with other nations, has compounded the felony of her profligate-partner by holding a substantial part of her reserves in dollars, thus, in strict Currency School theory, adding much of the sterling area's reserve base to the pyramid of direct calls on America's gold.

The mechanics by which the French authorities claim that such 'unsound' international banking practice builds inflation into the international monetary system are simple, but may be worth following through a single trade transaction. A French company sells a mechanical digger to a New York construction firm, the dollars being deposited in a French bank. If that money is not then spent on a counterbalancing purchase of American goods, it will remain as a United States dollar debt to France. The dollars received represent assets in the French bank, against which loans can be made. But this American payment does not reduce America's supply of usable international money. The result: the French money supply is inflated, but the transaction produces no *automatic* pressure for America to protect its foreign exchange reserves.

The French have not been entirely consistent in their opposition to the Anglo-Saxons' Banking School principle of flexible credit creation. Sometimes (for instance at the press conference in February 1965, when de Gaulle proposed a greater international reliance upon gold) they would seem to deny altogether the validity of such discretionary credit-creating power at the international level. At other monetary conferences, however, the French have argued differently. They have proposed that other national currencies besides the pound and the dollar should be held as international reserves, so that the privilege of having a printing press for international money in the backyard should be extended to other nations. Such a reform would put no obstacle in the way of France, or any other reserve currency nation, from increasing liquidity at its own discretion. But whether this latter argument has been used simply as a debating point or not, it clearly runs counter to the mainstream of French hostility to the principle of the gold-exchange standard.

Because of General de Gaulle's monetary antics, attention has been diverted from the monetary conservatism of other continentals. Among the Six, the Dutch point of view on money is steered firmly to the right by the heavy weight of Amsterdam's banking and commercial community in the nation's political scales. This viewpoint is ably represented at the polished international top table by their orthodox central bank chief, Dr. Holtrop. Himself a leading authority and academic disputant on monetary questions, Holtrop is a powerful apostle of conservatism. As such he tries, like Montagu Norman and others before him, to exempt monetary measures, which he feels should be concerned solely with price stability, from any social responsibility. Responsibility for social progress and change, should, in his view, be restricted to other economic measures—taxation, trade controls and, where fundamental disequilibrium is involved, industrial re-organization. As a conservative, in other words, he inclines toward the more politically exposed and therefore inflexible tools of economic management. Holtrop's concern with the isolation of price stability as a first priority has generally placed him in the same camp as the Germans in international monetary discussion; both nations tending to see price stability as an end in itself, rather than a means.

GERMANY: THE POWER OF THE PIGGY BANK

In the light of 20th century history, Germany's almost pathological dread of inflation is not surprising. The psychological reaction to be anticipated after two total collapses of a nation's monetary system in little more than a quarter of a century is obviously overwhelming. But the fact that the German attitude is understandable does not protect it from resentment. Britain in particular tends to listen to teutonic homilies on the 'social crime' of creeping inflation with the charity of a slightly tipsy merrymaker being ticked off by a reformed alcoholic.

The irritation bred by Germany's hard anti-inflationary line has only been important in so far as it has added friction to generally delicate financial negotiations. What remains *vitally* important, however, is the way in which Germany's reaction to her hyper-inflationary past tends to restrict progress towards the creation of greater international liquidity. For Germany's key resistance to expansion of the international money supply has not only threatened development prospects of the poor nations (see Chapter 13) but has encouraged rich nations to grapple for a share of an international cash supply that is constantly diminishing in proportion to world trade: both effects threatening more economic nationalism.

Ignoring the currency collapses that have followed defeat in war, Germany's monetary history has been distinguished throughout by iron discipline and national self-control. Perhaps national character, though as vague an explanation for teutonic discipline as it is for French financial caution, is the essential, inexplicable ingredient. But in Germany's case, that character has been reinforced by the nation's peculiar pattern of economic development.

THE SOCIAL ORIGINS OF GERMAN MONETARY CONSERVATISM

For more than half a century before Germany came into being, the merchants, businessmen and industrialists of the Rhineland enjoyed the monetary benefits of the pan-European franc area. Indeed, when the German nation was formed in 1871, they pressed almost unanimously, despite France's defeat and aroused German chauvinism, to remain on the franc standard. But the Prussian bureaucracy, which ran the new German Empire, ignored the Rhinelander businessmen.

That Prussian bureaucrats should overrule the industrial interests of Rhinelanders came as no surprise to anyone. Clearly a German currency was essential for the task of welding the new Empire into an economic unity of mutual dependence. But another political angle was also involved: Prussia's bureaucrats also had in mind the monetary interest of other parts of Germany. From 1815, when political control of the Rhineland passed into the hands of the Hohenzollern monarchy, a classic clash of monetary interests existed in the enlarged kingdom of Prussia. Indeed Prussia's feudal-agrarian structure produced a sort of populism in reverse. Prussia's 'Junkers', the landed aristocracy who drew their rents (and cannon-fodder) from the plains of East Prussia and Pomerania, were anxious to restrict the note-issuing power of banks, so as to protect the value of their rents.[7] Such a restrictionist monetary policy was, however, diametrically opposed to the interests of the Rhineland communities for whom industrial expansion depended on plentiful credit. Prussia's monopoly of the note issue thus meant that the Anglo-America solution to early industrial financing—the issue of bank notes—was largely unavailable to the financiers of Germany's industrial revolution. It was replaced by the technique of overdraft financing, and by 'acceptance' and discounting of bills of exchange, the net result of which was to involve banks intimately in the industrial investment structure. By contrast, banks in England and the United States, who made loans through the issue of banknotes, had little hold over the borrower, who was free to cash the banknotes for coin on demand.

Prussian hostility to Rhenish monetary requirements was thus one fundamental cause of German banks' close control over industry. A more important one was the march of technology. Again in contrast to the English industrial revolution, German industrialization took place during, rather than before, the railway age. Capital sums required to build a railway network were simply too large to raise by the slow processes of accumulation which fired England's industrial revolution. The result was that the wealthiest merchants and bankers 'doubled up' their capital-raising capacity by making large direct investments, while at the same time promoting companies and themselves offering their customers' stock. Railway-age industrialization thus helped produce a more dynamic domestic role for banking in Germany than in the Anglo-Saxon world. And while English and American bankers emerged from the industrializing experience primarily as financiers of trade and as providers of financial services, German private banks played the combined role of the finance and planning ministries in a present-day industrializing under-developed country. They actively organized new enterprises, often owning a substantial share in the businesses to which they supplied finance, and kept an important say in companies' policies and activities. This historic pattern of centralized banking control over German industry has continued to the present time. Its effect upon both official and private sector monetary attitudes remains immense.

THE GRIP OF THE GROSSBANKEN

Today, Germany's banking system is dominated by three giants, the Deutsche, the Dresdner and Kommerz. Because they had all backed Hitler solidly from the early 1930's, the Big Three were broken up after World War II into thirty-three separate 'compartments'. But as with the Krupp empire, it was not long before they re-emerged in their original shape. Today they not only hold large blocks of shares in the companies which they promote or finance, and act as 'retail bankers' handling consumer credit, they also act as brokers for the German stock exchanges as well.*

This uniquely central position of Germany's banking giants naturally gives the views of bankers extraordinary influence in the economy. Almost every respectable-sized German company will include at least one influential bank director on its board, and in many cases the banker will be board chairman. This practice by no means always tends to maximize efficiency or profitability, however. The classic example of Germany's banks being forced by their own involvement to go on propping up an ailing industrial structure was the House of Krupp itself. For years Krupps had been wobbling along selling an increasing proportion of their steel and steel products in the less competitive markets of Eastern Europe, financed by a lengthening string of short-term credits from the great banks which allowed themselves to get more and more deeply involved for fear of default on outstanding loans. Early in 1967, however, the situation became insupportable. Then, with full governmental acquiescence, an 'administrative council' was established to

---

* In Germany, as elsewhere in the Common Market, stock markets are, when compared to their Anglo-Saxon counterparts, narrow, and turnover is often lacking. At the same time, there is poor knowledge about transactions, insufficient reporting on the part of companies, and share denominations tend to be so high as to seriously hinder the extension of stock saving.

supervise all major Krupp management decisions. Inevitably the leading figure of this 'administrative council' was the dominant figure of German banking and business, Hermann Abs.

Abs personifies the centralization of German economic decision-making, and its domination by the banking mentality. It was Abs, as Chairman of the Deutsche Bank (largest of the Big Three), who had precipitated the Krupp crisis in the first place, by refusing the firm's fifth-generation one-man ruler a $25 million advance. After an uncomfortably prominent role in the Deutsche Bank's financing of the Third Reich, Abs had re-emerged from enforced retirement on his Rhineland estate in 1948 to manage the distribution of Marshall Aid to German industry. In the intervening years, his short, rotund and trimly moustachioed figure cropped up everywhere in German economic life, his vast personal conceit and incorrigible conservatism proving no hindrance in his progress to the undisputed doyen-ship of German banking. Though retired in 1967 from active banking, Abs continues on the board of Germany's largest companies, including Daimler-Benz, Lufthansa and the Deutsche Bundesbahn, the state-owned railway. The pervasive conservative influence of Abs and his colleagues of the banking establishment encourages many in Germany and outside to see big bank control as an alarming force. Significantly, such a system of comprehensive 'mixed' banking which puts so much real economic power into the hands of a few private individuals is forbidden by law not only in the Anglo-Saxon countries, but also all other major industrial countries including France and Italy.

Germany's banking system forms a structural block against inflation at the top of the political pyramid. But other re-straints against inflation that run all the way down to the pyramid's base assure the banks of anti-inflationary support. The post-war political necessity for Western Germany to absorb a steady inflow of immigrant labour has been one anti-inflationary bulwark. Originally, arriving escapees from East Germany and Poland conditioned Germany's labour unions to accept the principle of permitting a steady influx of cheap man-power into the economy. And, since World War II, the stream of refugee or expatriate labour, with its restraining influence upon labour's bargaining power *vis-à-vis* management, has been maintained. When the Berlin Wall cut off an ebbing stream that had provided 11 million skilled and already culturally integrated refugees from the East, with only the shirts on their backs, the labour supply was augmented by successive waves of Italians, Greeks and Turks, whose number totalled over 1,300,000 by the end of 1968. This influx was made tolerable to indigenous German labour by the nature of the work permits granted to the immigrants. When jobs become scarce due to a slackening in the economy, these new migrant workers are the first to be laid off, and when out of work are forced to return home. At the time of the 1966 German recession, 900,000 of these immigrant labourers from Mediterranean lands were sent packing. But the vast majority have since returned with the revival of demand and hence of job opportunities.

The two-decade experience of a tendency to over-supply in the German labour market has been a powerful stimulus to expansion, offering management higher profit margins which the national drive for expansion above all other objectives has turned into high levels of saving and investment. Thus, indirectly, this plentiful labour supply acted as an effective alternative to the need to buoy profits with greater monetary expansion.

A CONTRAST OF IMAGES: 'THE CITY' AND THE GERMAN BANKS

The other broad-based check on inflationary pressures is, of course, German labour's folk-memory of inflation. Here the divergence of experience between Britain and Germany, the two economies of Western Europe whose structures otherwise most resemble one another, is total. This difference is perhaps most vividly encapsulated by the contrast between British and German shop-floor attitudes towards their respective nations' monetary managers. Germany's savings banks and above all, the Bundesbank (central bank) are looked upon by the average German labourer as the working man's defender and friend. The British worker is, by contrast, inherently suspicious of the City.

The Bundesbank, particularly, has an indelible image in the

German public mind as the guardian of that formidable electoral figure 'the small man'.[8] The small man in Germany is a big saver, and the savings bank lobby, characteristically one of the most powerful pressure groups in the Federal Republic, has statutory authority behind it. This authority was the result of 'safeguard' monetary and fiscal regulations drawn up by American and British financiers at the end of World War II, and incorporated as Fundamental (unalterable) Law in the federal constitution. The regulations were designed to prevent irresponsibility in the management of the money supply and the national budget. Under them, representatives of the savings banks sit on the board of the Bundesbank where they can actually outvote its President and the Bank's executive officials. The Bundesbank president in his turn is empowered to ignore the instructions of the elected government in safeguarding the currency: meanwhile a provision in the constitution, that the federal government's budget must be kept in balance, prevented Germany from employing 'Keynesian' fiscal and monetary tools to ensure full employment in the German economy.[9]

These orthodox legal restraints on an already conservative institutional structure have proved a hefty rod for Anglo-Saxon backs. For by encouraging Germany to run a perpetual surplus in its national budget and its overseas payments balance, they had the effect of forcing deficit countries into the position of having to take on the whole burden of correcting international disequilibrium by deflating their economies, instead of giving encouragement to the Germans to reflate theirs. This situation became acute in the German recession of 1966. The Erhart government found itself without the legal machinery to intervene quickly and decisively with deficit spending. As a result, an easily correctable economic sag was allowed to drift into recession before the Keisinger government, coming into power in January 1967, managed to circumnavigate the constitution and pump nearly three billion dollars of deficit public expenditure into the ailing economy. This was a dramatic transformation of German economic philosophy. It occurred only under heavy diplomatic pressure from the United States, whose Federal Reserve analysts had calculated that German unwillingness or 'inability' to reflate in 1966 had, in that year, cost the United States $1 billion and the United Kingdom $600 million in exports.

The provision that the German federal government must stay in surplus had more than one ironic effect. It meant that the massive task of reconstructing credit in the post-war period of very rapid growth was left solely to the private sector banks, the reamalgamation of the Big Three thus becoming essential. Meanwhile, throughout the period of the German 'miracle' the government was in fact putting deflationary pressure on the economy, each year raising considerably more in taxes than it spent. This deliberate and enforced building of a surplus did, however, suit German political purposes. For the government devoted the bulk of this surplus to building the *Juliusturm*, the reserve fund named after the Berlin Tower in which Imperial Germany used to hoard gold at the request of the Prussian General Staff, and set aside to finance eventual rearmament.

German pursuit of a budget surplus for future spending emphasizes the point that neither German nor American officials had absorbed the message of Keynes in the early post-war years. For apart from the fact that the accumulation of a large surplus put a mild dampener on German economic recovery in the 1950s (Germany in those early days still had a considerable over-supply of labour which could have been put to work on government-financed reconstruction without inflationary damage to the economy), spending of the *Juliusturm* when Germany began to build up her military forces again in 1958–59 at once began to threaten price stability. For then the economy was already at full employment, and Germany's war chest could only be emptied into the economy at the risk of inflationary overheating.

Despite all the forces that encourage the government to stamp on inflation symptoms wherever they appear, Germany has by no means escaped from the universal post-war decline of money's buying power. However, between the 1948 currency reform and the year 1957, concern over the mild inflation that occurred was more psychological than social or economic. The colossal task of post-war reconstruction produced a situation in which demand for capital greatly exceeded supply; but at the same time consumer demand remained limited and the labour supply plentiful. Any inflation occurring under these conditions was thus channelled back via profits into capital investment, *i.e.*, it was 'profit-led'. This meant in practice that prices rose faster than wages, so that businessmen were spurred on to greater investment and enterprise.

THE ALLIANCE OF MISTRUST

To sum up, the monetary outlook of both Frenchmen and Germans may be characterized as one of profound mistrust. In France's case the cause is a desire for independence: in Germany's the fear of inflation. The policies chosen by each have been different but the international result has been the same. Each nation has built up trading surpluses, and held these surpluses in 'liquid' form although France has since spent the great bulk of her reserves, as an alternative to extreme deflation, in defence of the franc. This 'liquidity preference' was adopted as a conscious alternative to the path of more spending on investment, or consumption (producing faster growth though inevitably with more domestic inflation) or, alternatively, of more lending abroad, either of which would greatly boost the world's production of wealth.

Italy, on the other hand, with a vast degree of monetary discretion in the able hands of her young and independent-minded central bank chief, Guido Carli, has remained, throughout the rough monetary passages of the 1960's, remarkably co-operative with the United States. Carli was, from the beginning, a leading exponent of currency swap arrangements for neutralizing flows of capital from one currency to another. This greater degree of co-operation reflects a broad strategic decision by the Italian Government to stick to the path of expansion in preference to that of political independence. This same strategic outlook is reflected in the fact that successive Italian governments of various political complexions have done everything in their power to welcome American capital, have been generally obliging in agreeing to reflate the nation's economy, and have been sympathetic to measures proposed for new forms of international liquidity.

To the mistrustful among the Europeans, however, whether they were governmental officials, politicians and/or central bankers, America's massive overseas dollar debt has represented the spearhead of a double threat—a source of inflation and the principal feed-line of the American world business empire. Meanwhile, however, European private bankers and corporate chiefs who use or invest these dollars are more than content to do so; for they represent a uniquely unrestricted international vehicle for storing, transferring and investing wealth. The growth of the Eurodollar market, concurrently with official worries over the health of the dollar, illustrates this paradox which is examined in the next and final chapters.

To what extent, then, have the monetary crises of the past decade been purely political or diplomatic, reflecting little real economic anxiety on the part of business? It is impossible to answer with real precision; but the following chapters describe the great Atlantic divide and how it may be bridged.

10

Gold War

1. THE DOLLAR DEFIED

By 1965, the demand by European conservatives for restraint of the dollar invasion could be contained no longer. The alibi for counter-attack was immaculate in its respectability. No orthodox banker, under the prompting of businessmen and politicians, would deny that, in orthodox 'Currency School' terms, the dollar's soundness came into question.

So the European counter-offensive began. In the first six months of 1965 $2·5 billion of American dollars were turned into gold, or gold convertible claims of the International Monetary Fund. France was, of course, in the van of the switchers, converting nearly $900 million dollars in this period alone. But France was not alone. Italy switched $475 million into gold in the same six months, Germany $276 million, Belgium $175 million, the Netherlands $132 million. The Six were by far the outstanding, but by no means the only, switchers. All the other industrialized countries (with the exception of Britain) together converted $365 million into gold, while the less-developed countries collectively changed $50 million in this period, according to Professor Triffin.[1]

The gold war was on. At stake was the division of power within the Western Alliance; at issue, the monetary price of gold. On the European side the war was fought by proxy. Behind the scenes were the politicians and public officials. But the shock troops of these 'Old Europeans', their mercenary armies, were the speculators; for as deflationary European policies and the hints of politicians aroused distrust of the pound or the dollar, the speculators scrambled out of the suspect currency, and in ever-increasing numbers bought gold.

THE GENERAL'S MONETARY WAR

The intellectual father of European hostility to the reserve currencies, hammer of the Anglo-Saxon profligates, and grand strategist of the European forces in the gold war was the quiet-spoken but intense French economist named Jacques Rueff then aged 62. Rueff has long been a national figure in France; indeed he enjoys the rare distinction, for an economist, of membership of the Academie Française. Twice in his lifetime, Rueff has advised authoritarian French presidents to undermine the odious gold-exchange standard by scooping in Anglo-Saxon gold with an undervalued franc. In 1926, the 30-year-old Rueff made a study for Poincaré of the level of franc exchange that France should adopt. Thirty-two years later, while putting the finishing touches to an article describing the episode,[2] he received a call from another authoritarian president, equally determined upon stabilization of the franc. For the second time Rueff came out for an undervalued exchange rate for the franc, this time recommending a 17·5 per cent devaluation less than twelve months after M. Bourgès-Maunoury's 20 per cent reduction of August 1957.

Rueff's logic was irreproachable. In 1958 he was again able to exploit France's enviable freedom from reserve responsibilities, which permitted her to take unilateral action without fear of toppling the world monetary applecart. The near-revolutionary crisis that ushered in de Gaulle and the Fifth Republic had left France with less than $600 million of gold in her reserves. But Rueff knew French psychology. He knew that the authorities could be counted upon to use France's resulting healthy export surplus to rebuild the nation's reserve.

To de Gaulle, groping for the path of destiny, Rueff's solution shone like a beacon. The General was quick to absorb the point stressed both by the veteran economist and Couve de Murville (Rueff's deputy of thirty years before, later to become finance minister) that the key to the extension of American power abroad was the international position of the dollar.*

* In 1958 M. Rueff headed the committee that prepared the reform plan for the franc. He was not thereafter publicly associated with the French government until January 1965 when de Gaulle began his monetary offensive.

By January 1965 the bulk of the competitive advantage gained by Rueff's low franc valuation of 1958 had been eroded by inflation. But, as Rueff had planned, seven years of economic striving with a favourable exchange-rate had built the General a $6 billion gold reserve. Now, with his armoury well stocked and with nothing to gain from further delay, it was time for France to take the monetary offensive.

The General opened his campaign with a play to his peasant gallery. Not content with large-scale conversions of dollars into gold, he insisted that the metal be shipped to Paris. Today, official transfers of gold rarely involve its physical movement. Central banks hang on to a last ditch emergency holding, but at least 30 per cent of the world's monetary gold stock lies stacked in battered 400 ounce bars in the cages of the New York Federal Reserve Bank beneath lower Manhattan 'under ear-mark' for a host of countries, the IMF and the Bank for International Settlements. One day early in January 1965, however, the General asked where France's gold reserve was actually located. On hearing that a large part of it was in London and New York, he remarked that if he were the man responsible he would hardly sleep soundly under such an arrangement.[3] A few days later, gold bars were being crated in soft pine boxes and air-freighted off to Paris—de Gaulle's answer to 'American neo-colonialism' to the loss of French control over her industry.

The classical authoritarian phase of the French political syndrome was repeating itself. An *assainissement* of the currency (a phrase coined in the 1920's suggestive of Hercules in the Augean stables) leaving it heavily under-valued internationally accompanied by a sternly deflationary policy at home which, of course, redistributed wealth in favour of the national redeemer's solid base of middle class support. Meanwhile a heavy foot on wage claims helped to preserve the competitive edge needed to boost French exports and achieve the surplus which was to be locked up in the national gold hoard. France, to borrow the General's phrase, 'became France again', her middle class able once again to hold its head high.

THE LONDON GOLD MARKET: SORE POINT WITH AMERICA

Throughout the gold war the American position remained as intransigent as that of France. The United States Treasury was determined to hold its ground and in doing so to continue reaping for America the benefits of automatic international credit, so that the American military and business establishment might go on spending and investing more abroad than America earned through the sale of its exports. America's strategy was thus as straightforward as her purpose—to honour her 35-year-old commitment to buy and sell gold at $35 an ounce. Hence the determination of successive secretaries of the Treasury to parry the upward transatlantic pressure on the gold price with its implicit downward pressure on the dollar. Standing pat was not easy. America has had to work hard for the international co-operation necessary to defend its currency's unique gold link and has not always achieved full co-operation from her Anglo-Saxon ally.

For nine years following World War II, central banks dealt in gold exclusively with the Federal Reserve Bank of New York, the IMF in Washington and the Bank for International Settlements in Basle (although gold markets for the private hedger and speculator continued to flourish).* Then, in 1954, against a background of opposition from American officials, who saw no need for an additional pressure point against the dollar, the London gold market was re-opened. At 10.30 a.m. on Monday, 22 March, of that year, representatives of the five British bullion brokers, Rothschilds, Mocatta and Goldsmid, Sharps Pixley, Samuel Montagu and Johnson Matthey foregathered at the N. M. Rothschild premises in New Court to recommence a City activity abandoned since Hitler's invasion of Poland closed the market fifteen years before.

It was generally anticipated that London would only slowly, if indeed ever, regain its former pre-eminence as an international gold market. Sterling was still, in the early 1950's,

* These were, principally, Paris (almost exclusively a domestic market in coin and small bars centred in the basement of the Bourse); Zürich for the nervous rich of Europe and the world in general, and a string of trading centres, Beirut, Kuwait, Bahrain, Cairo, Saigon, Bangkok, Macao and Hong Kong, feeding the appetites of Middle and Far Eastern investors.

hedged about with controls, and was freely convertible into neither dollars nor gold. At the same time, Commonwealth gold production had been flowing for many years to other markets throughout the world. Yet within a year of London's re-opening, it was handling over 85 per cent of all the new gold coming on to the free market and the Bank of England was able to declare London again to be 'the largest and most important gold market in the world'.

Behind London's instant return to pre-eminence were the classic economics of the market-place. London's world-wide contacts both on the demand and supply side produced a market of sufficient breadth and depth to enable it to offer a stability of prices not found in other centres. Furthermore, not only did London offer quotations within a narrower range than other countries, but its world contacts soon enabled it to absorb large quantities of the metal, while its excellent physical facilities for gold handling made it possible for London's bullion brokers to offer the cheapest commission rates available. Swayed by both its cost competitiveness and convenience, central banks began to conduct their gold transactions through London after 1954, the Bank of England becoming, as formerly, their agent. In fact, London's focal role, though disliked by the Federal Reserve Bank of New York as a convenient centre for applying gold pressure to the dollar, also helped to stabilize the free market price for gold; for when the London gold price fell below $35 an ounce, it paid central bankers to buy gold with which to fulfil their international commitments.

By removing the uniqueness of the American currency's gold pledge,* the return of Western Europe to convertibility in 1958 further weakened America's monetary leadership by causing an increasing number of foreign-held dollars to be converted into gold. Two years later, during the Kennedy–Nixon presidential contest of October 1960, still more serious doubts over

---

* 'Convertibility' of European currencies still did not put them in the same category as the dollar, however, for their link to gold was only via the dollar. Thus, the answer to 'what is the pound sterling worth?' was, after 1958, $2.80 or 2·48828 grams of fine gold (today $2.40, or 2·13281 grams) and the French franc 20·255¢ or ·180000 grams (today 18·004¢ or ·160000 grams) the value of gold being defined in dollars.

America's future gold commitment appeared. Not only had the American payments deficit widened considerably in that year, but the uncertainties of new American leadership added to the growing doubts. Reflecting this anxiety, demand for gold so outran the supply released to the market that the London gold price lifted for the first time above $35 an ounce, moving in a rapid surge up to $40. As agent for the American monetary authorities, the Bank of England beat back the speculators with large sales of American gold. But this gold scare had its effect. It forced the United States to secure the co-operation of the central banks of the West in reinforcing the foundations of the monetary system.

In the year following the 1960 gold scare, at the annual IMF meeting in Vienna in 1961, the Americans brought strong informal pressure to bear for the closing down of the London gold market. What went on at these meetings has yet to be revealed, but it is known that the Bank of England, standing staunchly behind the City's bullion-dealing interests and its vital gold ties with South Africa, flatly refused. As an alternative approach to the dollar's defence, the Americans reluctantly turned to reliance upon a collective support agreement—an informal arrangement for sharing the burden and responsibility of the dollar–gold link. The result of this approach was the formation in that year of the London Gold Pool. With the Bank of England as their agent, the United States, Germany, France, Italy, Switzerland, Holland, Belgium and, of course, Britain, all pledged themselves to this gold stabilization syndicate. When speculative market pressure on the gold price forced it up, they would sell their gold in agreed proportions so as to keep the market price within the narrow band between $35.08¾ and $35.20. They also agreed to take in, as a syndicate, any newly mined South African gold not needed to satisfy demand on the market, and to do the same with the periodic Russian gold sales.

The motive behind the Bank of England's resistance to American log-rolling in Vienna now became clear; for from the setting up of the Gold Pool until the gold crisis of 1968, London, with the Bank of England acting as agent for the South African Reserve Bank, the Federal Reserve System, and the six other central banks in the Pool, remained assured of the profits and prestige of being the primary world market for gold, from which other secondary 'retail' markets were fed.*

STERLING TRIGGERS THE GREAT GOLD DRAIN

For six years the Gold Pool arrangement worked well. But sterling's fall from grace of November 1967, which threw the viability of the entire monetary system seriously into question, proved too much for the syndicate arrangement. In the week following sterling's devaluation, private demand for gold rose to ten times the normal level. A second gold rush of similar proportions, which followed in December, was also staved off by official gold sales. But the central bankers' syndicate was finally overwhelmed in the great gold stampede of 11–14 March 1968. In that four-day period alone, $850 million worth of bullion was snapped up by private buyers, climaxing with the private purchase of over $200 million worth on Thursday, 14 March, alone. On the Friday, amid a Cabinet crisis which resulted in the resignation of Foreign Secretary George Brown, the British government closed the London gold market temporarily at President Johnson's request. Those four March days represented de Gaulle's Austerlitz, the high tide of his monetary campaign. The spreading from Paris of news that France had secretly withdrawn from the Gold Pool back in July 1967, and of rumours that the Italians, the Swiss and the Belgians were doing the same, was the final French salvo aimed at triggering an overwhelming anti-dollar stampede. For a while, as United States gold reserves and those of America's collaborators took staggering losses, it looked as though de Gaulle had won.

* The arrangement continued unaltered when South Africa left the Commonwealth in 1961, the Bank of England having kept up its close working relationship with the South African Reserve Bank. Meanwhile, even since the break-up of the London Gold Pool, Union Castle Line ships, equipped with special vaults, were able to offer a freight rate for gold shipments which has continued to deter dealers from airfreight shipment direct to Europe from Johannesburg.

FRENCH STRATEGY'S FATAL FLAW

The French monetary syndrome of the 1920's, coinciding with a period of weak international demand and over-production, had precipitated and helped to deepen the ensuing world depression. Happily for the world, the syndrome of the 1960's occurred amid a buoyant tide of international prosperity. That is the reason why the gold crisis, which the French did so much to provoke, could be checked and coped with. The urge to preserve prosperity produced, in the 1960's, a level of international co-operation which contrasted vividly with the weak co-operative efforts of 1931–32. Indeed the spectre of 1931 was a leading factor in foiling the General's plans for monetary conquest. For as wave after wave of crisis overwhelmed sterling, and then broke over the base of the dollar, governments recoiled rapidly from the brink while their central bankers fought with unprecedented unity of purpose to prevent the speculators from winning the day. Overnight, currency swaps and loans of unparalleled size were agreed: the grimness of the money men's determination to weather the storm suggesting that this time they realized that it was they and their quasi-autonomous institutions which were on trial just as much as the politicians and electorates whose vagaries they were labouring to offset. Political pressures may have brought them to the brink, but just as Hiroshima and Nagasaki have, since World War II, apparently helped to hold the superpowers' leadership in check, so the hungry thirties may have galvanized the central bankers to resist the ultimate folly.

Ironically, however, it was French students and workers who stepped in, or rather sat down, to relieve the pressure and prepare the way for monetary truce; for in May 1968, two months after the peak of the anti-dollar stampede, and just as it seemed that the psychological ingredients of the monetary system must be ground to powder by the Paris 'rumour mills', de Gaulle's own monetary breastwork suddenly began to give way.

De Gaulle's problem was simple. France's political structure of 1968 would no longer sustain the weight of gold roof that it had borne in Poincaré's day. In order to grasp the monetary independence necessary for his grand design of European hegemony, de Gaulle had been forced to run the French economy on a distinctly short rein since 1960. But despite this deflationary restraint, and the sizeable pool of unemployment which it had helped to deepen, the General had been unprepared to take the still sterner measures necessary to curb a 3 per cent creep of inflation. Meanwhile the French worker, although enjoying actual gains in buying power because improvements in productivity in important sectors of the economy kept ahead of the creep of prices, was beginning to grumble noisily against the absence of wage increases.

'*Les evenements de Mai*', the French worker's angry outburst after the 'seven lean years', was not so much a case of his feeling the inflationary pinch (which on the whole he wasn't) as of his overall sense that his share of the national cake was too small (which, compared to the British and German worker's, it was). *Denouement* was not long in coming. The wage increases of up to 30 per cent necessary to get the nation moving again at once caused a dumping of francs by frightened Frenchmen and foreigners that brought the currency down to its 'floor'. The Bank of France was now forced to dip deep into the nation's reserves to protect the exchange rate. The franc, however, was in little immediate danger. France's enormous reserve which (if we include her IMF drawing rights) totalled over $7 billion at the time, represented about seven times the total value of francs held abroad.* But ten months later, when the deferred negotiations with the unions were due to take place at the *rendezvous de Mars* in an atmosphere of renewed international monetary crisis, more than one half of de Gaulle's monetary armoury was expended; and fifteen months later, with de Gaulle himself receding into history, reserves had reached a point where the franc was once again forced down.

When his gold-based 'Free France' campaign was first threatened, the General had hurried home from Rumania to face the rioting strikers and students. "*La reforme oui*," he had announced, "*la chie en lit, non.*" But his prompt capitulation before the strikers' demands and his refusal to devalue ensured that this time France would choose to foul her own bed, rather

---

* By comparison, sterling held abroad represented at the end of 1968 about 20 times the reserves of the Bank of England.

"Vive la France! Vive le General! Vive la gloire!—And don't forget to buy me as many Deutschmarks as you can lay your hands on before the market closes!" 19.xi.68.

than inaugurate a *chie en lit* of international proportions. So the General was forced by the events of May to succumb to a brand of reform more distasteful to him than anything that he had promised at home—a reform of the international monetary system that would leave the 'privileged' positions of the pound and the dollar intact, while taking the pressure from them. The General's staunch rearguard resistance to the creation of Special Drawing Rights, or 'paper gold' as they were derisively

named in Paris, was fatally weakened by his own loss of the real
article, and his own prospect of possible future need for international support.

The backlash of the General's gold campaign was even more
humiliating. For early in 1969, with an inflationary outcome to
the *rendezvous* on the horizon, the French government began to
feel rising alarm over the huge amounts of money that would be
pumped into the French economy if owners of France's $7
billion private gold hoard decided to take their profit at the
prevailing ($43) free market price. A meeting of the central
bankers in Basle on the weekend of the 8–9 March 1969, with
its official announcement that the French government no longer
believed that there should be an increase in the official gold
price, marked the conclusion to the French gold campaign with
the Bank of France suing for monetary peace. The policy of
quietly encouraging the paper-doubters of France had come
home to roost.

So ended France's monetary offensive of 1965 to 1968. With
his currency put temporarily in the nursing home by the
French student and worker, de Gaulle was forced to call off the
campaign. His extraordinary sallies and manœuvres to encourage speculative attacks upon the pound and the dollar, his
repatriation of GI dollars from Vietnam via the Banque d'Indo-
Chine for presentation at the United States Treasury, his
attempts to strike at the foreign exchange jugular of the Anglo-
Saxons—their income from Middle East oil—with a campaign
aimed at undermining the British and American concession
system, all had been foiled in the end by the traveller on the
Metro.

But the greater irony was that the effect of France's monetary
antics was the precise opposite of the General's intention. For
in face of the French monetary offensive, a new and unprecedented level of co-operation and understanding among central
bankers in defence of the *status quo* had occurred.

2. VICTORY FOR THE DOLLAR IN SIGHT

The avalanche of private gold buying in those four days of
March 1968 had robbed Pool members of 10 per cent of their

remaining reserves. Apart from Parisian monetary warfare, this run on the West's official gold reserves had been unintentionally nudged along by a proposal made in late February by Senator Javits of New York, that the United States Treasury should immediately halt gold sales and allow the dollar to float, keeping its value stable by the 'European' method of using the New York Federal Reserve Bank's exchange stabilization fund to buy and sell other currencies. When the top negotiators of the Gold Pool countries (minus France) met hurriedly in Washington on the weekend of the 16–17 March to plan an alternative strategy for the gold price's defence, this may indeed have been the background threat wielded by Treasury Secretary Fowler in order to ensure co-operation. At any rate, with the notable exception of France, central bank solidarity was maintained. The Pool was to be abandoned, its members declaring that they were satisfied that they jointly held sufficient gold stocks for inter-governmental transactions and saw no need to add to them further. Meanwhile Fowler re-emphasized that while America's obligation to sell gold at $35 an ounce to official foreign dollar holders 'for legitimate monetary purposes' held good, this did not include any obligation to make such gold sales to central bankers who were prepared to sell their gold on the free market.

So the two-tier gold price was born. Since March 1968 it has worked with remarkable success. For not only did central bankers abstain from the very substantial profits to be had by taking advantage of the average 25 per cent differential between the official and the free market price over the year, they also abstained from buying South African gold in an attempt to force the Republic's newly mined metal onto the free market, and hence depress the 'free' gold price. So far, the insulation of the two prices has, despite persistent monetary jitters, been maintained intact, though it has not yet been tested by a full-scale crisis involving one or other of the reserve currencies. Furthermore, a compromise settlement with the South Africans over the disposal of their gold appears to be in sight. After a year in which the United States has successfully blocked South African attempts to sell gold to the IMF and maintained the central banks' boycott, and in which the South Africans have acquired needed foreign exchange by use of their automatic drawing rights at the Fund, European bankers appear to be prevailing upon Washington to agree to central banks' buying a small fraction (say 10 per cent) of South Africa's offerings, provided that 90 per cent is channelled to the free market. Henceforward, the Americans, believing that the two-tier situation is now fully under control, have apparently agreed in principle to official authorities' buying gold from the free market if and when it sinks to the $35 an ounce official monetary price.[4]

By refusing to upvalue gold in relation to the dollar (or to devalue the dollar in relation to gold, depending on the political point of view) the Americans have carried the rest of the world far towards their ultimate monetary objective—the final banishment of gold, and its replacement with a total dollar standard.

But the fact that the dollar's gold price has already stood for thirty-six years has added peculiar strain to the politics that surround the price of gold. Thirty-six years of inflation would have to be covered if gold were to be restored to its former value relative to other prices and world trade. This meant that, for gold alone to provide the bulk of necessary international liquidity for the foreseeable future (and with the present rate of technology-fired trade growth, the foreseeable does not extended very far), at the very least a doubling of its price was considered essential. Anything less would only have meant an early resumption of argument over its price, as the growth of world trade brought liquidity shortage back again. Herein lay the basic argument against any monetary solution based on gold—that the world economy would once again be slave to the vicissitudes of the metal's discovery and production.

A second politically compelling argument was that periodic up-valuing of the metal to meet world monetary demand would be preceded by such hurricanes of private (and public) speculative buying that the international monetary system would remain subject to acute periodic crises and the constant danger of collapse. Gold revaluation would then at best be merely a time-buying expedient, solving nothing in the longer run, while enabling nations to loosen the ties of economic co-operation that bind them in the short. This is why revaluing gold was opposed by so many who put continuing international prosperity before national prestige.

But by no means all the opposition to gold's revaluation was so altruistic. There was opportunism on the side of $35 an ounce as well; for the up-valuing of gold would considerably redistribute financial power among nations. How would it affect the international situation? First and foremost it must be emphasized that the United States would *not* lose reserve power in relation to the world as a whole. The United States' gold reserve is still massive by other national standards, and with a 100 per cent up-valuing of gold it would of course be doubled in dollar-value like everyone else's.

The point is rather that financial power would be redistributed both among America's Western allies and also between East and West. Those who had trusted the United States and held on to their dollars would see their dollar reserves devalued at a stroke by 100 per cent. Those who had disliked American financial power and wanted greater national independence from dollar influence would reap a 100 per cent up-valuation of their gold in dollar terms.* The change in distribution of international reserve strength would therefore look as shown in the table overleaf.

Beyond the obvious implications of these figures, the fact that close to 90 per cent of annual gold production is accounted for by the Soviet Union and South Africa encouraged dollar defenders of both liberal and conservative persuasions to join forces in rejecting a solution which would offer massive bonuses to their respective political anathemas.†

Regarding the bonus that a doubling of the gold price would

---

* This is especially important in the case of Japan (see table) which has agreed to hold mostly dollars in its reserves instead of behaving like France and Germany and demanding American gold instead. Thus to up-value gold would deal a very serious blow at the Japanese economy apart from smacking of a level of ingratitude with which the Americans do not wish to be charged.

† Somewhat hard for liberals to swallow, however, is the fact that the artificial depression of the price of gold has forced South Africans to employ cheaper immigrant labour from Malawi, Angola and East Africa in their gold mines rather than the more highly paid domestic black labour force.

provide to the Soviet Union, American authorities have long found themselves in a dilemma. Presumably for political propaganda purposes, the CIA appears to have purposely under-estimated Soviet gold production. In 1963, the Agency issued a report revising the US Bureau of Mines' estimates for Soviet gold production in the 1950's and early 1960's downwards by over 75 per cent (from around 12 million ounces to the range of 3·5 to 3·9 million ounces annually). On the basis of these CIA figures, a doubling of the world gold price would only have raised Russian gold reserves from $1·5 billion to $3·0 billion, clearly not an advantage of earth-shaking importance. European gold dealers, however, have consistently come up with far higher estimates for recent Soviet production. Franz Pick, a veteran and highly respected gold authority, estimated Russian gold reserves in 1964 at $10 billion. If this estimate were to be believed, the prospect of handing the Soviets a like sum in additional foreign purchasing power would indeed begin to take on the dimensions of a significant foreign policy decision.

Distribution of International Reserve Strength (a) at $35 an ounce and (b) at $70 an ounce. Reserves shown for end 1st quarter 1968 in billions of dollars. (Source: *International Financial Statistics*, October 1969)

	(a)	(b)
United States	13·4	24·4
United Kingdom	2·7	4·2
France	6·0	11·2
Germany	7·4	11·4
Italy	4·4	6·8
Benelux	4·3	7·4
EEC	22·1	36·8
Japan	1·7	2·0
Other 'Group of Ten' (Canada, Sweden)	3·1	4·3
LDC's	12·7	15·8

Such wide divergence of estimates illustrates the density of fog that continues to surround Russian gold production and holdings. Yet some things may be deduced from what is known of Soviet monetary practice. First of all, despite the communists' theoretical scorn for gold, it is evident that a large gold reserve is important to the Russian authorities. Russia is not, after all, a member of the International Monetary Fund. Nor does it have access to any of the other credit facilities available to Western trading nations. The Soviet government is therefore motivated to use its gold very sparingly, and as a last resort in peacetime (*e.g.*, in the event of a major crop failure) because the metal could represent a vital factor in the event of emergencies such as foreign military operations. Moreover, ironically enough, the Russian authorities have consistently shown a degree of financial conservatism beyond that of the American Congress. They still maintain a legal minimum of 25 per cent gold backing of their currency note issue, a measure that the United States Congress waived in March 1968 in order to release the balance of its gold reserve to meet international commitments. Thus, despite the fact that it undoubtedly costs the Soviets considerably more than $35 an ounce to dredge and refine their alluvial gold deposits, it is clear from this official preoccupation with the metal, as well as from other hints that filter through, that they are working hard to expand their gold holdings.[5]

Quite apart from questions of national financial advantage involved in the gold price, however, there has also been the obvious distaste shown by the more puritan-minded among Anglo-Saxon monetary officialdom that the private sceptics and gold gamblers would be so richly rewarded. Speculative profits may be unimportant as a political issue beside the question of the international distribution of financial power, but their effect upon the thinking of a veteran puritan warrior like ex-Federal Reserve Board Chairman, William McChesney Martin, with eighteen years of outwitting and, where possible, punishing foreign currency speculators behind him, should not be underestimated.

On balance, though, the struggle over the price of gold was over prestige more than over substance. For while there are advantages for the United States in the continuation of the present status of the dollar, the prestige victory of the gold revaluation, for which General de Gaulle was driving in his campaign of 1965–68, would in practice almost certainly have meant a vast increase in America's real financial power relative to that of gold-favouring nations. A universal increase in the price of gold would leave the dollar in the same parity-relation to European currencies. At the same time, however, the United States would have far higher gold reserves in relation to its outstanding dollar IOUs. The dollar would therefore return again to the position of unquestioned strength that it commanded in Marshall Plan days.

So we arrive at the anomalous situation that if the Americans swallowed their pride and submitted to political pressures on gold, they would *strengthen* their monetary position *vis-à-vis* Europe and the world. Furthermore, America's revaluation of gold would also have had the effect of forcing European pressure against the inflow of American capital out from behind the skirts of the speculators and into the open political arena. In itself, this fact puts the tacit alliance of politicians and businessmen, who comprise the gold-minded continental conservatives, into an awkward dilemma. For the electoral spectacle and drama of being able to threaten the Anglo-Saxons with monetary embarrassment is quite a different matter from trying to push through a national assembly legislation designed directly to check the inflow of American capital—a move which could, and would, be identified by pro-American and anti-protectionist forces as a direct bias towards indulging non-competitive national industries at the price of diminished national prosperity.

TOWARDS THE LIBERALS' DREAM: DEMONETIZING GOLD

So much for the short-term political issues of the gold price. But it was the peculiar fascination of the gold war that in it, short-term politics and long-term philosophic issues became inextricably blended. In terms of immediate power considerations alone, and the extra freedom of manœuvre that $70 an ounce gold would bring them, the Americans might be thought to be in two minds on the price of gold. The vast majority of them see no dilemma here however because $35 an ounce has become the foundation of an American-led international crusade for monetary reform. Supported by monetary liberals internationally, Americans see the maintenance of the present gold price as the most realistic and practical way of weaning the world onto a more stable and rational monetary order.

American long-term as well as short-term interest therefore dictates that the Treasury should play for time. For, if they can keep gold's official dollar value stable for long enough, five or ten years from now, they believe, the world will come to accept a man-made dollar standard, managed by a committee of nations, on which the United States would have, of course, a major, though not necessarily a predominant, voice. Recent international agreement to create a new form of international credit (the SDR) was a very important step in this direction, and thus a clear victory for the Anglo-Saxon or 'liberal' view of monetary management. If the SDRs work as planned *i.e.* if they prove acceptable even in times of political strain and crisis, and are increased from the extremely modest level of $3 billion per year planned for the coming three years to a more significant figure, then they will provide a third alternative to the present system whereby an increase in international liquidity can only be accomplished by a rise in the gold price or an increase in Anglo-Saxon debt.

SDRs can thus defuse the political tensions of the present dollar system while putting the world gradually onto an internationally supervised dollar-equivalent standard. In such an event, gold will remain to back the dollar and guarantee the SDRs for some time to come. But as the constantly rising 'intrinsic' (non-monetary) value of gold, propelled by new demand for gold in industry, rises to exceed the metal's artificially depressed monetary value (a date projected by *The Economist* as likely to fall sometime at the end of the 1970's),[6] the final demonetization of gold could occur quite naturally.* Then private

* As the monetary use of gold has tended to decline, its industrial and artistic use has been rapidly expanding. Gold is today used in most transistor systems including transistor radios, apart from finding more spectacular use as a plating for the umbilical chords of astronauts. Additionally, the artificial holding down of gold's monetary value has made man consider it

individuals, despairing of the likelihood of a really massive re-valuation of gold for monetary purposes (a move that will be increasingly widely resisted as impossibly disruptive) will, it is hoped, gradually take whatever profit they could get, selling their hoards onto the industrial and artistic market. Finally, with new production matching the growth in gold's industrial and decorative uses, these private individuals may be followed by the central banks and the international monetary author-ities. In this way, American officials hope, the metal may finally be tamed out of primordial fetishism and into logicality.

However, the demonetization of gold by this process is likely to be very much less rapid than of silver, where demand for the metal for photographic film expanded at such a rate that the United States was unable to demonetize fast enough. After a thrilling race between the American authorities replacing silver coinage with nickel 'sandwich' coins just in time to forestall massive meltings of the old coinage, the free silver price went through the roof and forced the American Treasury to redeem millions of 'silver certificate' dollar bills backed by the metal at up to a 60 per cent premium. Silver, however, is now largely out of the monetary game, the United States government having officially ended silver redemption in July 1968.

A gradual retirement plan for gold, if it could be made to work at all, is liable, however, to be a most expensive policy for the American people. As George Bernard Shaw once put it, 'the world has to choose between trusting to the natural stability of gold and the honesty and intelligence of members of the govern-ment'. Many mistrustful people in the United States, as well as in the world beyond, agree with Shaw when he concluded that 'with due respect to these gentlemen, I advise you, as long as the capitalist system lasts, to vote for gold'. Shaw put his finger on the reason why gold need not be expected to exit from the monetary scene without a mighty and protracted struggle. Gold pressure on the dollar is therefore liable to continue to force Americans to curb their foreign held IOUs, either by

for all sorts of new industrial uses, perhaps the most spectacular of these being coating glass buildings (rolled to 3 millionths of an inch) to reflect the sun and thus replace far more costly air-conditioning. (See Timothy Green, *World of Gold*, New York, Walker and Co., 1968, Chapter II.)

greatly restrained public policies abroad or continued deflation at home.

The implications of such future deflation, the many billions of dollars worth of lost potential growth and the heavy strain which this may place on America's political structure, are the subject of chapter 12. By sticking grimly to the magic totem of $35 an ounce, Americans may be subjecting themselves to a period of steadily intensifying international monetary pressure before the final release of natural demonetization arrives, if indeed it ever does; for pressure on the dollar via gold-buying speculation may well intensify as it becomes more and more unlikely that the gold price will ever go down and more and more certain that industrial and artistic uses will ensure that it eventually rises. This may be an unnecessarily gloomy view. But it is incontestable that a more or less mystical belief in gold remains, in Europe, South America, and especially in India and the Far East, deeply embedded in cultural and social life. In fact it forms an integral part of patterns of behaviour, formed over the millennia, which it will take much more than immediate expectations of profit or loss to change. Backward societies, therefore, as well as the economically less sophisticated or more reactionary groups in the advanced nations, are powerful battalions on the side of those national or regionalist politicians who would continue to use gold as a defence against American 'economic takeover'.*

* India alone is estimated to contain *private* gold hoards, mostly in the form of jewellery, worth over $4·5 billion at the present monetary gold price (see Paul Ferris' Pelican *The City*, 1965, p. 164). One of the few 'liberal' arguments for gold's revaluation is the fact that such a move could give India a windfall in foreign purchasing power of double this amount, which would go far to meeting her needs for development capital in the present plan period. But this, of course, assumes that the Indian government would prove capable of charming the gold out of India's possessors. This is highly disputable, even in return for a 100 per cent profit. Indeed, if their payment for the gold were in rupees or government securities, as it would probably have to be, it seems almost certainly impossible. Of course, the converse argument could be applied: the demonetization of gold could rob India of an immense potential reserve asset.

3. GOLD AND THE STRUGGLE FOR EUROPE

So much for the objectives and strategy of the gold price defenders. What could the opposition really hope to gain from a new victory for gold?

The opposition to the dollar's dominion comprises a diffuse and varied group. It is not made up only of *laissez faire* conservatives. Others on both sides of the Atlantic, who see themselves as the hard-eyed realists, men who respect the lessons of history regarding the perennial fate of man-made money, also want to see a continuing role for gold. Whatever their political persuasions, all these 'realists', who watch on the sidelines, prepared to step in and buy gold if they see the tide of battle going against the dollar, are the reserve battalions of conservatism. But, consciously or unconsciously, this 'realist' group is used by a more active group of men with whom antipathy toward the dollar is an active force. As combatants this group regard themselves as defenders—defenders of the political and cultural integrity of Europe. Their target is the American presence in Europe, the influx, not so much of American money, as of American management and technology, almost impossible to measure accurately in financial statistics, that has grown massively with the prospects of European prosperity that follow the continent's economic integration.

Jean-Jacques Servan-Schreiber called Europe the new American frontier. This phrase scarcely seems an exaggeration in the face of a tripling of United States investment on the continent (from $2 billion to $6 billion) in the 1950's, followed by a second astonishing tripling between 1960 and 1967. Schreiber went on to illustrate how Americans have so far been the only people able to muster the organization, resources and will to take advantage of a European economy. The French learnt between 1963–66 that *direct* national resistance to American investment is futile; for the incoming American corporation can simply replan its location to the benefit of his antagonists' neighbour.[7] Upon de Gaulle's famous imposition of foreign investment restrictions in 1963, the Ford Motor Company switched their proposed plant site from Thionville in France across the border into a grateful Belgium; Phillips Petroleum switched from Bordeaux to the Benelux, and only a reversal of the General's edict in 1966 prevented a vast new General Motors plant from being relocated from Strasbourg in France to the German side of the Rhine.

A particular source of hostility among continental business leadership and bankers is the fact that America's superior technostructure has enabled her industry to capture the commanding economic heights—computers, electronics and chemicals in particular—the high growth sectors of European business where capital may expect a return of 10–15 per cent instead of the average 5–7 per cent return common in Europe's slow-growing traditional industries. It is this more glittering prospect of rewards that has attracted European capital away from European-run enterprise and into American-backed firms. As Servan-Schreiber put it, 'nine-tenths of "American" investment in Europe is from European sources. In other words, we pay them to buy us.'[8]

When one remembers the narrow limitations of the European capital market, the lingering preference for '*auto-financement*' in French business, the oligarchic control of German industry by the *grossbanken*, the tradition of close-to-the-chest secrecy which keeps company reports utterly unrevealing—and often downright misleading—to the would-be investor, and the preference of European managements for the principle of giving the shareholder a 'fair return' on his money rather than the principle of maximizing shareholders' capital appreciation, it is scarcely surprising that the European investor should prefer the 'glass house' principle of American company reporting to the intentional obfuscation which conceals the relative efficiency of even some of the largest European concerns.* Such preferences were amply demonstrated in the rise in popularity of 'Eurobonds' offered by American companies at handsome rates of interest, generally convertible into ordinary shares so as to make them inflation-proof, and denominated in dollars. The volume of Eurobond issues, which went from some $760 million in 1967

---

* It struck nobody in Germany as odd or surprising, for instance, when in 1966 the Chairman of Mannesman, Germany's third largest steel producer, publicly objected to a bank even making an estimate of his company's true profits.

to over $3·1 billion in the course of 1968 (of which American
companies issued $1·5 billion)[9] does much to prove that when
European investors are given a choice they will tend to ignore
traditional investing habits and look for the best buy.

NEW EUROPEANS VERSUS OLD

But the European politics of the gold war cannot be summed
up as one group of Europeans putting pressure on the dollar to
dissuade another group from financing American takeover by
holding dollar balances and dollar securities. The invading
American technostructure is welcomed by many Europeans as
a force helping to speed progress toward the high mass-con-
sumption way of life. Faster growth produces a higher level of
investment, more mass-production and a quicker rise to
American-style affluence for more people. But such rapid
growth will inevitably produce economic dislocation. There
will be widening contrasts between the growth areas (geographical and economic) and the inevitable pockets of stagnation, redundancy and high unemployment. Politicians are
the first to appreciate that votes, unlike productivity, conform
to the distribution of population. They also realize that shop-
floor level discontent caused by such growth-sponsored dislocation will readily ally with management of the afflicted industries in an effort to bolt the door on further disruptive
change. Furthermore, entrenched forces opposed to change
naturally tend to find plenty of allies in a business structure
peppered with family-based businesses ripe for take-over on
account of low capitalization, low productivity or uncompetitive size. As the American sharks enter the pool, all but a
few of the largest and toughest fish are bound to swim somewhat scared.

Still, these forces of suspicion and hostility face growing
opposition within the European body politic. First, of course,
they are opposed by the direct beneficiaries of the American
presence. Euro-American business is very largely managed and
staffed by Europeans. Together with United States-oriented
European investors and the great majority of consumers, they
represent a growing body of support for American 'fertilization'.

Thus, the 'old Europeans' find themselves more and more directly in conflict with a new pan-European economic force which may indeed come increasingly to hold the balance in European dollar politics. This force is well described in Anthony Sampson's *The New Europeans*, as the European claimants to the heritage of Europe of whom M. Servan-Schreiber has emerged as the mouthpiece.

The generation gap between the Old and New Europeans is also significant. Younger than the conservatives who have marinated in their respective nationalisms for too long to adopt a continental perspective, the New Europeans see themselves as a newly emergent élite. Springing from government, industry and the professions, remarkably mobile between these hitherto watertight compartments, the new men coalesce under the banner of continental integration, with their New Europe to be formed in America's economic image. The vision of the Moderns is expressed vividly by Servan-Schreiber. They see the creation of Europe-wide industrial and commercial units capable of competing with the American giants not merely in size, but in dynamism and efficiency. In order to achieve such competition, they want an enormous new concentration of effort on major enterprises in advanced technology. They see a need to transform present haphazard relationships between business, the university and government into a series of giant team efforts. They would mount vast and concerted campaigns to broaden and intensify all levels of education, and to project it as a continuing process into adulthood. To enable such a transformation to occur, they favour an organizational revolution involving every aspect of Europe's life, to be conducted along American lines. But above all, they press for the foundations of a federal European power capable of promoting and moulding the new business society.

EUROPEAN CIVILIZATION—THE CENTRAL STAKE

In their approach to the promotion of genuinely pan-European enterprise the New Europeans confront a basic political dilemma—a crossroads with implications for their monetary attitude. One road is labelled free international competition, the other, regional protection. The first is fraught with uncertainties, but its followers hope to gain the benefits of competitive stimulus and cross fertilization from an expanding American presence. The other road, regional protection, runs the risk of becoming taken over by those more interested in protection of smaller precincts—the nation, the province, the family firm: people whose fears of competition include their European neighbours as well as the American behemoth.

This European dilemma is not restricted to economic and social policy. With the mentality of protection goes a philosophy of life, a concern for the preservation of non-economic intangibles, stress on personal relationships and the belief that beyond a certain (undefined) point, quality of life surpasses in importance any aggregates of material wealth and power. If the price of European viability means embracing cost/benefit analysis to the exclusion of traditional patterns of thought—maximizing efficiency rather than cultivating relationships, gobbling a sandwich at the desk rather than commuting home to lunch with the family—viability may be achieved at the price of being European.

Here is the essential paradox of Europe—two instincts at war within one continental breast. The instinct for world power and mastery of the continent's destiny opposes the instinct for an identity, a way of life, a social order. The first promises a wider, deeper spread of a higher (in American values) standard of living. The second offers, for a while at least, preservation of traditional character and style, founded on the continuation of a social order and the traditional distribution of wealth. The real irony of Europe today is that it is appreciation of this way of life that fires the European desire for autonomy. Indeed, for most Europeans there can surely be little other purpose in hankering for continental independence. To the élite in Europe's capitals, who may control the continent's future industrial colossi, autonomy, for purely economic gain, may seem a burning issue, but to whom else? It is of little consequence to the unemployed worker in Trieste or Bordeaux whether the decision to lay him off was made in Brussels or New York.

The question of European autonomy will continue to divide Europe. Those who have noted how far concern over American

dominance has helped oil the wheels of Common Market agreements, believe that a dramatization of the American 'takeover'
can galvanize Europeans into Federation. But this, too, is a
potentially dangerous strategy. For aroused electorates, having
chosen the type of protection that encourages relative economic
stagnation, may well rue their decision as the gap between
East and West Atlantic living standards begins to widen
dramatically. They may have second thoughts about their
choice of impoverished gentility over affluent helotry. Those
who prefer to emphasize that Europeans who, after all, will be
the owners and employees of Euro-American business will be
the prime beneficiaries of the American challenge; those who
stress that, after all the ringing of alarm bells, only 10 per cent
of European assets are currently under American control;
those who note that pressure upon the Americans to correct
their balance of payments deficit has already curbed their
foreign investment, may have grasped the better part of wisdom, whatever their ultimate political motives.

THE NEW ROLE OF GOLD

In the last resort, no monetary manipulation, no juggling
with the price of gold can long neutralize the magnetism of a
single continent-sized nation's economic power. Only direct
political action—tariffs, quotas, exchange controls, in fact the
whole apparatus of protection with its open invitation to
retaliatory action—can insulate any nation, or region, from
American influence.

Gold may have been valuable to Europe as an instrument of
pressure, but it is useless in the longer run as an anti-American
prophylactic. Gold pressure on the dollar may have forced the
United States, given the high priority which it sets on preserving
the present role of its currency, into measures of self-limitation
such as controls on foreign investment, restraint of growth at
home, the re-examination of its military posture and even the
moderation of its anti-communist crusade. Wholesale return to
gold via revaluation, even if it could have been forced upon the
United States (which it could not), and even if the redoubled
value of the American gold reserve had been used for paying off

foreign-held IOUs, might initially have limited American spending power abroad. But it would not have touched the productive capacity which is the real source of American economic power. America's technical and scientific lead would, once again, have built for the United States a massive trading surplus, another great pile of sterile gold, against which she would have begun to lend, so that the whole cycle of profligacy would naturally recur.

Useless as a prophylactic, gold was nevertheless sufficiently effective as a pressure point to bring the world to dangerous deadlock. American officials and politicians, with their grand design for a perpetual dollar standard, and irritated by France's monetary hostility, have turned $35 an ounce into a citadel of national prestige, to be defended at almost any cost. The pressures behind this deadlock are still sufficiently dangerous, though recently eased by short-term capital flows from Europe to the temporary relief of the American balance of payments and the exacerbation of European monetary problems, to threaten a major monetary rupture. Signs of this rupture, ominous cracks, appeared in early 1968 with the break-up of the London Gold Pool and the emergence of the two-tier gold price system. These cracks could widen as today's blueprints for European monetary federalism draw closer to reality. Another reserve currency scare might yet cause the two-tier system to topple. Such a predicament could not be allowed by the United States Treasury to continue. As soon as American officials became positive that their gold was being fed to the speculators, the Treasury would be bound to snap shut the gold window, and allow the dollar to float.

Such action would signal another great turning point in monetary history. All indications are that under the ensuing speculative storm, the Atlantic monetary fault would become a split. Just because sub-surface political struggle would be involved, any one of many unexpected twists could then occur to confound prediction. By the same token, just because each nation thinks it so unlikely that foreign bankers would risk a financial Armageddon, the danger of unstoppable tailspin still lurks in the background.

INTERNATIONAL CURRENCIES AND
NATIONAL POLITICS

11

Sterling's International Twilight
—a Dawn of Hope

1. STERLING—THE LAST BRITISH EMPIRE

In the lean years that followed World War II Britain's sterling war debts helped to speed her recovery. Indeed the demand for British goods which they financed enabled Britain easily to exceed the Labour government's target of increasing her exports to a value 75 per cent above that of 1939 by the year 1950. They also led to a financial bargain that was even more useful to Britain; for under a series of informal bilateral arrangements—in true British fashion the club had no written rules— the sterling area became a dollar pool, with members handing their dollars into the Bank of England in return for sterling deposits with British banks.

As British economist Sir Dennis Robertson described this pool:

> It meant that each country, as a country, agreed to hand over its surplus dollar earnings to Mother in exchange for sterling, and to go to Mother when it wanted extra dollars to spend. Naturally the degree of confidence with which it exercised or presented claims on the dollar pool depended partly on its political status: the little black children who were often the best earners could be smacked on the head if they showed too great a propensity to spend dollars, while the grown up white daughters, who were often pretty extravagant, could only be quietly reasoned with.[1]

The 'little black children', the poorer and least-developed club members, which in those pre-independence days had little import-hunger, ran surpluses in their balance of payments and dutifully deposited these foreign exchange earnings in London, because they were told to. Meanwhile, the 'grown-up white daughters', the fast-growing and independent white Dominions, bought more from the North American continent than they sold to it and thus ran dollar deficits financed from the poor countries' dollar pool contributions. Britain, of course, also had use of the dollar pool when she needed it; and in the early post-war years, she drew great advantage from the fact that sterling was backed by reserves which included the foreign exchange earnings of a whole group of sterling-using nations.

This British advantage did not, however, come free; for the dollar pool of the sterling area was a *quid* in exchange for a *quo*. In return for the right to bank other people's foreign exchange, Britain had to offer the other aspect of a banker's services—capital for her clients to borrow. British capital exports, in other words, were to continue, as they had since the 1870's, to finance imperial demand for British goods. It was an arrangement which, albeit informally, institutionalized the traditional structure of the British economy. That was the snag. And it was precisely this characteristic which made it so burdensome in a fast-changing world.

What actually emerged from the hurried series of piece-meal arrangements made between a dollar-hungry Bank of England and sterling-using countries after the 1947 failure of convertibility, was an attempt to use a monetary device—the pound— to unite the entire group of countries economically (and also, in so far as was possible, politically) as though they were one vast nation. But the trouble was that the sterling area's industrial base was too limited and too localized. As a result, its source of capital, the City of London, was far too small. In short, if the whole 'sterling commonwealth' was viewed together as one country, it was an under-developed country, itself needing outside capital and technology if it was to achieve rapid growth.

Britain's inadequacy as a source of capital and technology became increasingly apparent as more and more British overseas possessions achieved their independence and the strings which controlled their foreign spending were released from tight fists in Whitehall. The experience of India furnished the clearest example of this change of outlook and its result for Britain and her banking role.

INDIA'S FINANCIAL REVOLT

The first Indian Five Year Plan, conceived in 1950 with a large measure of British guidance, had assumed that India would, by and large, continue to live within its means. And in fact, in the first years of independence, India generally speaking did. In the course of their first Plan's execution, the Indian government fairly consistently underspent the foreign exchange at their disposal. During this time, Indian planning officials were held up by Britain to other members of the sterling commonwealth as models of prudence and moderation, the ideal clients, in fact, for a banker with limited resources. But India's second Five Year Plan, drawn up in 1955, was conceived under the intellectual influence not of London but of the Soviet Union, and other high-investment, fast-growth economies. Its approach was characteristic of the new mood of developing nations. Now that the Indians themselves were planning their rate of growth and the amount of investment needed to meet it, they began to look beyond traditional sources for the necessary investment capital, and India's sterling balances were obviously an asset which could be used up to help fill her investment gap.

The Anglo-Indian financial crunch came in 1957, exactly a decade after independence. By the end of the first year of their new Plan, the Indians had run through their reserves of sterling to the point where the remainder of their pounds represented no more than the reserve cover of their currency. They therefore turned to the British government for a £200 million public loan. It was Britain's refusal to grant this loan which precipitated India's financial revolt. Her finance minister Mr. Krishnamachari promptly announced that he would hence forward be prepared to use the whole of India's sterling balances to meet the nation's import bills necessary to fulfil the goals of the Second Plan.

Britain's bluff was being called as a banker because she could no longer afford to act as one. Ever since World War II, it had been the City of London's tacit assumption that Britain's sterling debts were really more of an asset to Britain than a liability, because a large proportion of them would never be presented as claims on Britain, as they represented the effectively frozen currency backing of client countries. The significance of India's financial revolt was that it shattered this basic assumption behind the sterling bargain.

2. THE WATERSHED YEAR FOR STERLING

India's decision to use her sterling balances was one of several events in the year 1957 which encouraged people in the City to re-examine the sterling area bargain. Another was that by 1957 it was becoming clearly evident that Britain's pattern of trade had, since World War II, undergone significant change. Between 1946 and 1951, Britain's trade with the sterling area had grown rapidly, while her trade with war-smashed Europe had scarcely got back to its pre-war level. But since 1954 the growth pattern was sharply reversed, Britain's Commonwealth trade expanding by only 16 per cent, while trade with Western Europe grew by almost 60 per cent. At the same time, bilateral bargaining over tariffs had greatly reduced the effectiveness of imperial preference, so that the United States, Japan and West Germany were all rapidly increasing their exports to the Commonwealth, partly at the expense of the British share of the market.

Thus by 1957, it was becoming evident to a number of observers that the sterling arrangements of the 1940's were perhaps becoming a drag on British growth rather than a prop to the pound. Britain's own dollar earnings in 1957 exceeded those of the whole of the rest of the sterling area combined, and, taking American military aid into account, came very close to balancing British dollar spending. Meanwhile, as these observers pointed out, the sterling arrangements themselves, producing as they did a heavy haemorrhage abroad of British capital, represented a fearsome burden on the British balance of payments. Put another way, in the early post-war years British exports to the sterling area were largely financed by British capital exports. This meant that though exports increased, Britain did not see an increase in her reserves or liquidity position as a whole. Furthermore, in playing her part as international banker, Britain was, allegedly, depriving her own industry of capital, and thus inhibiting the growth of British export capacity on which the strength of sterling ultimately depended.

It was just as the domestic implications of Britain's capital-supplying liability were being grasped that a new and unprecedented kind of sterling crisis arrived to produce a climacteric in British monetary theory. It was by no means Britain's first monetary crisis since World War II,* nor was its scale such as to make it a landmark. Many others, before and since, were more phrenetic and more costly to the Bank of England in gold and foreign exchange. But with the benefit of a dozen years of hindsight, the sterling crisis of 1957 emerges from the agonizing sequence of Britain's financial melodrama as a portentous watershed.

What was new about the crisis of 1957 was that it was the first sterling crisis to occur *in spite of the fact* that the British economy appeared perfectly healthy at the time, and with no balance of payments deficit in sight. All of a sudden, the pattern of the modern-style sterling crisis appeared. Suddenly, in June, began a now all-too-familiar rush to get out of pounds and into a safer currency, either the dollar, or, preferably, the mark, which it was believed might shortly be revalued. Delayed reaction to the Suez adventure of the previous November, which had shattered both Britain's and France's Great Power pretensions, had begun to set in. The year 1957, in fact, saw a preview to the monetary crises of 1968–69, with the weakness of the pound and the franc adding to the glow of the obviously under-valued mark. At once rumours of an impending sterling devaluation ran hot and heavy. But on this occasion the pound, not seriously overvalued in fact, was successfully defended *without* a major international rescue operation. Chancellor Peter Thorneycroft managed the situation by hoisting bank rate from 5 per cent to what was then a forty-year high of 7 per cent, and, when this proved inadequate to staunch the outflow of hot money, imposing direct controls on capital export. What emerged in the process, however, was the realization that Britain was now vulnerable not merely to declines in her own

* Sterling crises of greater or lesser severity had occurred in 1947, 1949, 1951, 1955 and 1956.

earnings relative to her imports, but also to her *relative* weakness, and to any waves of preference that might develop in favour of another currency.

THE RADCLIFFE REPORT, AND DISILLUSION

The 1957 sterling crisis shook even some diehards' confidence in the value to Britain of sterling's international role. It also helped to change the Conservatives' basic ideas on the whole subject of monetary management.

Indeed the experiences of 1957 so completely shattered the government's confidence in its understanding of how the monetary mechanism really worked that a Royal Commission was set up, under Lord Radcliffe, to examine the working of the British banking and monetary system from the ground up. The monetary confusion climaxed at the year's end. A deadlocked policy confrontation at the Treasury resulted in the resignation of Peter Thorneycroft, together with his two top advisers, Nigel Birch and Enoch Powell, in an open Cabinet split over economic policy.

More than three orthodox, City-oriented Cabinet ministers were ousted in this split. It spelt final Tory rejection of the traditional concept that the 19th century mechanism of bank rate was sovereign against the economy's ailments, both internal and external. For while Thorneycroft's 7 per cent bank rate of the previous autumn had successfully stamped the remaining life out of Britain's stubbornly resistant investment boom, it had signally failed to hold foreign-owned sterling in London. This was why it had been necessary, on top of a record-high bank rate, to use exchange controls to halt speculation in favour of the mark. By the year's end, therefore, the weakness of the traditional sterling defences in the face of foreign strength was fully exposed.

Doubts about the effectiveness of the traditional role of bank rate were clearly inseparable from doubts about the value of the international role of sterling itself. The Radcliffe Committee's Report, which appeared in August 1959, helped to confirm these doubts. In fact it openly questioned the assumptions on which Britain's monetary policy continued to operate.

The Committee had heard evidence from exporters who pointed out the vicious cycle of Britain's banking responsibilities. By keeping British reserves so slim in relation to Britain's liquid debts, these men asserted that the government continually forced itself to stop new investment in productivity as soon as an import-led boom threatened Britain's scanty reserves. Some experts therefore proposed that British capital exports (including to the sterling area) should be further restricted. This would, they claimed, enable the government to increase Britain's economic autonomy. It would permit the building of substantially larger reserves and release more capital for domestic investment. The Committee assented to the general desirability of such a course, but concluded that Britain was not free to pursue it.[2] She could not, in Radcliffe's opinion, unilaterally wind up the sterling area bargain on discovering that it had turned out to be a trap.[3]

At the same time Radcliffe pointed to two important facts which it felt in the long run let Britain out of her monetary dilemma. The first was that the international role of sterling was itself gradually fading away. Official holdings of sterling, it noted, had fallen by about 60 per cent between 1945 and 1957. Meanwhile the share of world trade financed in sterling had declined since 1949. The second was that, contrary to fondly held belief in the City, the City's foreign exchange earnings (estimated by Radcliffe at an annual £125 million in 1959), were scarcely affected by foreigners' growing preference for holding their reserves in dollars, gold or other 'safer' currencies.

This last blow at the most sacred of all British monetary assumptions was another result of the pivotal experience of the sterling crisis of 1957. For when, in September of that year, the Bank of England had clamped strict controls on London banks' sterling credits to borrowers outside the sterling area, these banks began offering dollar loans instead, bidding for dollar deposits from overseas to finance them. As an *ad hoc* device at a moment of crisis, this new dollar dealing hardly seemed to be a matter of shattering significance. But the birth of the Euro-dollar market, which it in fact represented, destroyed the final national argument for continuing to bear the sterling burden.

The weakness of the other arguments for a special sterling role was brilliantly revealed in Andrew Shonfield's widely influential Penguin, *British Economic Policy Since the War* which appeared the year before the Radcliffe Report. Shonfield had analysed the political assumptions on which the sterling area was based, and how the rationale for the post-war sterling bargain had vanished for all concerned. From every point of view, Britain could no longer afford to meet the growing demands of the sterling club. Not only had the price in impediment to her own growth become unacceptably high, but the corollary of this lagging growth and flagging competitiveness made sterling an increasingly risky vessel in which to store international wealth. Thus, in circular fashion, Britain was continually lowering her potential as a supplier of development capital.

In 1959, with sterling newly convertible, and thus more vulnerable than ever, the writing on the wall was perfectly clear. Yet the Radcliffe Committee and the City fathers equivocated on sterling's future role. For a dozen more years Britain, increasingly bowed with debt, contracted in support of her overvalued and vulnerable currency, was to continue handing out Danegelt to her friends, a ransom paid not to buy freedom from the bonds of a dead Empire, but to preserve those imperial shackles.

In part, the reason for this continuous self-imprisonment was the inevitable slowness of the readjustment process—the time it takes for the political penny to drop. But another pressure for resisting change came from across the Atlantic.

3. THE ATLANTIC TRAP

It was Britain's peculiar misfortune that, just as she was coming to terms with her post-imperial destiny, the demands of world power on her Atlantic partner's balance of payments, produced powerful American pressure to keep her active in a supporting role as international banker and policeman, for fear that total responsibility for both these functions might topple the dollar. So the sterling area, which throughout the 40's and 50's had served to finance Britain's survival and her post-war recovery, was projected into the 1960's in support of American world power.

In November 1967, a remark by United States Treasury Secretary Fowler that 'Devaluation of the pound puts the dollar in the front line in the defence of the world monetary system'[4] was designed to alert and brace an American audience for the coming speculative impact in the wake of the pound's retreat. Reported in Britain, however, the remark prompted many to enquire why the Americans had not been in the front line before. Why, people wondered out loud, had Britain, in her well-known state of economic weakness, for so long been exposed in the 'forward positions', using her precious reserves as cannon fodder to protect her much more powerful sister currency?

No one would question that the basic decision to continue the defence of sterling for those four grim years, 1964–67, was at root a British one, based upon a British government's view of national self-interest. Yet it was also true that other commitments undertaken by Britain in the early 1960's, which directly affected sterling, were compromising the British government's independence of view, and enormously increasing their dependence on the dollar and American financial support.

This shifting monetary relationship between Britain and the United States reflected their shift in political roles. Britain's post-Suez instinct was to question her overseas military commitment. America's post-Dulles posture was to fill every power vacuum in sight. The meeting point of these ebb and flood tides was the whirlpool vortex of Southeast Asia. In the far-flung strategy of global power, the fate of Indonesia linked the Anglo-Saxons' interests. Sukarno, while making threatening gestures towards British-protected Malaysia, was drifting towards alliance with Southeast Asian communism in a manner which spelt trouble to Americans in Saigon. Thus the growing American involvement in Vietnam brought heavy United States pressure on the British to build up their defence of Malaysia and Singapore, the other half of an Anglo-American nutshell in which Dulles' successors planned to contain Asian communism.

Malaysia's confrontation with Sukarno in the early 1960's was the last straw for sterling. What was supposedly an era of retreat from Empire, and of subsidence in the cold war, saw a major build-up of Britain's overseas bases and a doubling of the number of servicemen abroad.[5] Astonishingly, the British government's net current expenditure overseas *trebled* from £147 to £449 million between 1957 and 1967. If one went back further to 1952, when the net figure was £54 million, the increase was eightfold. At one point in 1963 the Malaysia–Indonesia confrontation alone was costing Britain over £1 million a day. Even after the Wilson government's foreign military expenditure cuts in 1964–66, Britain was still spending over $1 billion annually in foreign exchange abroad. For the sake of comparison, the next largest expenditure by a European nation (France) in the same period was a mere $46 million; meanwhile Germany's balance of payments *benefited* by other nations' overseas military expenditures to the tune of an annual $300 million net.

The pressure from Washington to maintain this level of British commitment was clear and constant. The reward for doing so was continued support of the pound. The full extent of British attachment to America's financial apron strings will not be revealed for years to come. But from all contemporary reports and accounts* this dependence, which had anyway been lifted to a new level as far back as December 1958, when sterling finally returned to convertibility, was virtually complete by the time of the Malaysia–Indonesia confrontation. Such dollar support soon proved to be a mixed and highly questionable blessing. It blurred the stark alternative that Britain would otherwise have had to face. It perpetuated the illusion that Britain could manage her modernization and expand her welfare state while playing a global role.

America's need to keep sterling in the front line in one sense gave Britain a little more latitude in her straitjacket, but it also served to ensure that she remained in it. At the time, however, it was argued by Conservatives that dollar support served as an alternative to brutal 1957-type use of the monetary weapon, and to the destructive frustrations of 'stop–go'. In the next

---

* Two of the most revealing of these emerge from on-the-spot reports by journalists, Henry Brandon's *In the Red, The Struggle for Sterling 1964–66* and William Davies, *Three Years Hard Labour*.

major sterling crisis after 1957, that of 1963, the need for a sky-high bank rate was sidestepped by a three-month $250 million credit from the United States and continental central banks.

On returning to power in 1964, Labour, like their Conservative predecessors, faced the choice between devaluation plus drastic use of bank rate or continued dependence on foreign borrowing. Wilson's attempt to get the country moving and eschew 'stop–go' was, however, bound, like Maudling's similar effort of 1963–64, to increase Britain's indebtedness and dependence on foreign financial support. Thus by November 1967, when Labour were finally forced to bow to the inevitable, a combination of party politics and egregious foreign generosity had put the Exchequer deep into the red with foreign bankers.

Enforced devaluation finally revealed how pointlessly foreign support for the insupportable had mired Britain down in debt. For in December 1967, the British faced the world with repayment commitments undertaken in support of the $2.80 rate amounting to over $4 billion, a debt load which was itself largely responsible for the need for other continuing loans.

Meanwhile more and more people were awakening to the fact that while the dollar was supported by other nations out of their own self-interest, the pound was ultimately supported only by the British taxpayer. When the dollar sank close to its floor at Frankfurt (for example), which it did consistently in the spring and summer of 1968, the German Bundesbank would be bound to support it by buying dollars with marks, because a dollar devaluation would have the same result for the German economy as a revaluation of the mark. But when sterling dropped near *its* floor, it was the British government which had to come to its rescue, raising huge foreign loans in support. Thus every rush out of the reserve currencies, while regarded as merely a nuisance in Washington, represented an additional burden on the British taxpayer.

HOW CLOSE TO TECHNICAL BANKRUPTCY?

By the spring of 1968 it had become unavoidably obvious to even the blindest that sterling was being forced out of its world role by the fact that Britain was running out of credit.

Since before Labour's return to power in 1964, many people, notably among the Left-wing of the Labour Party, had been in favour of hoisting Britain out of her permanent plight of inadequate reserves by the sale of part of her still large foreign investment portfolio. The Bank of England and City's reaction to these suggestions were along predictable lines. Liquidation of long-term assets, they pronounced, amounted to 'eating the seed corn' because these investments yielded a considerable foreign income which helped the overall balance of payments. But after all, if a sensible parent will spend savings or capital to ensure his child an education that will produce greater future earning power, why shouldn't a nation challenged by advancing technology in the international community be prepared to spend some capital so as to afford the technical training and re-tooling which will ensure future competitiveness and prosperity? Such a measure would, of course, mean the compulsory sale of private portfolio foreign investments in return for government stock. It would *not* necessarily, however, mean, as City Tories suggested, a massive capital levy.

But despite the strong arguments in favour of such a course from left and centre, Labour in practice chose the path of conservatism. True, in the aftermath of the sterling crisis of 1964, Chancellor Callaghan did take steps to start liquidating the government's own $1,250 million portfolio of dollar stocks acquired from private investors during World War II,* but this represented less than 5 per cent of Britain's estimated £13,550 million-worth of private overseas assets. Meanwhile, in the budget of April 1968, the scheduled raising of the school leaving age from 15 to 17 was deferred as one of the economy measures to defend the pound. This scheduled extension of schooling represented in fact, if not in national accounts statistics, an additional national investment which in the longer run would undoubtedly pay off in increased foreign earnings for Britain. It was postponed for the short-run reason that it would

---

* The process of converting these stocks into short-term bonds and then into ready cash took two years to complete so as not to disturb the market against the sales and was conducted in the strictest secrecy, an approach which helped the conduct of the operation, but which largely thwarted its psychological purpose of adding to the visible strength of the pound.

involve a greater absorption of resources in a process without immediate productive result, which would put further temporary strain on the labour supply, and hence prices, in the years of transition.

When this national belt-tightening proved insufficient to correct the balance of payments while Britain continued to expand her overseas investments, the government became compelled to borrow more heavily abroad. By July 1968, the *reductio ad absurdum* of such a policy was reached; for Britain, in acquiring the $2 billion standby credit for the purpose of stabilizing the sterling balances, had come to the verge of technical bankruptcy, with her total of foreign debts approaching for the first time in history, the total of her foreign assets (see breakdown of UK Overseas Assets and Liabilities at December 31st, 1968, page 240).

DEPENDING ON THE SHEIKS

Meanwhile the character of the sterling area had changed during the 1960's in such a way as to reduce still further the advantages which it brought to Britain. During the mid-60's, as more and more Commonwealth members left the club, their places were being taken by a more volatile group of depositors, who felt little loyalty to London as such, but only to the extraordinarily high interest rates which Britain was forced to maintain both to restrain her economy and to attract short-term foreign deposits. India, Egypt and Argentina, the original big sterling holders, had, of course, spent the bulk of their sterling long ago. But their place had been taken by the flourishing banking centre of Hong Kong, and more especially by the deposit of oil royalties paid by British and American oil companies to the rulers of the Persian Gulf states. Surprisingly, therefore, though the level of *officially held* sterling balances continued to decline (from £2,252 million [old series] in 1951 to £1,726 million [new series] in 1966), *private* overseas holdings of sterling rose from £333 million in 1951 to £614 million in 1966. Thus though their composition changed, the overall level of sterling balances in the late 1960's was almost the same as that of the immediate post-war years.[6]

UK OVERSEAS FINANCE: SHORT AND LONG TERM ASSETS AND LIABILITIES, AT DECEMBER 31st, 1968

(Sources: *Bank of England Quarterly*, *United Kingdom Balance of Payments* (Central Statistical Office) and *International Financial Statistics*)

Short-term assets	$ million	*Short-term liabilities*	$ million
Gold and foreign exchange reserves	2,422	Private claims against UK (Total)	9,435
Private claims against foreigners	6,101	Official debt to IMF	2,723†
		Official debt, other bodies	706†
		Claims in sterling, official holders	5,081*
	8,523		17,945
			− 8,523
		Net short-term liabilities	9,422

Long-term assets		*Long-term liabilities*	
Private (UK investments overseas)	32,532	Private (overseas private investment in UK)	16,416
Public (inter-government loans etc.)	2,671	Public (inter-government loans etc.)	5,380
	35,203		21,796
	− 21,796		
Net long-term assets	13,417		

Balance of long- and short-term net assets and liabilities:

Net assets (long term)	13,417
Net liabilities (short term)	− 9,422
	3,995

*This figure does not include central bank debts incurred on central bank 'swap' lines, which are not officially disclosed. Confidential central bank 'swap' credit added an estimated $1,000 million to $2,000 million to foreign official claims in sterling. This estimate is derived from the statement of Mr Jenkins, Chancellor of the Exchequer, that $1,000 million, or what he described as 'between a sixth and a seventh' of short- and medium-term official debt, had been repaid in the first six months of 1969. From this it follows that the total outstanding at December 31st 1968 must have been between $6,000 million and $7,000 million. Of this, $5,081 million is accounted for by the officially disclosed debts, so the balance of approx. $1,000 to $2,000 million must represent the then outstanding swaps. The total of short-term liabilities must therefore be an estimate only.

†The maturities of medium- and short-term indebtedness (excluding the confidential central bank debts) were as follows:

	$ million		
IMF	1,200	1968/70	
	123	1969/71	
	1,400	1971/73	
US Exim Bank	527	1969/75	
Swiss National Bank	26	1968/70	
Bank for International Settlements	103	1968/69	Official indebtedness to other bodies.
Deutsche Bundesbank	50	1972	

The confidential central bank 'swap' credits are technically granted for periods of three months, with one automatic renewal for another three months. In practice the six-month maturity of these 'swaps' is not insisted upon.

But these Arab balances, as was proved during the Arab–Israeli war in 1967, represented one more potential thorn in Britain's side and one more area of vulnerability in the politics of sterling that could precipitate a run on the currency, and force the British taxpayer to pay out even more tribute in the form of interest on foreign loans.*

WASHINGTON BARS LONDON FROM BRUSSELS?

Apart from helping to ruin Britain's international finances and producing a new depth of bitterness in her domestic politics, the protraction of sterling's world role at the behest of Washington was also tipping the political balance of Europe.

America's need to shield the dollar by protracting the agony of sterling not merely helped to weaken Britain's bargaining power *vis-à-vis* the Continent. In a more direct way, it helped to secure her exclusion as well. For not only did continued dollar–sterling collaboration provide the pretext for de Gaulle's last veto† but, as the October 1967 report of the EEC Commission on Britain's entry emphasized, the reserve role of the pound added an extra dimension to the already immensely intricate problem of matching British economic patterns and institutions to those of Europe. This report strongly implied that the pound must be devalued (which it was, barely two months later). Much more alarming to British decision-makers, however, it suggested that Britain's entry into Europe would

* During the six-day war, a number of sterling area oil sheiks, acting under political pressure from their poorer Arab socialist neighbours, withdrew their sterling from London, so as to embarrass a supposedly pro-Israeli Britain. The money soon returned to London. But, gallingly enough for the British, in the form of that much publicized £37.5 million credit, offered by a Swiss banking consortium in October 1967, in an eleventh-hour attempt to stave off devaluation. With the British bank rate at a crisis level 6 per cent, the crafty 'gnomes' were turning a very handy 2·5 per cent on the Arab money, for whose use they would only offer the sheiks 3·5 per cent; meanwhile they obtained from the Bank of England a 'gold-clause' guarantee in their loan agreement, thus insuring themselves against devaluation.

† In his press conference of May 1967 the General cited Britain's financial vulnerability caused by the special relationship between the sterling area and the dollar as the principal barrier to her entry into Europe.

be impractical without a transfer of sterling's reserve responsibilities onto a multilateral basis. The feeling was strong that the maintenance of a reserve currency by one member of the Community was incompatible with the Community's development into anything approaching 'full-blooded economic and political union'. Thus, as *The Economist* put it at the time:

> So long as sterling is a reserve currency, run from London . . . British chancellors will tend to side with American secretaries of the treasury in international financial questions. Nor is it enough for Mr. Wilson to explain that Article 108 of the Rome Treaty (mutual aid to a member state in difficulties) will not be invoked in Britain if, say, Australia runs into trouble. A member of the community which happens to have a reserve currency cannot have one policy for its interests inside the community and another for those outside. If sterling needs support and none is sought from Europe, Britain will be even more dependent on backing from the United States—adding to the problem of evolving common European policies.[7]

The transatlantic trap was a tender one. True, a scattering of British political commentators and a sprinkling of politicians continually described the harshness of its concealed realities. But most of the time, almost all of Britain's leadership, under the influence of suave assurances and veiled threats from service chiefs and the financial community, preferred instead to gaze at the more flattering side, the 'special relationship', the side that enabled them to bask a little longer in the fast-dying glow of imperial glory.

The easy solution to the dilemma of sterling and Europe was to avoid the agonies of change now and to have the electorate pay, in cash, the price of self-delusion later. Unhappily for Britain, this was the line of both political parties, despite the mounting evidence of its dangers and costs.

4. BREAKING THE VICIOUS CYCLE

The 1967 devaluation removed the last vestiges of advantage in Britain's role of beggar-banker.

With the increasing threat of a lower sterling parity, most of the overseas sterling countries had long been anxious to switch their reserves out of pounds and into dollars. Now, with the fall of the pound, the remaining members of the sterling area had taken a 14 per cent capital loss while watching the industrialized nations' central bankers (and even some private Swiss banks) obtain gold guarantees against that fate when they lent funds to support the pound. Meanwhile Britain's rich-nation creditors, though their loans to Britain were safe, saw that sterling's weakness was putting their own currencies in jeopardy. At last both the rich and poor among sterling's creditors simultaneously found reasons to press for an ending of sterling's reserve role.

Britain too was at the end of her tether. The need to defend her balance of payments with savage deflation had raised unemployment to a post-war high, and caused yet another postponement of her timetable for economic expansion. How was Britain's transformation from avuncular imperial metropole to competitive industrial society, the necessary precursor to steady and rapid growth, ever to be achieved under a permanent régime of deflation? The only industries left unscathed by Labour's post-devaluation clamp-down were the consumer durable manufacturers who were supposed to lead a cut-price export boom. But these industries, for the most part, were not situated in the depressed industrial areas of the North, Scotland, South Wales and Northern Ireland which were in such urgent need of reconstruction. Cuts in British government spending announced at devaluation time were, therefore, bound to give a proportionately heavier knock to just those parts of the British Isles which in the absence of technological innovation were already turning to political revolt.

Thus, amid furious vituperation from every quarter of the political compass, the spotlight was finally turned full onto the anachronism of international sterling itself. After a decade of questioning and argument among financial and economic professionals, the prospect of an international monetary reform from which sterling would emerge minus its international responsibilities, ceased to be a taboo subject even in the most conservative crannies of Throgmorton Street. Instead it became a keystone of British policy.

But the first priority was release from the Atlantic trap. An early indication of new British determination to break loose from this entanglement came with the December 1967 decision to evacuate Singapore by 1971 instead of 1977, as previously planned. In removing the immediate threat to Malaysia and Singapore, the Indonesian counter-revolution had helped cut the bars of sterling's cage. But the question remained, could this relatively smooth transition in the Far East be duplicated in the monetary sphere?

Some form of 'funding' of the sterling balances had always been seen as the alternative to the threatening overhang of Britain's liabilities. The most logical step, and one favoured by many, would clearly be for Britain to make her sterling debts over to the IMF in exchange for a single, consolidated long-term debt, which Britain would owe to the entire world central banking community. An almost equally logical, and perhaps more attractive solution, would be to use the sterling debts to link Britain to Europe.

For a long time, President de Gaulle's abiding veto on Britain's Common Market membership combined with a quiet rearguard action by Bank of England and City conservatives to rule out such a solution. Political deadlock thus forced sterling to continue to play the dying gladiator in the centre of the world financial arena. Devaluation had momentarily removed the heat of speculation from sterling, but soon the troubles of the dollar and franc and the stubborn refusal of the British trade account to show a surplus pushed sterling once again to its floor.

Britain was now left with no alternative but to move ahead alone. In July 1968 Sir Leslie O'Brien, the calm and dapper Governor of the Bank of England, returned from a visit to Basle with the first step of sterling's international dismantlement taken—the $2,000 million medium-term standby credit arranged with the Bank of International Settlements. At this point, the only feasible way out of the sterling straitjacket was an expensive insurance policy on top of all the other debts into which Britain's beggar-banker situation had landed her so as to guard against the danger of large-scale conversion into dollars of the remaining sterling balances.

But the sterling area wind-up would not grant any substantial or early release. For the Old Lady of Threadneedle Street, continuing to indulge her traditional taste for bilateral and secret dealings, insisted upon doing the rounds with sterling area governments, telling them that they could, if they wanted to, convert part of their balances into some of the proceeds of

"Now suppose we drop the term 'overdraft' altogether and start talking about 'a new facility for sterling'?"
10.vii.68.

the $2,000 million credit, but not too much. This was seen as a nice compromise formula. It allowed those who so wished to regard the move as a measure to bolster up rather than dismantle the sterling bargain. The sterling area was, after all, to be kept in being: the carrot of British capital still dangled in return for depositors' informal agreement to leave their reserves in pounds. The City had won one more battle against the forces wishing to limit Britain's foreign financial entanglements. As usual, they had won it at the expense of the British economy as a whole.

HAVE THEY REALLY LEARNT?

If 1957 marked a turning point in British monetary politics, 1967 marked the end of a road. But the long agony of a decade of financial enslavement to her imperial past was not altogether without purpose. For, by the close of the decade of the 60's, the hard realities of modern economic life had penetrated the thinking of all but the extremist fringe of both political parties.

Progressive Tories had learned the lesson that the shift of emphasis in British exporting from traditional and protected to sophisticated and competitive markets required not only vastly more investment in efficient production, but an unburdening of the currency which would permit a new freedom of choice in behaviour and thinking.

The realists of the Labour Party had also been clearing their cupboard of skeletons. They had been forced by the hard facts of life in office to acknowledge that a handful of shop stewards could be just as stultifying and reactionary a force as the cohorts of Montagu Norman: that in Britain an inverted pyramid of obstruction hindered national progress just as surely as the beliefs of the traditional pyramid of power.

By the end of their second post-war term of office, there were signs that Labour's leadership had bridged the traditional chasm in socialist doctrine, and were facing up to the classic socialist dilemma between a tendency towards economic nationalism while supporting international political action. This meant facing the fact that Britain, as an export economy earning a quarter of her national wealth abroad, is so interlocked

248 Sterling's International Twilight—a Dawn of Hope

with other socio-economic systems that her range of choice
as to her national distribution of wealth must be limited by the
choice of a wider community.

Over all, Labour had shown, however, that such intellectual
food could not be stomached by the band of doctrinaire
socialists that grew up in the depression and dominated the
Party in the 60's. These men, prisoners of their past, in just the
same way as was Philip Snowden in the 1930's, were forced into
the same invidious position. Their own rigidity condemned
them to defend the *status quo* with all the weapons of orthodoxy
because they were debarred from revolutionary change by lack
of a mandate, and from the path of compromise by an excess
of ideology.

In the one area where Labour could have found more latitude
for social renewal and high government spending, that of getting international agreement to an expansion of liquidity, they
were unable to push the international community, or the City,
with sufficient speed. For this they had to pay the penalty of
increasing Britain's liquidity by borrowing from other nations
on high interest terms.

Release from the sterling bargain, together with the overseas
military burden with which it forms a parcel, will provide,
when it is fully accomplished, a new sense of freedom. But
whether Britain's financial problems are solved in a European
or a world context, their solution could aggravate the difficulties
of her erstwhile clients in the developing world, unless very
specific provisions are made for their new needs. This final
dimension of international monetary politics, and the problem
which it poses for the reformers of the world monetary system,
is the subject of the penultimate chapter.

The Price of the Dollar's Defence

1. DOLLAR MANAGEMENT FOR AN EMPIRE OR A NATION?

In very rough terms, the United States accounts for one third of the annual wealth-production of the entire world, the other capitalist industrial countries together accounting for another third, and the rest of the world for the rest. This sort of scale in a single national economy produces important differences in kind. Indeed, can an economic entity which accounts for so much of the world's wealth-production be meaningfully looked at as just another, albeit vast, national economy? Is it not more sensible to regard it rather as something qualitatively different —the powerhouse of an international capitalist system? Politically, of course, other nations' leaders must purport to see America as the former. But most now also realize that there is a compelling case for looking at America the second way: as financier and energizer of an international prosperity.

Americans themselves feel the same ambivalence. Those who, like Senator Fulbright, fear the implications of policing ever-increasing global interests, tend to stress their economy's self-preoccupation and its high degree of self-sufficiency. Foreign trade, it is pointed out, accounts for a mere 4 per cent of American GNP, compared with 25 per cent for Germany, 22 per cent for Britain and 16 per cent for France, and balance of payments deficits of $3–4 billion that get Washington so upset represent less than half of 1 per cent of GNP and only 5 per cent of America's international trade. Such people may accept the fact that the international monetary system hinges upon the buying power of the American dollar. But they would oppose domestic monetary restraints in response to international pressure on the dollar because they realize that this involves increased unemployment, fewer job opportunities for blacks and further postponement of assaults on rural poverty and urban decay. To these people, giving such priority to international claims on the dollar is comparable to the famous piano-playing clown, who always insists on adjusting the piano in relation to the piano-stool.

Moreover, it is not necessary, they argue, to maintain the dollar's reserve role by deflation as Britain had to do with the pound, because, unlike Britain, who had trouble paying her way commercially, pressure on the dollar abroad is a result of two decades of overseas expansion and the political backwash it has brought. Hence their answer to attacks upon the dollar is to check international expansion, either by curbing overseas military spending, foreign investment, or aid, or by raising tariffs to check imports.*

Americans who prefer to stress the United States' integral involvement in, and dependence upon, the world economy, on the other hand, recoil from such controls. They believe that, apart from inviting economic nationalism and retaliation elsewhere, their proposers mistake the true springs of America's stable prosperity. It is, they point out, utterly fallacious to suggest that America's involvement in the world economy is in any way indicated by the small part of her wealth gained in foreign trade. Her close intermeshing in the international economy is much more the result of the unique scale and nature of her export of capital and technology since World War II.

It is, in this connection, important to grasp the difference between America's late 20th-century financial hegemony and that formerly wielded by London. In the 19th and early 20th centuries, the British (apart from their wholly owned colonies) lent abroad to finance trade, or to draw rent from government bonds. By contrast, America's foreign investment has been technology-led and used to set up American production facilities all over the world. The expansion of this foreign production has been staggering. It has grown at an annual rate of 10 per cent in the 50's and 60's compared to an annual average growth of 7 per cent in foreign trade. Thus by 1968, while American exports amounted to an annual $32 billion, the value of

* John Kenneth Galbraith and many other liberal economists have consistently advocated this last alternative.

foreign production based on direct American investment was about $120 billion a year, and as high as $150 billion if production associated with American investment other than direct is included.[1]

In day-to-day terms this massive American investment is familiar to everyone. American-owned firms hold over 50 per cent of Britain's petroleum, computers, refrigerators and agricultural machinery markets, and over 20 per cent of pharmaceuticals. Well over three-quarters of foreign capital investment in Britain, over half in Germany, over a third in France, is American.[2] Jean-Jacques Servan-Schreiber startled Europe by pointing out that fifteen years from now the world's third industrial power would be American industry in Europe. What he omitted to mention, however, was that America's *total* foreign production was *already* the third industrial power.

In February 1967, the Research Director of the United States Council of the International Chamber of Commerce pointed out that:

> The earning capacity of this entire productive structure has reached the point where it is capable of remitting earnings to this country at the level of some $6 billion a year after allowing for the very substantial retention of earnings to finance expansion of capacity—the expansion of which constitutes, it should be noted, the country's most promising source of additional foreign exchange to finance the urgent cost of military operations in Vietnam.[3]

Yet, not only isolationist Americans but internationalist Americans, who took a sanguine view of the freedom of action, yielded by American self-sufficiency, still felt able to maintain that even $150 billion in American foreign production was dwarfed by the nation's imposing gross domestic product. But here, as Harry Magdoff has pointed out in a fascinating series of essays entitled *The Age of Imperialism*,[4] they probably deceive themselves. For to assume that all types of productive activity have a similar degree of influence upon policy-makers is almost as naive as to believe that all men are equally intelligent or honest.

America's foreign commercial operations speak with a relatively louder voice than her domestic commerce in the councils of government for several reasons. In the first place, their high profitability adds greatly to their vocal power. In 1950 earnings on foreign investment represented about 10 per cent of all after-tax profits of domestic non-financial corporations: by 1964 such foreign sources accounted for no less than 22 per cent of such profits.[5] In no foreign sector was profitability greater than in banking. In the 10 years to 1967, deposits in the foreign branches of New York banks rose from $1·3 billion to $9 billion, a rate seven times greater than deposits at home. The foreign business of one of them, the Manufacturers' Hanover Trust, rose from 10 per cent of its total business to 25 per cent during this time, while its international division's profits doubled in 5 years.[6] As one New York investment banking house put it in their 1962 annual report, 'suffice it to say that life for the Edge Act banker [one type of American foreign subsidiary] begins at something well above the customary 6 per cent of his domestic cousins'.[7]

More important than its compelling profitability, however, American foreign business was becoming recognized as a vital prop and re-insurance against domestic cyclical instability and a worrying absence of dynamism in the domestic economy.* In a decade (1951–61) of sluggish domestic performance, United States-owned factories abroad showed a 110 per cent increase in sales compared with a mere 50 per cent increase in manufactures at home. By the mid-1960's, indeed, the United States, though on balance an importer from its foreign subsidiaries, sold them about one quarter of all its exports. Lower foreign wages and material costs were thus being used to fuel both continuous expansion at home and widening domination abroad. The treasurer of the General Electric Company, in an address to the American National Industrial Conference Board in May 1965, made the point succinctly:

> In this respect, I think business has reached a point in the road where there is no turning back. American industry's marvellous technology and abundant capital resources have enabled us to produce the most remarkable run of peacetime prosperity in

---

* The United States GNP showed an average growth rate of only 2·4 per cent over the years 1954–60.

the nation's history. To keep this going we have for several years sought additional outlets for these resources in foreign markets. For many companies, including General Electric, these offshore markets offer the most promising opportunities for expansion that we can see.[8]

This would mean, according to another authority, Hoyt P. Steel, Chairman of the United States Council of the International Chamber of Commerce's Committee on Commercial Policy, that ' . . . the future will probably find us trading increasingly with ourselves throughout the world'.[9]

The extent of the role of sales to foreign subsidiaries as the fly wheel of the United States economy is revealed not so much by their overall volume, as by their support of America's economic foundations, its capital goods industries.* Exports which, as we saw, account for only an average of 4 per cent of total goods and services (GNP), account for an average of 11 per cent of America's annual output of investment goods (excluding the housing industry). Meanwhile such exports combined with Federal government purchases (almost all for military, hence foreign policy-oriented, purposes) account for over 35 per cent of investment goods output.[10]

One other characteristic of America's foreign economic involvement adds to its influence in domestic economic management—its concentration. Two statistics will suffice to make this point. One is that 40 per cent of American foreign investment has been made by just three companies: Esso, General Motors and Ford; the other, that by 1965, 700 of the 1,000 largest

---

* These 'producer goods', as opposed to 'consumer goods', industries are the true foundations of an industrial economy whose expansion or contraction transmits, with leveraged effect, the forces of the business cycle to the vast consumer goods superstructure. If demand for 'capital' or 'producer' goods falters, demand for consumer goods can be sustained considerably by such devices as unemployment relief, or reduction of consumer savings. However, as businessmen will not invest unless they expect a handsome profit, it is possible, except for essential replacement needs, for expenditures on investment goods theoretically to go down to zero. This, in general, was what occurred in the Depression Era. In the United States between 1929–33, consumer goods purchases declined only 19 per cent; but expenditure on residential construction fell by 80 per cent and non-residential capital investment by 71 per cent.

American corporations had establishments in Europe. These companies, plus the great 'money centre' banks, form an internationally oriented monetary interest-group of such power that the nation's construction industry, the consumer and municipal government are increasingly outweighed when it comes to management of the dollar.

2. EMBRACING STRENGTH THROUGH STAGNATION

The world banker role of the United States, and the reserve role of the dollar on which it depends, are the mechanism which enables the United States not only to enter the industry and markets of its chief trading partners, to maintain a dominant world military position and to provide aid and private capital for the less developed countries, but also to maintain domestic prosperity and fend off depression. And determination to defend this role of the dollar as the lynch-pin of the necessarily internationalist American economy did indeed cause the American government up to the early 1960's to 'remain satisfied with relative stagnation which is one of the main reasons for the flight of capital abroad'.[11]

John F. Kennedy, in his celebrated inaugural address of 6 January 1961, spoke of the 'idling' economy that he had inherited. As President he took several steps to increase its growth rate. Johnson's skilful coaxing through Congress of the tax cut that Kennedy had inaugurated in 1963 was the main step towards that goal. This 10 per cent cut, unaccompanied by any equivalent cut in government spending, opened the taps of demand sufficiently to hold the momentum of a resurgence that began in 1961–62. At last, it seemed, the vaunted fiscal tool of the New Economics, hailed by Kennedy's and Johnson's advisers, had slipped the economy into top gear.* More encouraging still was the fact that the economy's new burst of vitality was *not* accompanied by a rise in inflation. Price rises were contained in the region of 1 per cent, so that the vast bulk of the new national wealth created in those four

---

* The 'New Economics' being the old Keynesian economics of 'managed demand', *i.e.* varying government spending and interest rates so as to maintain a high level of economic activity, writ large.

years represented real gain, and not just higher figures on paper.

This happy state of affairs was achieved by a mixture of incentives and controls, or rather 'self-controls'. The White House's success at maintaining the newly inaugurated wage price guidelines was dramatized by President Kennedy's successful 'staring down' of Big Steel's attempt to raise prices. Meanwhile his 7 per cent investment tax credit, though at first scorned by business, soon restored to fashion the Victorian habit of reinvesting the surplus rather than consuming it. As a result of this two-pronged fiscal attack, although wages did continue to edge ahead, improvements in productivity easily outstripped the level of the increases.

Unfortunately, however, despite this apparent arrival at the gates of economic paradise, the dollar's strength continued to deteriorate; for while the United States' trade balance improved, the overall payments balance continued to show a deficit, and the pile of dollar IOUs in foreign hands continued to rise. Nor did imposition of unprecedented governmental deterrents to the export of capital narrow the payments gap and check the gold drain. The problem was that America's foreign earnings, instead of being remitted, were increasingly being reinvested abroad.

At the same time, Kennedy's non-inflationary boom did not turn out to be the great cure-all for domestic problems that his advisers had proclaimed. The albatross of unemployment continued to hang around America's neck. In fact, the President's New Frontiersmen turned out to be remarkably timid pioneers. Their target for the reduction of full-time unemployment was not brought below 4 per cent. Indeed throughout the boom years of the 1960's, until the Vietnam War inflation really flared up in 1968, full-time unemployment scarcely fell below that figure.

Here was the fissure that ran through the American body politic. Four-fifths of the nation were experiencing, year by year, new heights of prosperity, while the bottom fifth, statistically half black and increasingly urban and slum-dwelling, were left to stagnate.*

---

* Conservative protestations notwithstanding, the link between unemployment and poverty is clear and undeniable. In 1967, 4 per cent full-time

IN DEFENCE OF THE DOLLAR

Since it first came under the speculative fire of gold buyers in late 1960, the dollar has been defended by basic action of two types. The first category of defensive measures might be described as the 'visibles'. The need to defend the dollar from foreign danger being altogether strange and new to American experience, some dramatic measures were deemed necessary, partly to bring the dollar crisis vividly to the businessman's attention. Apart from Kennedy's 'interest equalization' tax on foreign portfolio investment, voluntary restraint on direct foreign investment was called for. Also among these 'visible' measures were others which John Kenneth Galbraith has labelled 'cosmetic'. Ploys such as the proposed tax on Eastern Hemisphere tourism, savings bond campaigns designed to mop up overseas GI dollars and trade fairs for the promotion of American goods abroad. All were aimed at hammering in to affluent America, the people who thought in terms of European vacations or foreign investment, the seriousness of this strange and unfamiliar crisis.

These 'visible' dollar defences, then, were in effect curbs on the rich. The simple fact of these 'cosmetic' measures' visibility naturally made them highly vulnerable politically; and because a close correspondence exists between the affluence of an interest group and its degree of articulateness, it is scarcely surprising that all the above-named controls came under frequent and withering attack.

The second, and less 'visible', line of dollar defence had no

---

unemployed together with their dependants, represented about 9 million Americans. But that level of 'full time' unemployment represents a true unemployment level of $5\frac{1}{2}$ to 6 per cent. Taking account of dependants, this '4 per cent' level therefore affects a real total of $11\frac{1}{2}$–13 million people. In a year when the full-time unemployment rate averages 4 per cent, it is estimated that 12 per cent of the labour force is unemployed for an average of three months, the consequent loss of income dragging most of them below the officially designated 'poverty line'. So it is probably fair to say that at least 40 per cent of the 32 million Americans below the poverty line owe their poverty to full-time or part-time unemployment. (See Leon H. Keyserling, 'Employment and the New Economics', *Annals of the American Academy*, October 1967.)

such vociferous opponents. It took the form of restraint on the economy's growth as a whole in the period 1964-67. The progressive hoisting of interest rates and the curbing of credit, the attempt to stabilize the price level by reducing job opportunities for the marginally employed: this was the sacrifice in defence of the dollar levied upon the inarticulate poor.

The monetary weapon, which the Democratic administrations were forced by the opposition to use with greater and greater force (the fiscal weapon being withheld by the Congress), was, as usual, only rarely expressed as a solution favouring one part of society at the expense of another. 'The rate of interest', in Professor Galbraith's words, 'can only be understood as the one price that has been in some sense sanctified.' He goes on:

> Producers of wheat, copper, cotton, and even steel are assumed to prefer higher prices for the larger revenues they return. Those who lend money, in contrast, are permitted to urge higher interest rates not for the greater return but as a selfless step designed to protect the nation from the evils of soft money, loose financial practices, and deficient economic morality. An economist who sees the need for a higher weekly wage may well be suspected of yielding to the unions; one who urges an increase in the rediscount rate is, however, invariably a statesman. This should not keep anyone from penetrating to the fact. There is a lively, insistent, and durable preference by the money-lending community for high rates of return; this is related to an intelligent view of pecuniary self-interest. It would be astonishing were it otherwise.[12]

Apart from enriching the financial community at the expense of the debtor classes, this second line of defence of the dollar cost the United States an estimated $30 to $50 billion *per year* in lost output in the decade since 1958.[13] A few hundred millions transferred into rentier pockets under régimes of tight money may be of little general social consequence in an economy of the American scale. But the loss of $300 to $500 billion of national wealth, forfeited over a decade, is not by any measure a negligible cost to a nation desperately in need of vastly expanded social programmes. America was not short of uses for the dividend offered by fuller use of her economic capacity. During the decade the part of that dividend for which balance of payments considerations was responsible could, without depriving any person or programme of the spending power that they enjoyed, have made a start on rebuilding the ghettoes, restoring the crumbling school and hospital systems and begun to raise the present dank and debasing floor of welfare for under-privileged Americans.

CONTEXT OF THE DOLLAR'S DEFENCE: ECONOMIC LEADS AND SOCIAL LAGS

Those who support the present reserve role of the dollar naturally make light of this problem of the social cost of the dollar's defence. The fact that the scale and productive power of the American economy is so great as to be of a different order from any other Western economy is supposed to enable America to sustain its reserve burden unbowed. The problem with this conventional wisdom is that it takes insufficient account of international differences in the relative pace of economic and social development.

America's historical tendency to more rapid economic than to social integration forms a mirror image to the present-day trend of Western Europe. For today the nations of Europe, long since integrated socially at the national level, and with compatible levels of social development on a continental scale, increasingly find themselves incomplete economically. The clearest manifestation of these cross-currents—the different Atlantic rates of economic and social integration—is provided by a comparison of their differing tolerances to unemployment.

The experience of the last two decades suggests that the politically tolerable level of worklessness in the United States today averages roughly double that of Europe. The reasons for this vast difference in social emphasis are not far to seek. America's sheer size, and the diffusion and decentralization which that size has engendered, when added to its fragmented ethnic composition, may explain much. Its political decentralization, and the presence of a great under-privileged black minority, have produced country-sized pockets of poverty and stagnation within a prospering economy. The same factors that enable America to tolerate high unemployment have enabled it to lag on the development of social services, offering, as an alternative to state welfare, an ideology of social Darwinism in a context of illusory opportunity. European nations, on the other hand, have, since Bismarck's day, gradually been forced, for the sake of domestic tranquillity, to embrace the welfare state.

America could, perhaps, more easily have handled the burden of the dollar's defence had her social development more closely paralleled that of her chief client states in Western Europe. The trouble was, however, that the drive for social reform, lower unemployment and higher social benefits, picked up momentum in the United States just as the defenders of the dollar in Washington had to face the maximum pressure for monetary restraint.

3. JOHNSON'S TRAP

In the face of a classic war inflation the Johnson administration found its hands tied. Moral opponents of the war joined hands with budget balancing conservatives to stay the President's hands from the remedies. Lacking a mandate for full-scale emergency measures, a rigorous system of wage, price and balance of payments controls, Johnson could deliver both guns and butter only by delivering inflation, too.

Not the least of the Vietnam war's mischiefs has been its identification of full employment with inflation in the public mind. The axiom that the cost of reducing poverty is inevitably rising prices was ridden hard by Nixon's conservative advisers as the vehicle that would carry them back in from the cold.

Indeed, in the election year of 1968, the conservatives' bogeymen lined up as neatly as a set of ninepins. First the Democrats could once again be labelled the war party who had led the United States into every war it had fought in the century. Then there was that solid core of Democratic support, the 'aristocracy' of organized labour, whose industry-wide bargaining power could be labelled inflationary, while their restrictive practices could be represented as keeping the able-bodied on the relief rolls. Finally, with over 3 per cent unemployed at the height of the war boom, conservatives could proclaim that while expansion inevitably brought inflation, it could not solve an essentially structural unemployment problem and they sounded extraordinarily persuasive when they claimed that the price of 3 to 4 per cent more inflation for 1 to 2 per cent less unemployment was altogether too high.

To the charge of mistaken theories conservatives could add that of mismanagement. In Congress, the determined Democratic Chairman of the House Ways and Means Committee, an Arkansas xenophobe named Wilbur Mills, demanded cuts in the federal budget before he would pass on Johnson's 10 per cent tax increase. It was this political friction, delaying Johnson's use of the fiscal tool for the better part of a year, which forced the Federal Reserve to bear the full burden of enforcing economic restraint. The resulting sky-high interest rates did little other than line businessmen's pockets while the economy, unstoppable without the retarding jerk of a tax rise *plus* drastic 'open market' measures by the Federal Reserve to freeze the total money supply,* continued to roar onwards with lending rates of 9 and 10 per cent.

Over-reliance on interest rates rapidly produced its own distortions. Public borrowers—states and municipalities—being unable either to offer equity participation (so that investors in their bonds could fight inflation) or any return on investment that would offset the enormous cost of borrowing, were particularly hard hit. Thus the local public sector suffered severely and had to postpone socially essential investment in schools, hospitals, etc., while the federal government, by contrast, enjoyed a fattening of its purse, as taxes rose proportionately to the growth of the economy. The sky-high price of borrowing also hit hard at the younger generation of young married mortgage seekers and credit buyers, while assuring high rewards to the saving and investing group, their parents. A monetary policy so favourable to the older and better-heeled in a country filled as never before with young marrieds setting up house hardly served to bridge the generation gap.

* See pp. 171–76.

Thus by the election campaign of 1968 the expansionary vision of the New Economists seemed to have run into a wall. But in fact it had simply been caught in a trap made up of the military on the one hand, and a hostile, war-weary electorate who would not countenance wartime controls on wages and prices on the other. Once in this trap, there was no alternative to persisting with attempts at deflation as the price for maintaining America's foreign power structure. Unable or unwilling to alter its priorities, Washington was thus forced to heed the threats of European bankers rather than the voice of American liberals who asked why 'millions of unemployed and their families should be the insurers of the affluent against somewhat higher prices on their third cars, extra steak dinners and additional fur coats'.[14] Did the unemployed and the slum and ghetto dwellers always have to be the ammunition in the war against inflation? After the experience of Detroit, and proto-civil war in a score of other cities, would Americans remain so strait-jacketed by the ideology of greed that they would shun wartime controls of wages and prices and further progressive taxation to damp demand for the superfluous and the secondary and permit bigger social programmes without an excessive penalty of inflation?

America's problem in the late 1960's was that she was fighting a war too unpopular and undignified to permit wartime measures. World War II experience had proved that with a full panoply of controls, both guns and butter *could* be financed together. In World War II, the volume of consumer goods did not fall as war outlays increased; their *distribution* changed, with ration cards allowing more goods to go to the lower bracket and less to the upper. But by opting against any measures of wealth redistribution, while maintaining their imperial priorities, Americans in the 1960's allowed the crowding pressures on the dollar to block the most friction-free path towards social regeneration—that of rapid inflation-free growth.

4. THE AMERICAN MONETARY CLIMB-DOWN

For the first time in their history, Americans were discovering that defence of national prestige could cost their nation its prosperity. Historically, the American economy had always 'emerged triumphant and reinvigorated' from successive wars.[15] But the new American pastime of self-styled world cop, and self-accused domestic robber, threatened the nation's very unity; some thought its national viability. The growing disenchantment of Wall Street with the war during 1967–68 clearly indicated business's rejection of this propensity to auto-cannibalism.

Inevitably the growing discomfort of the dollar's dilemma produced a softening of Congress's former hard line over the dollar's international role. Significantly, it encouraged the liberal monetary internationalists to surface on Washington's interest-group ant-heap. Now that other nations held the monetary whip-hand, Congress moved rapidly from its nationalism of the Bretton Woods era to tread the path of monetary compromise.

No more telling gauge of the effectiveness of the continentals' dollar squeeze can be found than the degree of liberalism and internationalism towards the dollar problem shown by an otherwise conservative House of Representatives. As early as 1965, the year, it should be noted, when the great switch out of dollars took place, Representative Henry Reuss, the Chairman of the House Subcommittee on International Exchange and Payments, proposed a set of 'guidelines' for sweeping monetary reform. Harry White's shade was no doubt smiling as these Congressmen pressed the Treasury earnestly to find ways of sharing the burden of responsibilities that weighed upon the dollar. The Subcommittee indeed was energetic in pressing for the early creation of new international monetary reserves along the lines of the IMF's 'paper gold', later agreed upon; and it demanded to know whether there was any good reason keeping the Treasury from pressing for international agreement over greater flexibility for currency exchange rates. Why, Reuss asked, should the dollar not be permitted to ride more freely on the tides of demand and supply, and thus free officials from the uncertain pressures of speculative betting over the likelihood of the sharp break of a devaluation?

From 1965 onwards, by recommending wider support margins round currency parities, Reuss and his Subcommittee were pressing the Johnson administration to permit limited depreciation of the dollar as an alternative to placing further restraints on Americans' freedom both at home and abroad. Indeed, Mr. Reuss's committee went further than that. In its anxiety that American policies should shake free from the dictates of foreign financial preferences, it proposed that steps be taken by the Administration to press foreign surplus countries to 'harmonize' their monetary and fiscal policies in relation to the United States, that is, to return, in fact, to something like the gold standard's 'rules of the game' and inflate their money supply in proportion to their swollen reserves. This would, of course, be asking the Europeans one-sidedly to abjure their national monetary advantage, to forswear use of the political pressure that their possession of dollar IOUs could now bring to bear, without any binding guarantee of American co-operation should the payments seesaw reverse itself in the future.

To European officials, this *volte face* of Congressional attitudes from the time of the dollar's undisputed dominance was all too transparent. But continental determination not to let the senior Anglo-Saxon get away with it was tempered by the realization that their own bluff, too, could be called. Foreign central bankers were well aware that elimination of the American payments deficit would deprive the world of over three-quarters of its annual increases of liquidity, and force them to choose between parting with some of their gold or facing the consequences of world trade recession.

These, then, were the parameters of monetary compromise. By the autumn of 1968, the anticipated creation of at least $2 billion of 'paper gold' in 1969 put an important psychological light at the end of the dollar's dark tunnel. After years of wrangle a deal had been struck. Veto power over the issue of the new international credit money had been the Common Market countries' condition for acceptance of the new paper gold.

5. AMERICA'S NEXT FRONTIER: ITS BACKYARD

In the spring of 1969 the *Wall Street Journal* assessed the effectiveness of the European central bankers efforts at checking America's foreign expansionism. They had, according to this newspaper, prevented a punitive response to the North Vietnamese Tet offensive; they had ensured that the American response to the *Pueblo's* capture was limited to words; they had even perhaps forced the resignation of an American President.[16] Stated more modestly, they had been strongly instrumental in bringing a colossus to its senses. For the first time, perhaps, since the days of its infancy, the American Republic had lost the unqualified mastery of its destiny.

Was external discipline saving America from itself? Were the responsibilities of their currency forcing Americans to break with their tradition of always pushing on to new frontiers, never looking back at the mess to be cleaned up? The American frontier experience—new space and new resources with which to expand and resolve—had not ended as Frederick Jackson Turner had claimed, with the official closing of the frontier in the 1890's. The frontier had simply moved on: Canada, the Far East, Europe, space. In its wake, it left decaying cities, polluted waters and poisoned air. The ever-widening ripples of American venture-capital appeared to flee the tasks of reconstruction back in the domestic pond. American capitalism has continuously gained vitality from lush markets and broad profit margins. But can this vitality be maintained if the profit-levels are thinned as social overheads rise? While the American technostructure has gained ground abroad it has ignored problems at home, with the result today that, like ancient Rome, America's gravest threat comes not from outside challenge, but from within.

International monetary crisis has helped force America to face priorities: priorities among frontiers. The United States needs 'paper gold', and other monetary change besides, to buy time, to give it latitude for further domestic expansion and flexibility within which to meet the bill for renewal and repair. If it fails to use this latitude however and instead prefers to continue expansion abroad while maintaining the dollar foundation of its foreign power with deflation rather than controls at home, it may lose both the capacity and the will necessary to set its house in order. In this respect the lesson of the 1960's is clear. If it is to keep the leadership of the West, America must make it's next frontier its backyard.

LAST BARRIER TO WORLD GOVERNMENT OR FIRST STEP

13

Development Aid and the Monetary Bottleneck

1. SOCIAL LEFT FOOT, MONETARY RIGHT SHOE

The world monetary system under which we live is a product of the age of imperialism. As such, it is dangerously incapable of responding to the economic aspirations and political assumptions of today. For all its recent streamlinings, swap agreements, 're-cycling' and drawing rights, the gold-exchange standard cannot escape the fact that it evolved in a world in which industrial nations related to non-industrial as a feudal manor to its estate.

Within a colonial empire, the question of balancing national payments did not arise because the colony usually fell within the mother country's monetary system. But even where independence had been won, and ex-colonies managed their own currencies and kept their own reserves, a harmony of mutual needs prevailed. A foreign investment in Bolivian tin-mining, for example, was repaid by the export of tin. Similarly, British investments in Argentina railways—the classic instance beloved of textbooks—were financed by the grain and cattle exports which the railways made possible. Like feudalism, then, occidental trade was, until the middle of the present century, a comfortably balanced relationship; comfortable, that is, from the lordly point of view.

But also as with feudalism, this balance was upset by scientific and technical advance. The missionary may, symbolically, be blamed for causing the upset. For the literacy and medicine which he disseminated were the seeds of future upheaval. Today's world has reaped their fruit—the new nation, fired with knowledge of the good and evil life; the independent state in which reduced infant mortality has given population growth a running start on the production of food and other resources.

THE MIRAGE OF ABUNDANCE

Today the basic issues of politics, of who gets what, how and when, are raised at the global level. This is the achievement of the African's transistor radio and the Peruvian shanty town's communal television set. The parched South has sighted the oasis of incredible abundance defined by the North Atlantic's shores.

But technology is cruel to those without it. It allures but it then denies. Lack of the tools of technology make the prospect of reaching that oasis a continually receding mirage; for, year by year, science, technology and compound interest decrease the Atlantic worker's reliance on the southern poor. His greater productivity enables him to buy all that he needs from his Southern neighbour with an ever-decreasing proportion of his time and effort. Meanwhile trade with his wealthy fellows becomes more and more rewarding, his wants for sophisticated goods increasing in a dizzying spiral with his own productivity and purchasing power. His technology has also made him less and less dependent on the Third World's raw materials. Where previously he imported nitrates from the soil of Chile, he now literally pulls them from the nitrogen in his native air. His wife buys a vinyl coat where before she bought cotton or wool. Nor has the productivity explosion of the Atlantic rich confined itself to their industry. For two decades French peasants have been migrating in droves from the land, yet the output of French fields increases yearly. Europe, whose demand for cereals to feed its rising population opened up the temperate zones of North and South America a hundred years ago, is now self-sufficient in wheat. Even the farmers of England, where proverbial insufficiency of home-produced food was the original engine of Free Trade, now look to the time when the British Isles will be agriculturally largely self-supporting.

The good old market mechanism, whereby, as the Atlantic nations grew so did their demand for raw materials, has been diverted not just by the *possibility* of substituting synthetic for natural, home-grown for imported, but by a *conscious policy* of protection. Where Atlantic products are competitive, beet sugar with cane, soy beans with groundnuts, the domestic farmer is protected. The supply side also works in favour of the rich. Developing countries, each aspiring to increase its export earnings, must compete not merely with Atlantic substitutes, but with each other. African nations struggle with India and Ceylon for a share of the tea market while they compete with Latin America in the production of coffee.

Thus while the poor South tries to lift itself by its own efforts, its bootstraps are slit both by the rich North's drive for efficiency and its instinct to protect its own. Under such conditions, how can the world's Southern poor hope to sell enough of their cocoa, their jute or their sugar in a relatively stagnant world market, to afford to buy the scientific knowledge and the tools of technology which alone can save them from remaining a mediaeval majority in a space-age world? Clearly there is only one alternative to the poor nations' permanent submergence in hopelessness: they must import a vast and constant flow of knowledge and resources.

Japan, whose unbelievable progress in technology and wealth has been fueled in the past decade with a derisory amount of domestic research and development, is the all-time classic example of wholesale imports of science and technology. The Japanese have reached the stage, enviable from the point of view of the Southern poor, but worrying to themselves, where they have completely closed the 'technology gap' with the Atlantic countries. Where then is their technology going to come from? A massive shift in resources towards domestic research and development is going to be needed.

But for the Southern poor not even in sight of industrialization, here is where the monetary problem enters the scene. For the inflow of investment that is needed to modernize the hungry two-thirds of mankind, unlike flows of mercantile capital for such things as tin mines, railways or oil, which generate the export to balance them, can be balanced by no immediate, and little medium-range, counter-flow. The vast bulk of the investment needed to prevent the rich–poor gap from widening disastrously is 'social overhead' capital, by which is meant investments in education, health, sanitation, family planning, housing, etc., which are the 'first-stage' inputs required to make people productive beings whose activities can then yield a monetary return. Such social overhead investment produces little or no financial return for many years. It may, then, represent a *net* drain upon an aid-giving nation's balance of payments. It is a type of capital transfer unheard-of in the era when the present monetary system evolved. Not surprisingly, then, the gold exchange standard system, unless drastically modified, is incapable of responding to it.

2. ATLANTIC MONETARY POLITICS AND AID

After World War II, this impediment to global development was largely swept under the carpet for a decade. Lack of any provision for a one-way transfer of wealth to the developing world was dealt with by the ostrich-like technique of insisting that any transfer of resources (aside from the small proportion of transfers that took the form of grants) be made on a normal repayment basis. The poor nations, accordingly, were lent development capital at, or close to, market rates of interest.

This was not, of course, the intention of most of the 44 signatories of the Bretton Woods Agreements. But subservience of the World Bank to Wall Street orthodoxy had been ensured in Washington's post-Bretton Woods anti-liberal purge. At that time, the Bank's original President, the liberal ex-publisher of the *Washington Post*, Eugene Meyer, had been hurriedly replaced (within six months of his appointment) by John J. McCloy, a Wall Street lawyer. At the same time, the World Bank was so short of paid-up capital from governments that it was forced itself to borrow in the capital markets of Wall Street and Europe and thus to lend on near-commercial terms. Meanwhile, in their bilateral aid transactions, the rich nations often proved much less scrupulous lenders. All too often they transferred the tools of modernization on short credits at high rates of interest and much of what was called 'aid' in the rich nations' accounting* was really loans on pawnbroker terms.

Soon the inevitable and foreseeable began to happen. The poor nations' development plans ran head-on into trouble, as profit-seeking development projects failed for lack of a solid

* According to the OECD Development Assistance Committee's aid publications.

social base. Meanwhile, where social overhead investments financed on commercial or near-commercial terms had been undertaken, there was a painful choice to be faced. Either new debt must be contracted to repay the old, or the development process would grind to a halt. By 1961, the year in which the United Nations 'Development Decade' was launched, counter-flows of capital from the world's poor to repay the rich were actually decreasing the outflow of aid in real terms. And by mid-decade the World Bank found it was taking back with one hand almost as much as it was lending with the other.

The hard-nosed Wall Street approach simply did not meet the situation.* Accordingly, in 1961, a 'soft loan' window, the International Development Association (IDA) was opened by the World Bank. 'Soft loan' is a euphemism for grant. Virtually interest-free (a ½ per cent 'service charge' was generally attached) with fifteen-year grace periods and up to fifty years to repay, no realist, taking account of the post-war record of international inflation and the political risks involved, could call lending under such terms anything other than donation. The difference between soft loans and grants was one of ideology more than of substance. It circumlocuted the banker's phobia for 'hand-outs'; that was the important thing.

However, soft lending only partially resolved the resource transfer problem. True it eased the Third World's repayment problem. But since the IDA received no short- or even medium-term return on its money, rich nations' contributions to the Agency still represented a net drain on their balance of payments. So when the time came round for the rich nations to replenish IDA's resources, argument broke out between deficit Anglo-Saxons and surplus continentals as to who could afford to give most. The continentals argued that the burden should be measured on the basis of national wealth, the Anglo-Saxons

* Significantly, the Bank's current President, Robert McNamara, takes a strongly anti-Wall Street view of World Bank operations. He is, incidentally, also firmly opposed to high-technology projects in aid programmes, and believes in a high level of Bank loans for agriculture and education, with little commercial return in the short or medium run, but, he believes, good long-run dividends. He is also emphatic about such direct foreign-exchange earners as tourist projects, to help countries with debt-repayment problems.

argued on the basis of national surplus. Thus in the mid-1960's, with replenishment from neither side forthcoming, the chill of Atlantic monetary cold war, exacerbated by de Gaulle's attack on the dollar, froze a vital pipeline of international aid. For almost two years the supply of even a part of the $1 billion called for by former World Bank President George Woods was held up over the balance of payments issue. Here, in vivid terms, was demonstrated the monetary bottleneck to the transfer of resources.

Of course the bottleneck occurred with bilateral giving, too. But in this case politics played a more overt part. Nineteenth-century Britain had financed her massive capital 'aid', to the then developing world, out of continuing surpluses on her commercial account. But defeat in war has given West Germany and Japan, the countries with comparable trade surpluses today, the smallest pre-disposition towards foreign aid.* Deprived by conquest of their old imperial spheres of influence in Eastern Europe, East Africa and Southeast Asia, the Germans and Japanese preferred to preserve their monetary strength for hard bargaining with the Anglo-Saxons over defence commitments. Rather than narrow their overall payments balances and expend their reserves in lending to countries whose markets are anyway unimportant to them, the former Axis nations (Italy may be included here too) prefer the bargaining power that comes from a strong currency and uninterrupted growth.

France, the other important surplus country of the 60's, though by far the largest giver of development aid on a *per capita* basis, may have gained herself a monetary advantage with her financial generosity. For France has continued to devote her development assistance almost exclusively to French Africa. The new French African nations all fall within the franc area, and like some former British territories referred to earlier, they

* This situation, however, is gradually changing. Germany has recently been offsetting some of her embarrassment of foreign short-term funds with more and more long-term export credits to the Third World—though the interest burden of these is generally high. Japan contributed $200 million, the same level of pledge as the US, to the recently inaugurated Asia Development Bank.

still tend to accumulate net payments surpluses with the non-franc world, which they bank in Paris. However, if the experience of the sterling area is anything to go by, the French cannot expect to enjoy this monetary advantage indefinitely. Not even France's Schachtian inducements, such as offering some ex-colonial territories twice the world price for their peanuts, will keep their fledglings indefinitely in the nest. Sooner or later, as their development momentum increases, the ex-French colonies, like the former British possessions, will begin to run consistent foreign payments deficits, thus possibly altering the present French attitude of relative largesse.

So the facts of political history tighten the bottleneck. The French, still possessed of their self-contained sphere of influence, can afford to point the finger at others who give less when the aid hat is passed round. Many influential Germans however persist in ignoring the hat when it comes their way. They believe that it was involvement in world war which showed the less developed countries how backward they were in comparison with the civilization of the West, a realization which they have utilized, according to Schacht, by 'making a mark on the bad consciences of these victorious powers, who now seek in feverish haste to make good the omissions of previous years'.[1]

Meanwhile the 'guilt-ridden' Anglo-Saxons are caught in a dilemma. With their payments balances put into deficit by 'white' overseas investment and defence spending, with their ex- and neo-colonial ties, and with the international monetary system's viability dependent upon their minimizing their payments deficits, they have been the nations with the greatest *political* motive to be generous, but the greatest *monetary* pressure to be mean. For Britain, especially, this dilemma has been a painful one, as abandonment of the sterling area by her former colonies threw new strains on the reserve role of the pound, without abating their political pressure for more development aid. Meanwhile the shift of former sterling countries into the dollar area, i.e., their decision to hold their reserves in dollars, added to Washington's monetary exposure.

By the mid-1960's America's balance of payments difficulties were strengthening the hand of aid opponents on Capitol Hill, and adding momentum to the wave of disillusion that followed the absence of a Marshall Plan-type response to the aid so far given. So the provider of half of the rich nations' development aid began to reduce its official aid budget while increasingly tying that aid to American goods so as to avoid any adverse effect on the balance of payments.

The logic of an imperial-era monetary system had come full circle. An increase of 'tied' aid grew with mounting pressure on the dollar and the pound. By 1968 the British and Americans were tying almost all their bilateral aid. This practice of tying greatly reduced the value and effectiveness of that aid. For tied aid prevents the recipient country from obtaining the goods that it most needs at the most competitive prices. To the layman, the disadvantage to the recipient of tied aid may sound unimportant when compared with the problem of getting the resources in the first place, but the 'cost' of tied aid to the developing countries rapidly mounts up. A recent study produced the estimate that tying may force a developing country to sacrifice anywhere from one fifth to one half of the nominal value of the tied aid.[2] And the higher cost to the poor nation is only part of the story. As the practice of aid tying grows, lending governments tend to become more and more involved in subsidizing their own export industries. For recipient countries this all too easily leads to embarkation on costly projects whose rationale is dictated not by the needs of the recipient but on the economic structure of the donor. Once again, under the present monetary system, what the left hand gives, the right hand is forced to take away.

The final twist to this sorry tale of diverted philanthropy is that tied aid, as a balance of payments protecting device, tends to be self-defeating anyway. Tied export orders, which do *not* add foreign exchange earnings to the donor's balance of payments, tend to clog the pipeline, getting in the way of 'genuine' export orders which *do*. Aid-tying is not, in any case, a cast-iron balance of payments safeguard for the donor. The recipient country can get round some of the effects of tying by playing around with his various sources of aid. He can sometimes spend the tied credits on things that he would be buying in the tying country anyway, while diverting his cash (foreign exchange-yielding) orders elsewhere. This order-switching ploy to counteract the effects of tying helped to harden the deadlock over the IDA soft loan replenishment in 1967–68. For the more of its aid that the United States tied, the more likely it became that any further untied multilateral contribution would be spent by the recipient on the lower-cost exports of a more competitive supplier country, such as Japan or Germany, and would thus represent a dead loss to the American balance of payments.

3. THE AID DEADLOCK

By the mid-1960's, the increasing shortage of international liquidity produced by American insistence on maintaining the thirty-five-year-old gold price, and the capital controls and deflationary measures undertaken by the Anglo-Saxons in their attempts to return to the payments surplus which such insistence necessitated, was threatening to depress international trade on which the developing countries rely for 80 per cent of their foreign exchange. And despite a very modest scheme for short-term loans by the IMF to carry poor countries over acute balance of payments difficulties* and the planned creation of several billion dollars' worth of SDRs, Britain's debt-repayment schedule, and the Americans' need to check domestic inflation presage an intensification of this liquidity shortage. Thus for the poor nations' economic well-being to improve significantly in the 1970's—the Second Development Decade—the international monetary system must undergo further substantial change.

Some idea of the scale on which such change will be needed is given by rough quantification of the 'liquidity gap'. If the developing countries are to repay their present debts and keep any significant impetus in their average growth rate, their future annual requirement of external capital, on top of their export earnings, will be at least $18 to $20 billion, or something close to the one per cent of the industrial nations' GNP which was agreed as the capital transfer target by both the rich and poor nations in the United Nations Conference on Trade and

---

* A more substantial scheme of 'Compensatory Financing' by the IMF involving the lending of $300–$400 million a year has been hanging fire since 1966.

PM—T

Development in 1968.[3] This figure looks extremely large compared with the $11 billion average net capital flow, 1965–68. But it looks even larger when one considers that this necessary minimum *annual* input of $18 billion represents almost *half* of the ten richest nations' present gold reserves. If the price of gold were *tripled*, to around $100 an ounce, the needed annual transfer for development would be reduced to around a fifth of the group of ten's gold reserves.[4] Such an expansion of international liquidity would give donors sufficient reserves to break the monetary bottleneck on aid. It would prevent the present shortage of international means of payment from driving the world back to the one-sided bilateral bargaining of the past. But creation of new international money on this scale is (as explained in Chapter 10) almost unanimously regarded by the rich countries as unthinkable; some stressing its inflationary effects, others the excessive political dividend to those nations who happen to produce, or already possess, large quantities of gold.

BRITAIN AND THE THIRD WORLD—AN IDENTITY OF INTEREST

Almost unanimous, but not quite. For Britain's own economic problems draw her close to the monetary interest of the developing countries. In the decade following World War II, Britain's problems presented, as it were, the reverse side of the development problem of the Third World. Britain was growing more slowly than most of her industrial neighbours, partly because she traded more with the developing world than other industrial nations. These assured markets for her traditional and comparatively low-technology goods helped cement the British into their 19th century role of financing others' trade and development. Thus in seeking the higher level of domestic investment necessary to raise her unit productivity to the level of her faster-growing industrial neighbours, Britain must do for herself what the less developing countries are attempting to do for themselves at a more elementary economic level: she must transform traditional sectors of her economy to modern-style industrialism, just as the poor nations must move from pre-industrial to industrial status.

Such transformations of the nature of an economy, like a

change of careers for an individual, inevitably call for high levels of reserves. For the transitional economy must expect to run into successive payments deficits while importing the tools or raw materials of change. If the need for extra latitude is particularly acute for Britain today, this is just because, ironically, she has borrowed herself into bankruptcy in a misguided attempt to preserve her traditional role.

Harold Wilson had this linkage of Britain's destiny with that of the developing world in mind when, as opposition leader, he inclined to support the proposal of a number of British economists that a linkage be made between international liquidity-creation and aid. The most obvious of these proposals, put forward by economist Maxwell Stamp, was for the IMF to create new 'reserve units' of international money which could be fed into the resources of the IDA. Such new reserves for the developing countries would be supplementary to, not a substitute for, present flows of development finance. One great attraction of them would be that they could relieve the strain on the present monetary system at the times when it needed relief most, *i.e.* when world demand was slackening, especially as a result of reduction of conventional liquidity produced by surpluses in Anglo-Saxon payments.

The obvious drawback of this scheme, and others like it, is of course its potential for increasing international inflation. For the bulk of new 'reserve units' given to the less developed countries would inevitably be rapidly spent on importing the tools of modernization. This would mean that they would pass into the economies of the donor countries, which, because they are already operating at close to full capacity, would feel the inflation effects of such foreign spending.

There is, however, considerable dispute as to just how inflationary the effect of such new international money would be. One argument is that it would not in practice increase the international liquidity supply *enough*. This argument runs that such new reserves would mostly be spent in the cheapest markets, which would mean that they would in all likelihood finish up in the most competitive (and therefore surplus) countries like Japan and Germany, who are in no need whatsoever of increased reserves, and who would therefore be inclined to 'sterilize' this unwanted increment in their surplus, for fear of its domestic inflationary effect. Thus the new liquidity-aid might perform only the aid part of its function, and would then disappear from international circulation.

Such objections could easily be got round, of course, given the necessary political will on the part of the international banking community. One ingenious scheme proposed by Mr. Tibor Scitovsky would match the needs of nations on both sides of the old imperial relationship. Britain, for example, might deposit a budgeted aid appropriation with the IMF. The IMF would then issue its own units against this British sterling deposit. These it would issue to a developing country, say India or Peru, to finance a development project approved and supervised internationally (say by the IDA). The recipient country could then spend this money only in Britain. For India or Peru, this aid would represent a tied grant. But when the tied grant actually returned to Britain it would become an international asset, like dollars or gold, acceptable anywhere. Such a scheme is an advance on the 'Stamp Plan' of simply giving newly created reserves to the IDA for aid purposes as it would provide the IMF with a usable international currency, sterling, which is transferable into dollars and/or gold. India or Peru, meanwhile, would get a tied *grant*, which though far from the ideal transfer from their point of view, is better than the present diet of tied loans.

Like all liquidity plans, such a system would need careful safeguards against abuse. For anti-inflationary purposes, there would have to be a limit on the amount of the new international credit that Britain or any other user could activate. The prices that the donor charged for the goods that it supplied to India or Peru under the plan would also have to be monitored by an international authority. But something like Scitovsky's scheme could, at the very least, be a most useful supplement to existing reserves, SDRs and conventional channels of aid. In a nutshell, it would create new international cash in the same way as gold mining in developing countries has traditionally created cash. But the initial effect of the new money would be to finance hospitals, schools and roads, instead of more profit in the hands of the owners of gold shares. The longer-term result would be a readily manageable quantity of interest-bearing paper reserves, in national central bank vaults. From both the short and long term points of view, this is surely a solution more in tune with the needs of the time than the haphazard and inequitable business of feeding the world its liquidity from the pockets of gold mine owners.

The monetary conservatives, of course, can still object that a Scitovsky-style creation of reserves would be inflationary. More serious than the inflationary concern, however, is their unhappiness at the relative loss of power that such a scheme would mean for the Atlantic rich. For to a greater or lesser extent, depending on the regulations governing the scheme's activation, direct control over the amount of resources to be handed over to the international needy—Britain as well as the poor countries—would escape from the surplus nations' hands. Like Keynes's wartime Clearing Union proposal, however, the Scitovsky scheme starts with the serious international bargaining disadvantage that it is obviously tailored with Britain's particular monetary problem in mind. Nevertheless, as with Keynes's scheme, hindsight may prove it to be wiser than more conservative offerings in the long run.

EMBRACING THE HENRY FORD PRINCIPLE

Indeed, conservative arguments against such reserve creation need to be seen for what they are, and squarely faced. The policy alternatives for global development today parallel those faced by the rich nations for their own growth in the last half-century. If the affluent classes of the rich nations had not been pressured from below via the ballot-box, would they not have continued to invest their collective wealth so as to increase the prosperity only of the already prosperous? Would they not have continued to ignore Henry Ford's revolutionary insight that greater long-term entrepreneurial profit was possible through raising the educational, health and general consumption standards—his famous five dollars a day wage? Would they not have ignored the far greater profits to be had from creating mass-consumer markets among the previously low-consuming poor?

Today, with almost no effective pressure from below through the international ballot-box, the rich nations are ignoring on a global scale the lessons of their own recent past. They are closing their eyes to future global mass-markets when, at the national level, such broader markets are the foundation of modern affluence. Instead they prefer to ignore the world's poor, and to do business on an ever-increasing scale among themselves.

What will happen if this attitude continues unchecked? Just a few years from now, these rich nations, with their apparently limitless appetite for each others' goods still unsated, will peer down from technology-built pinnacles of luxury to gaze with mingled guilt and horror at the dark-skinned mediaeval mass of mankind. The global rich–poor gap is already infinitely greater than when, in the 1840's, the young Disraeli in his novel *Sybil* identified two nations cohabiting Queen Victoria's kingdom. But today, lacking the bonds of world political union, we face a vastly greater danger than Disraeli, who was able, with his 1867 Reform Bill, to enfranchise the masses and hitch their votes to the euphoria of Empire. On a world-wide scale, the economic divide is already defined as white versus colour. It is perhaps the first human gap too great for the mustered forces of humanism to bridge.

One breakthrough desperately needed to prevent the final, fatal split of the planet into hostile racial camps, is monetary internationalism. This means the creation of sufficient new international money to finance the long capital-outflow-repayment-inflow cycle which distinguishes today's development aid flows from the exploitive inflow-outflow of mercantile capitalism. Suggestions for new reserve creation, summarized in the final chapter, have not been wanting. But because demand among the industrial nations is today so buoyant, and because these economies already suffer from inflationary pressures, the further creation of spending power for the developing countries is looked upon askance. Of course the result of printing money to enable the poor nations' latent demand to become effective *will* be somewhat inflationary for the industrial countries in times of normal 'full' demand. But the cure for global inflation, just like that for national inflation, is there to be used if the

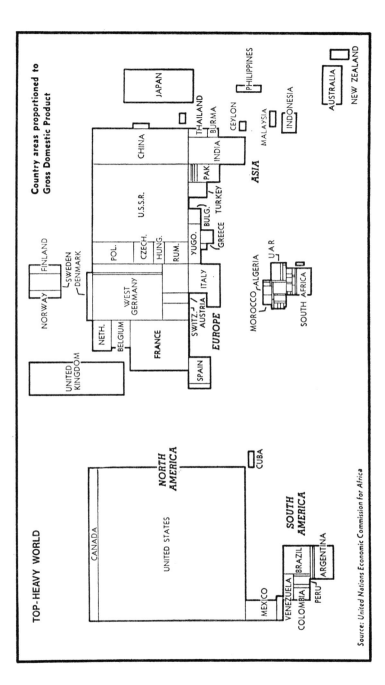

TOP-HEAVY WORLD

Country areas proportioned to Gross Domestic Product

Source: United Nations Economic Commission for Africa

political will to do so exists. It is simply a question of priorities. The annual $120 billion spent on armaments by the ten leading Western industrial nations is itself a prime cause of present inflationary overheating, apart from being a tragic diversion of potentially life-enhancing resources. If we want to keep *everybody* happy and have *both* undiminished arms expenditures and more development, without incurring inflation, then wage and price controls must be applied.

The inflation argument against expanding aid through reserve-creation is thus essentially a red herring. Objections to giving aid through creating more international money on the grounds that this might prove inflationary should be seen clearly for what they are. They are no different from refusing aid because it would mean higher taxes. They are simply another way of saying 'we don't want to pay'.

14

Reforming the World Monetary System: Political Choices and Prospects

Parts one and two of this book traced the political evolution of our present world monetary system from its historical origins. Parts three and four tried to expose the forces that sustain it. Two tasks remain to this final chapter: to look at the myriad proposals offered by the experts for world monetary reform, and to examine the immediate prospects for monetary change.

1. THE POLITICS OF PLANS FOR REFORM

No attempt will be made here to go into technical detail or to offer a Bædeker tour of the many more or less complex and sophisticated plans for monetary reform. A number of books* devote themselves expressly to this task. This chapter will concentrate solely on highlighting the political assumptions that lie behind broad categories of proposals for monetary change.

The sheer variety of plans and proposals that have proliferated in a decade of repeated monetary crisis testify to the amount of disagreement among economists and monetary theorists as to both means and ends. Unfortunately, this extraordinary variety of solutions—the spectacle of so much ink spilled by rational men in persuasive argument for often opposite approaches to the same problem—baffles the layman and makes him suspicious. It also tends to devalue the amount of attention given by the interested public to any one proposal. Instead the intelligent layman tends to reject what he regards as an endless flow of obscure and technical 'bafflegab', and to express scorn at academic fractiousness rather than interest in the variety of possible expedients.

Public impatience also stems from the fact that the political

* A selection of some of the most concise and readable is offered in the bibliography.

preferences and social priorities of the proposers often remain implicit and therefore obscure to the layman. One reason for this state of affairs is that economists' social priorities and political assumptions are often only subconsciously held. But this is surely all the more reason why an effort should be made to expose them and spell them out. For clearly the ideological roots of any plan to alter the central controls of our economic life ought to be widely and clearly understood.

It is the intention of the following section to make some contribution in this respect, so that the interested non-expert may make his own political judgement.

Proposals for change in world monetary arrangements may be placed in four broad *political* categories.

i. *The Conservative-Internationalist Approach* is that held by the bulk of the international financial establishment, or what Keynes called 'the apparatus of conservatism'. It has as its first concern the prosperity and security of the 'haves' among the rich industrial nations. It is less concerned with the retarding effect that a deflationary preference must have upon the weaker sectors of the international economy. Of course this general approach to monetary change comes in varied degrees of conservatism. Clearly at the right-hand extreme is M. Rueff, who would have the world return to the absolute rule of gold. However, as a return to the pure gold standard would be on a social par with repealing the Factory Act, M. Rueff's fondness for gold may be seen primarily as a rationale for upvaluing the profit and prestige of France and the rest of the gold-owning axis.

Defence of the present gold-exchange standard based on a new and higher price for the metal represents a liberalized version of the traditionalist-internationalist position. The politics of the gold price were dealt with in chapter 10. Suffice it here to recapitulate in summary. Leaving aside the short-term strategic transfer of prestige and power to the dollar distrusters, up-valuing gold, on the positive side, would effectively liberalize the monetary system in the short term by giving deficit nations a greater margin of reserves and hence greater latitude for fundamental economic readjustment, industrial regrouping and resource reallocation—measures which are made harder and more painful to take by conditions of deflation. It would also have a liberalizing potential in another direction. It would enable the rich nations to transfer resources to the Third World, and, if private hoarders in countries like India can be induced to realize a windfall profit on their personal gold hoards, it would provide at least some poor nations with increased international purchasing power for their own development.

On the negative side, the move would simply postpone tackling the problem of building international economic government. It would ensure that at some not so distant future date the dangers of world trade collapse through monetary shortage and monetary brinkmanship will occur all over again.

As an alternative to raising the gold price, many conservative-internationalists have looked to a process of bilateral bargaining as a means of shoring up (or strengthening, in the language of their political perspective) the present system. This was the rationale for the system of credit 'swaps' set up by United States Treasury Under-Secretary Robert Roosa in 1962, and extended with each major currency crisis since. Roosa also opened another avenue of co-operation at about the same time. This was the decision of the American government to encourage moves to a multiple currency reserve situation, a multilateralization of the bilateral reserve roles of the dollar and the pound. The plan, as explained by Roosa, was for the United States to start accumulating other convertible currencies (pounds, marks, francs, yen and lire, for example) when it achieved overall surplus in its balance of payments, instead of simply paying off its liabilities to the foreign authorities. This was an eminently sensible solution, but as a cure for the international monetary problem, it suffered from two drawbacks. The first was that other currencies, though convertible in theory into gold, are, in fact, only convertible into gold through the dollar (hence their parities always being expressed in dollar rather than gold terms). Thus in a moment of international financial panic, dollar claims on the United States gold reserve would still be presented. The other was that, although the Americans did actually start to hold foreign currencies in addition to gold for the first time from 1962, they never achieved a sufficient surplus in their payments for this practice to get very far.

Meanwhile, other suggestions for multilateral bargaining have not been wanting among the conservative-internationalists. One recent suggestion was for a *quid pro quo* arrangement under which the United States would agree to lift restrictions on export of American capital to any country that agreed to hold primarily dollars in their reserves, and that would co-operate with the United States Treasury in liberal swap arrangements to cope with panic or speculative short-term capital movements. But the snag with this approach is that, though it may help to cover the dollar's flank, it would clearly be unacceptable to precisely those countries that resist 'invasion' by American capital, *i.e.* that caused the dollar problem in the first place.

The most elaborate of all the conservatives' proposals for reinforcing the present system was the one first proposed at the time of the November 1968 franc-mark crisis by Henry Fowler to deal with a repetition of the wild avalanche of hot money that rushed from Paris to Frankfurt in anticipation of French devaluation. This was for central bankers simply to scoop up all the speculative capital that flowed over the exchanges in the crisis, and re-route it back to the exporting country (at the cost of a small percentage to the keepers of the weaker currency), so that no-one (except the authorities concerned) would know the degree of pressure to which the flow of capital was subjecting the currencies in question. How the speculative capital was to be separated from 'legitimate' investment was not explained. But the scheme, having been at first labelled 'impractical' by European central bankers was put into extensive use by the Bundesbank during the monetary crises of 1969 as a means of warding off revaluation pressures. That such a scheme, with its obviously arbitrary choice as to who should make a windfall profit and who should not, has been regularly resorted to, indicates the degree of desperation to which those who dread change, and prefer to tinker in the face of basic disequilibrium, have been driven.

ii. *The Progressive-Internationalists* are perhaps the modern heirs of John Maynard Keynes. Their right wing overlaps, to a great extent, the left wing of the conservative internationalists in their support of SDRs, though they would generally lay more emphasis on moving promptly and decisively in this direction.

Less preoccupied than conservatives with issues of prestige and special economic or strategic interest, they are prepared to envisage the gradual strengthening of the IMF's authority in world monetary management. A notable example of a cautiously pragmatic approach to the investure of the IMF with greater powers and responsibilities were the proposals put forward by Britain's Chancellor of the Exchequer, Reginald Maudling in 1962, at about the time of the Roosa proposals. The Maudling Plan called for the turning over of deficit nations' international debts to the IMF, where they would become gold-guaranteed international assets at the discretion of creditor countries. A more liberal version of the same concept, put forward by senior IMF official Edward Bernstein, would strengthen the Fund still further, but not simply at the discretion of the surplus 'hawks'. Nations would be permitted to count their total IMF 'positions', *i.e.* their gold deposits plus their credit entitlement, as part of their nations' reserves, usable without the need for IMF approval.

This proposal would be useful in realizing for everyday use the 'emergency only' central store of international cash (the IMF's gold) and credit (national drawing rights on the Fund). But it would do nothing to evolve the Fund into the international central bank that Keynes had envisaged. It is the advocates of the latter type of scheme that make up the most progressive wing of the monetary internationalists.

The most distinguished of these, and the prophet of international liquidity shortage ever since it emerged on the international horizon in 1958, is Professor Robert Triffin of Yale University. Triffin's Plan for an extended IMF (referred to by the experts with cloak-and-dagger crypticness as 'XIMF') has a wide constituency of international support among the more radical of monetary liberals. They support it because it provides solutions for their two principal monetary concerns. The first is to see that just as national central banks maintain a degree of domestic liquidity designed to encourage expansion, so a managed supply of international liquidity should be available to those national central banks. The second concern particularly stressed by monetary progressives more oriented to the problems of the Third World is that the new facilities for central money creation should be linked to aid to developing countries, and not reserved exclusively for the already relatively rich.

Progressive internationalist arguments face the national managers with a double dilemma. For apart from the ordinary considerations of national self-interest, abdication of a degree of autonomy in currency management in favour of some supranational authority would also imply a shift of power from central banks to treasuries, that is, from financiers to politicians. The ultimate weapon of the central banker is, as we have seen, the threat of adverse reaction on the part of foreign bankers on whose views the domestic bank chiefs are the undisputed experts. While their neighbouring nation's central banks continue to exercise autonomous choice, then the hands of central bankers everywhere are strengthened in dealing with their government at home. They can use the real or imagined threat of outside pressure to keep the management of money at least partially within their grasp.

The spectacle of the world's leading central bankers walking their political tight-rope may, depending on one's capacity for credulity, appear either astonishing or downright funny. After cosy monthly meetings at Basle at which immense credit swaps, amounting virtually to a temporary pooling of reserves, are arranged over cognac and cigars, these central bankers hurry home to assure their governments that their colleagues will stand for no more governmental profligacy, and are, even as they speak, sharpening their hatchets to sever lines of credit at the slightest future sign of governmental permissiveness.

But, somehow, the hatchet rarely descends. Instead, weeks later, the bankers are back arranging further stand-by credits. Yet the threat of adamancy on the part of those hard-eyed foreigners remains a powerful instrument for keeping their own governments in line, and the evolution of an effective central monetary authority would, some central bankers fear, remove the source of discipline, thus opening the floodgates to international paper ruin.

A domestic issue must therefore be settled before the rich nations of the West will be prepared to concede financial power to an international Superbank: are the central bankers to remain an international House of Lords, independent of the pressure of electorates, and with a special leaning towards the interests of creditors? Gathered together in a world central bank they could probably not survive in their present role as a restraining finger on the economic safety catch. Political pressures for expansion even at the cost of general inflation would almost certainly overwhelm them; for, in being forced under the spotlight of international publicity to take a broad economic view, they would be seen to be able collectively to place an effective check on government policy. Perhaps, under such enforced togetherness, the international House of Lords could not survive the composure of its national differences.

It is this uneasy realization, as much as anything, that makes the central bankers somewhat sceptical about the need for, or the advisability of, monetary supranationalism. It is this fact that encourages them, on the one hand, to co-operate to the maximum amongst themselves, while at the same time resisting pressure for greater international control.

Yet in fairness to these central bankers, it is disputable whether today they hold a significant degree of ultimate power beyond that which politicians have willingly—at times, perhaps, gratefully, considering their usefulness as electoral scapegoats—left in their hands.

iii. *The Traditional-Nationalist Approach* prefers the simplest solution to the problem of international money; that is to say, abolish the problem. This is what economic radicals at both the left and right extremes of the political spectrum, who have grounds for distrusting the pressures of internationalism, prefer to do. For if the international value of a currency is allowed to follow the laws of supply and demand, the need for reserves, for international liquidity, simply disappears.

The attractions of floating a currency have emerged in the narrative of this book. Floating its currency gives a nation independence to decide its own monetary and fiscal policy, its own level of consumption and government spending. Floating thus may hold strong appeal to a left-wing British economist anxious that socialism should be enabled to proceed in a single country, and equally strong appeal to Mr. Enoch Powell or a Right-wing American economist anxious to resist foreign pressures against America's policy in Vietnam. It was, for example, not solely domestic welfare considerations which led Milton Friedman, former economic adviser to Barry Goldwater, to propose to Mr. Nixon that he float the dollar. Pressure from foreign bankers works equally against staying in Vietnam and rebuilding cities.

Right-wing hawks and Left-wing doves may, therefore, both find reasons for preferring to float. If wages continue to rise faster than output, or if the government prefers to hasten ahead with public spending regardless of the nation's ability to earn its way abroad, then a floating exchange rate will simply allow the nation's currency to slip steadily downward in relation to others'; to devalue, in fact, gradually day by day, week by week to the point where equilibrium is reached—the point at which its exports are so cheap to foreigners that its export earnings balance the import bill. Any government interference with the exchange rate, with buying and selling of other currencies by the central bank so as to counteract the effects of the market, will of course immediately restore the need for reserves. But left alone both by government and speculators, an exchange rate based on supply and demand for a currency will arrive at a point where foreign payments balance and the economy is fully employed.

However, as is implicit in the above, floating has some very serious drawbacks. As might be expected, these are felt most immediately by those whose business concerns cross their country's frontiers, by foreign investors and all whose livelihood is closely linked with foreign trade. The fluctuation of the foreign purchasing power of the pound or dollar in your bank account, so that you could never be certain how much your exported machine tool or consignment of Scotch would earn in terms of your own currency, or of the yield and value of your overseas investment, is bound to discourage you from dependence on foreign trade and investment. Indeed, if freely floating exchange rates operated between all nations, the results would be akin to political anarchy.

But what tends to happen when an important exchange rate is allowed to float, as the pound was in 1931, is that closely related economies link their currencies in a fixed relationship to it. Thus fixed exchange rates are maintained on a limited regional scale, and trade blocs are formed. Unless the float of currencies is contained to within very narrow margins, and steadied by the operations of central banks, however, inter-bloc trade will be actively discouraged by the uncertainties involved. Internationalist opponents of flexible exchange rates often point in horror to the trade warfare that accompanied their use in the 1930's and that paved the descent into World War II. But in 1970, and particularly after the success of the Germans' upward float prior to fixing the mark at a new parity, there is renewed pressure from many quarters to loosen ties to fixed parities either temporarily, for adjustment purposes, or permanently. Conflicting national social priorities, different national preferences for government spending, different priorities for economic growth, have all primed the recent spate of demands that currencies be allowed to find their own level.

In the aftermath of the franc–mark war of November 1968, *The Economist* took the lead in advocating this course of action for the managers of the pound. 'The main object of such a move to floating rates [being] . . . to prepare the way for striking an agreement on world monetary reform with the incoming Nixon administration.'[1] *The Economist's* stance in arguing for removing support from the pound sterling and allowing it to float was, however, by no means simply one of chauvinistic support for Britain's high-consumption low-productivity way of life, and damn the consequences. At the same time as calling for a floating pound, this newspaper was agitating for further economic squeeze and freeze in order to strengthen Britain's position for striking a new international monetary bargain.

The weakness of this case, as of so many other strategies for British recovery, lay not so much in the prescription itself, as in the assumption of sufficient political will to make freeze and squeeze effective. This has long proved the weak point of British recovery efforts. And unfortunately it is precisely at this weak point of the recovery process that floating rates tend further to weaken the government's hand. For absence of need to defend a fixed parity would remove the government's ultimate rallying cry to complacent managements and intransigent

292 Reforming the World Monetary System

unions who, many people believe, need the external goad of attacks on the currency to keep them in the struggle. On this ultimate reckoning, then, the question boils down to a question of political psychology. On the one hand the threat of devaluation remains a powerful weapon for the enforcement of income and price restraint policies. On the other, the impact on a government and public opinion of a gradual subsidence of the exchange-rate would quite possibly soon become negligible. A clearly-defined battlefield, most observers feel, is a necessary device to stiffen governmental resolution against repeated surrenders when negotiating centrally bargained wage claims.

This last argument against floating exchange rates, as well as the criticism that they tend to produce economic bloc warfare, are largely got over by the supporters of a more moderate flexible exchange rate point of view.

iv. *The Progressive-Nationalist Position.* The fourth broad political category of reform proposals also prefers national freedom of currency manœuvre. But shunning the drastic qualities of the 'free float', their solution calls for various more sophisticated and restricted versions of exchange rate flexibility. In other words they provide for *limited* exchange rate variations.

The simplest of these expedients, the easiest both to administer and to get agreement on politically, is to widen the present maximum permissible float of 1 per cent either side of par (the traditional degree of flexibility allowed under the gold standard), to, say, 5 per cent or more. The great argument of those who pose this solution of widened 'bands' is that such increased flexibility would check speculation against currencies as national price levels move apart. The reason for this is as follows: if the 'band' within which currencies are allowed to float is widened to 5 per cent either side of par, the speculator who sells his weak francs, which an excess of supply over demand has brought to their 'floor', for marks, which an excess of demand over supply has driven to their 'ceiling' in expectation of a revaluation, will stand to lose up to 10 per cent of his stake if the devaluation does not come about, and his need of money in France causes him to shift back into francs. This may be compared with a maximum possible loss of only 2 per cent under the present 1 per cent bands system.

This argument has its theoretical appeal, but practical bankers and foreign exchange dealers argue that the problem is as broad as it is long. For great speculative profits may be made gambling *within* the 10 per cent range of permissible variation, if economic or political events within the countries concerned give rise to uncertainty. Besides, when the moment for devaluation seems really to have come, the much greater profits from the break could well make speculation far more overwhelming. The 'practical' men, then, still shake their heads. They point to the rapid and violent currency fluctuations that occurred after World War I, and again in the 1930's, as hot money poured back and forth over exchanges, tossing exchange rates about to the huge disruption of trade and investment.

The question, however, remains an open one. Flexible exchange-rate advocates can argue, with a good deal of justification, that the upsetting capital flows of the 1930's came as a result of the collapse of the fixed exchange rate system of the late 20's, and not as a result of the post-1931 exchange rate flexibility. Such arguments can too easily get bogged down in abstraction. But these finer academic points need not concern us here. If the international situation is sufficiently stormy and uncertain, then neither flexible nor fixed exchange rates will operate effectively, for *no* system which countenances the continuation of separate national currencies can isolate the monetary field from political life.

Other suggestions for controlling or checking the extent of currencies' float would, however, go further to allay the fears of practical men as to the degree of disruption that flexibility must cause to trade and payments. The most appealing compromise between fixed and floating rates is the horrific-sounding but descriptively named 'crawling peg'.* Under a crawling peg set-up, a currency would respond to the pressures of supply and demand, but the adjustment would be controlled in both timing and amount. For example, a shift in the pound's parity could be declared on a yearly, quarterly or even a monthly basis, but the permitted shift would be only decimals of a

* Such a system was first outlined in detail by Sir Roy Harrod in 1933, in his book *International Economics*.

percentage point. Such a solution would allow devaluation to occur gradually over a period of years.

As a compromise between fixed and floating exchange rates the crawling peg clearly has some of the advantages of both approaches. Greater certainty as to the future of exchange rates would both minimize deterrence to international trade and greatly reduce the incentive to speculate which is induced by a prospective change in the fixed rate system. Also, its flexibility in adjusting to disequilibrium would reduce the need for more international liquidity.

At the same time, the crawl would clearly also be heir to the afflictions of both floating and fixing. A crawling peg which moved slowly enough not to discourage world trade and investment might well provoke demand for the creation of more liquidity as well. But the main problem with this sophisticated compromise is its administrative complexity and its novelty, *i.e.* uncertainty as to its performance in practice. Its advocates can produce all sorts of graphs, charts and figures to demonstrate their understanding of the right amount of deci-points for each adjustment,* but the banking community remains sceptical.

Although perhaps the best available compromise between national and international needs, the crawling peg encounters criticism from those concerned over its gradualism. From a political point of view, enforced gradualness of change may seem not much better than violent deflation as a response to a sudden social upheaval, such as *les événements* of May 1968. In such circumstances the crawling peg may be thought to dawdle over the necessary adjustments insufferably. Thus from the point of view of national statesmen in an emergency, there is still a great deal to be said for the 'crisis flexibility' of conventional devaluation, the sudden break by any chosen amount in an otherwise fixed pattern. After all, the sovereign ability to devalue by any amount that national political or economic strategy may dictate, still represents the ultimate fail-safe device

---

* Professor James Meade has offered the suggestion for a 'sliding parity' whose maximum permissible move of one-sixth of a per cent a month could be required by the IMF of any country that was currently a net borrower from it.

of nationalism behind the internationalism of the present international monetary system—the ultimate flexibility that neither political nor financial leaders will readily give up.

By 1969, however, disequilibrium in national payments had produced such a degree of tension in the system of fixed exchange rates, that many believed the worst of all possible worlds had been reached. For national defence of the parities had caused deflationary pressures to build among the deficit nations, causing them to threaten international commerce with direct controls upon the movement of capital and trade in order to protect their unrealistic exchange rates. When such a situation is reached, then the ranking of alternative monetary systems according to which permits the freer flow of international commerce and investment, may become reversed. Under such circumstances, economists who would never have contemplated the use of flexible rates in times of reasonable equilibrium, feel forced to point out—as *The Economist* was doing in 1969—that short of a major war this may be the only way to bring about the realistic adjustment of currency parities which is the essential prerequisite of any new world monetary parley.

2. THE PROSPECTS FOR MONETARY CHANGE

The gold standard with its various modifications sustained the Free World economy, with brief hiatuses, throughout the era of international industrial trade. But that era is coming to an end. The logic of economic life has already, in the 1960's, left the concept of discrete national economies far behind. Today, the world monetary system faces the age of *international production*, for which it was never designed, and whose development it can do much to hinder. International production is unquestionably the outstanding economic phenomenon of the present age. Today, largely thanks to the overseas expansion of the United States, individual nations' growth outside their national borders is proceeding *at about twice the pace* of their growth at home. Since 1950, while the average growth rate of GNP has averaged about 5 per cent, the average annual growth in foreign investment has been about 10 per cent. At this rate

of growth, the total value of capital going annually into international investment will have surpassed that saved and invested
at home by the end of the century.

The logic of this international economy clearly points to some
form of world monetary federalism as the only solution to
future needs. But seen in today's political focus the outlook is
less certain. Indeed the experience of the United States federal
government in the last century suggests that world monetary
federalism still lies a great way off. America had to become
both a united polity *and* a unified economic entity before, in
1913, political pressures against a central monetary policy could
be finally overcome. However, there are many possible stages
in between the present one of sporadic co-operation within a
framework of national autonomy, and the emergence of a world
Superbank. What will the next stage be? Political rather than
economic considerations will answer this question. The interplay of political forces and monetary needs have been spelled
out in the course of this book. How they will in practice interact
for change it is not possible to say, but we must try to discern
the shape of events as they loom in the fog of the future.

BLEAK PROSPECT FOR A BRETTON WOODS II

There has been much recent talk of total monetary reconstruction. But the lessons of monetary history discourage optimism
over the prospect for a Bretton Woods II. Monetary officials
are not insensitive to the steady outpouring of new plans and
proposals, nor are they blind to the present system's obvious
and grievous failings. But they are inevitably concerned first
and foremost with the political realities of government rather
than the niceties of exchange rates and liquidity.

Beyond the gradual creation of Special Drawing Rights, over
which the Common Market countries hold a veto, a unified
solution to the world monetary problem seems highly unlikely
at the present time. The reason for this is not only a universal
unwillingness to relinquish individual national sovereignty,
already so compromised in the case of individual countries—
especially Britain—as to have lost most of its substance anyhow.
It is as much the result of basic differences in political and

economic philosophy between the continent of Europe and the Anglo-Saxons.

If the Americans' present growth pre-occupation continues alongside their external expansion of financial commitments, and if Britain continues to struggle out from under the burden of responsibilities that have long encumbered sterling, strains on the Atlantic monetary fault-plane may continue to build. Today, despite the quietude that has descended after a substantial up-valuation of the mark, a break along this fault-plane, a new monetary grouping which will take account of separate regional objectives, may yet be the force that produces the next stage of international monetary evolution.

The obvious parallels between the mounting crises that led to the great crack-up of 1931 and the monetary events of the late 1960's have been traced in the course of this book. But any move toward a Bretton Woods-type conference, involving as it would long and complex negotiations on, among other things, a new set of currency parities, even in the frenzy of 1968, never appeared remotely likely: for it is hard to imagine how the hands of the authorities could remain unforced as their currencies were subjected to overwhelming speculation. Thus it seems reasonably clear that a world monetary conference in the foreseeable future would almost inevitably end up more like the hopelessly abortive London Monetary Conference of 1932 than the Bretton Woods model twelve years later.

THE DOLLAR AND THE EUROPEAN COMMUNITY

Today, after a decade of monetary spasm, readjustments made to the parities of the three leading European currencies seem to many to presage a new period of quiet in international money. Thus the pressures for total monetary overhaul appear, at least for the moment, to have been largely removed. The fact that this return of calm has occurred while the worst dollar inflation since Civil War days continues in the United States, appears to many as an impressive indication that despite the anxieties of the Gold War, the world is by now so dependent on the dollar that to threaten its role would be to contemplate a form of multilateral suicide. Moreover, the recent agreement on the introduction over a three-year period, beginning in 1970, of $9·5 billion-worth of paper gold, the monetary moderation of de Gaulle's successor and the start of de-escalation in Vietnam appear to augur well for a substantial degree of relief for the dollar's dangerously exposed position.

Certainly, and especially if the Vietnam conflict is brought to an early end, much of the short-run pressure for monetary change will have been removed. Will, then, the convenience of the present fixed-rate, dollar-liquidity system, with its proven strength and flexibility in the face of great political pressures, cause it to survive basically intact into the 1970's and beyond?

For the moment, anyway, the liquidity-creation problem seems to have been resolved. European bankers, though they have so far seen few tangible results, have taken it on trust that the Nixon administration will use its will and authority to curb Johnson's war inflation and stabilize the anchor-currency. But if the Vietnam conflict is allowed to drag on and the dollar to continue dwindling at 4–5 per cent, then another bout of gold crisis, and thus a threat to the entire world monetary system, could very well suddenly occur. As it is, even if de-escalation continues as hoped, America's transition back to 'peace-time' monetary conditions is bound to cause anxieties. Recession in the United States economy under tight money restraints, produced an outflow of short-term European funds from Wall Street in 1970 which caused a massive deterioration in the American balance of payments.

As regards the fate of fixed exchange rates the future is even less clear. Parity changes in the pound, franc and mark have, here too, reduced short-term pressures. But as this book has tried to explain, the longer-term causes of exchange-rate tension among the major trading nations remain. At the time of writing, the prospect for general acceptance of some type of crawling peg relationship, at least between European currencies, seems increasingly good. The great problem of a universal crawling system would be the dollar, which, for some time to come, must continue its role of reserve currency and is therefore likely to remain fixed to gold. If the dollar remains so fixed, it would be able to depreciate, so as to offset domestic deflationary pressures, only if other currencies 'crawled up' on it.

But would their managers be willing to worsen their national competitiveness in this manner? Certainly, it remains highly doubtful whether countries will submit to the loss of sovereignty involved in a mandatory crawl. The rules must either be kept indicative, and rely on international pressure for their enforcement, or there must be major escape clauses built in to cover national emergencies. Despite such limitations, however, the crawling peg's widespread adoption in principle would be a great advance in monetary co-operation. Perhaps it is the best that practical men can hope for in the next few years.

At the same time, however, it must not be forgotten that the sources of 'European' antipathy to the dollar's dominion remain. At the time of the great gold crisis of 1968, it seemed possible to a number of monetary observers that a 1931-style return to monetary blocs could recur, with the Common Market countries all tying their currencies to gold, and that a dollar bloc, with or without the sterling area in fixed or crawling relation to it, might be allowed to float. Such a development today seems far less likely, for as subsequent events have shown, the monetary and commercial tensions within the community remain almost as great as between it and its Atlantic neighbours.

Indeed, the question of the future of fixed parities is inextricably involved with the wider political and economic questions of regional alliances and groupings. If the dollar were to be allowed to float, the pre-eminent position of the American economy would inevitably produce overwhelming incentives for many countries within its orbit—certainly Canada, Latin America and Japan—to fix their exchange rates to the dollar and use dollars in their reserves. A European currency bloc, on the other hand, would not have the natural focus of one pre-eminent currency. Instead, therefore, it would be bound to rely on the political and economic framework of the Community to develop its cohesion.*

This is why an American decision taken under extreme

*At present, despite this regional economic machinery, the Common Market countries discriminate against one another in favour of the dollar. They do so by fixing their currencies' parities to the gold dollar rather than each other. Thus, under the IMF 1 per cent 'band' rule, the exchange-rate of each currency can deviate from that of the others by *twice* pressure from Americanophobes in Europe could produce immense positive economic pressures for greater European integration. It is also, of course, the nub of the continuing dilemma confronting today's gold-dollar standard. Dislike of the American challenge, with such unpleasant results, from a European point of view, as the 'IBM hegemony' in world-wide competitive markets, makes separation from the dollar's orbit seem politically desirable to many continentals. Yet, because the result of a dollar depreciation in relation to the other currencies would be increased competitiveness for American goods, the proponents of non-dollar bloc ideas have little following. In the last analysis, the dominance in nationalistic thinking of the importance of a country's trading edge is the single unavoidable obstacle to cutting loose from the dollar.

The present international monetary system then, unsatisfactory to many, but tolerable to nearly all, will preserve the role of the Americans as the 'best Europeans', meaning the ones best-equipped and most willing to use the economic opportunities of the entire continent. But Europeans themselves must be under no illusions as to the results of their own continued parochialism and their refusal to behave as Europeans. Greater and greater integration and domination of the European economy by giant American corporations will, in the not too distant future, prevent any single European nation, and perhaps the whole continent, from pursuing the mix of social and economic priorities which it prefers. Must greater wealth, and more leisure for the mass, inevitably be accompanied by greater homogeneity, strip development, more ugliness and boredom?

Unfortunately, there appears to be a value-system built into America's offering of investment and technology which has so far borne these fruits without fail wherever they have been planted. Only European development under European control and in European hands offers the possibility of escape from the present appalling prospect of gradual 'mid-Westernization' of the European continent.

As this book has tried to show, economic and social sove-

the maximum possible deviation between any one of these currencies and the dollar.

reignty, the sovereignty to take such basic value decisions, must ultimately be based upon full political—which means full monetary—sovereignty for it to be effective at all. This is why in the longer term, when the implications of the de-Europeanization of Europe become more manifest, the continent may increasingly return to its lingering preference for autonomy. Such political pressures will lend support to plans for consolidation of the Community into a single monetary bloc.

BRITAIN'S MONETARY CROSSROADS

A 'two-bloc' monetary system would clearly be far from the ideal vehicle for the smooth expansion of world trade. But in permitting both continental Europe and the rest of the world to pursue the mix of political and economic policies that they prefer, it might very well help to achieve the uniting of Europe and the longer term enhancement of Atlantic harmony. At the same time, such a break would apply new pressure for a long overdue decision as to the direction—continental or Atlantic—in which Britain's future lies.

Since 1958, when the general European movement to non-resident convertibility in practice merged London's banking role in overseas sterling with her management of the Eurodollar, Britain's whole structure of international financial operations has become inextricably interthreaded with the dollar. In the event of an Atlantic monetary split, could London remain a monetary pontoon between America and the Continent? The agonizing question, if such a split became imminent, would be whether Britain's highly active role in the vast and volatile Eurodollar market would be feasible without American and Canadian support. The profitable position of entrepôt centre for so much of the world's trading and short-term capital leaves Britain with an ever-increasing exposure to sudden and massive capital movements. The kind of support so far given by European institutions to back this British entrepôt role has shown no sign of coming anywhere near the growing need. This is another reason why Britain has come to rely increasingly on massive doses of American credit to support London in its role as New York East, the dollar-financing centre for Europe.

In the past, schemes have been discussed (see chapter 11) between Britain and various European bankers for absorbing Britain's sterling debts into some European consortium in return for the shift of London's role of monetary entrepôt to the continent. Many in Britain who are anxious to be finally rid of the reserve currency mill-stone would favour some such settlement as part of a bargain over entry into Europe. Judging from the historical evidence, this would be an excellent bargain for Britain. For Britain's financial entrepôt role is not the kind of asset which can simply be transferred in settlement of a debt. It is a question of institutions, personal skills, temperament: in a phrase, a banking tradition. This tradition was acquired over centuries. It financed an empire's rise and survived its dispersal. In thinking that the City of London's function may be transferred to the continent, Europeans may be making the same mistake that the City fathers made themselves in fearing for its survival in the absence of an international role for sterling. Experience, however, has proved the contrary. London will remain a key financial centre in any open monetary system. Her unmatched tradition of sophisticated service and confidence, quite independent of the fate of the pound, will always bring her creditors and borrowers.

It would be greatly in Europe's overall interest—though not, perhaps, to that of some of her overseas bankers—if Britain brought these unmatched facilities into Europe as part of her dowry. However, as many of de Gaulle's successors still see Britain's external financial ties as a barrier between her and Europe, it may be that some official signs of British interest in joining a floating dollar bloc could strengthen the hands of those 'good Europeans' who are anxious to welcome Britain in. The prospect of confronting a monetary bloc including the United States, Canada, Britain, the Commonwealth, Latin America and probably Japan, whose goods were all highly competitive with those of Europe because their currencies were uniformly undervalued in terms of a European 'currency bloc', might encourage even the French Patronat to warm to the idea of taking Britain in.

THE INTEREST OF THE DEVELOPING WORLD

A NAFTA arrangement might have considerable appeal to the developing world. A North Atlantic monetary bloc in which sterling, the United States dollar, the Canadian dollar, the Swedish krone, etc., all offered each other automatic mutual support (for instance, by pooling their gold reserves to meet external payments imbalances) would break the aid-giving monetary bottleneck for precisely those countries most disposed to increase their foreign aid. British experts claim that she would also probably benefit from the removal of other nations' ties on their aid. In fact, it is widely believed in Whitehall that current United States (and other) aid-tying deprives Britain of a substantial volume of developing country export orders that she might otherwise win.

But the large-scale bloc would also have serious disadvantages for the less developed countries. Outstanding among these would be its shelving of the Bretton Woods monetary machinery with its wide representation and global terms of reference.

However, the happy resolution of the franc-mark crisis of 1969 and the inauguration of the first man-made reserve unit (SDRs) seems to have banished the spectre of rival currency blocs upon Anglo-Saxon/Continental lines. Yet the price of closing the Atlantic monetary rift has been serious concessions to Continental conservatism. A creation-rate of $3 billion SDRs a year will not long suffice for the kind of expansion the world economy must maintain if the rich nation–poor nation gap is to be significantly closed. Furthermore, the quota allotments in the IMF are not only still too small at the level of $28 billion established on 1 January 1970,* but their distribution, which matches national voting-power in the Fund, is still far too close to the Bretton Woods era of Anglo-Saxon hegemony (Britain's quota in the Fund remains twice that of Germany, more than twice that of France and four times that of Italy) and unnecessarily weighted in favour of the rich men's club. The recent quota adjustment did little to resolve this problem. Indeed it actually reduced the voting influence and power of

* Fund quotas, normally revised every five years, were raised from $21 billion at this date.

the Third World by demoting India from her position as poor nations' spokesman, with the fifth largest number of votes, in favour of Japan.

A new, more representative, monetary top table is badly needed, which provides seats for the poor nations instead of leaving them to scrabble for the rich men's crumbs. One fertile suggestion in this direction, championed by Professor Richard Gardner, is to make the IMF's Executive Directors into a policy-making Group of Twenty-One.[2] This proposed Group would consist of the twenty representative countries on the Fund's Executive Board, plus Switzerland, if she can be persuaded to shoulder a little of the responsibility that ought to accompany financial power. Professor Gardner proposes that this Group should meet at ministerial level once a quarter. Such periodic meetings at the top level, within the Bretton Woods framework, would recognize the danger of the increasing bypassing of Bretton Woods-type multilateralism by the members of the various rich men's clubs (Basle Club, Paris Club, OECD) when reviewing world monetary problems. A Group of Twenty-One, ministerially represented, would also help overcome a present weakness of the Bretton Woods machinery, namely that (as Keynes predicted in 1945) the practice of having Executive Directors of the IMF serve full-time in Washington, removes these national representatives from the seats of national political power and reduces their participation in top-level national decision-making. The Fund's and Bank's annual ministerial-level meetings fall far short of being an adequate forum for such discussion. Referred to colloquially as the 'fun and bunk' meetings, they tend to be just that: jamboree get-togethers of over 100 countries, plus guests, where little official business gets done.

Other institutional developments are also now becoming urgently needed to meet the changing pattern of international financial relations. So far international organizations have failed to respond to the problems raised by the emergent era of international production. Certainly these areas are today inadequately reviewed or monitored by existing bodies such as the General Agreement on Trade and Tariffs (GATT) and the United Nations Conference on Trade and Development (UNCTAD). However, it may be that entirely new multi-lateral institutions must be created to supervise international regulation of multinational corporations in such areas as balance of payments controls, liquidity requirements, concepts of competition and inter-country accounting and taxation. In all these discussions, the poor nations must have a greater role and voice. If they do not get it, the longer-term political and economic consequences will almost certainly be disastrous for all concerned.

3. SUMMING UP THE PROSPECTS: THE PERILS AND THE PRIZE

Any future world monetary settlement is inseparably linked with the question mark over Europe. Continental Europe has used its monetary whiphand to resist American economic invasion: but it has neither the financial institutions nor attitudes to replace the role of New York and the Eurodollar. The Common Market has made little progress toward its internal monetary integration, in part at least, because the financial facilities provided by the dollar have removed any pressure of need to do so. The inflow of dollars and gold from America in the 1950's and 60's gave the individual Common Market countries such strong payments positions that the need for monetary integration to cope with either internal or external payments problems has so far not arisen.

From 1970 onwards, however, if the original timetable of the Rome Treaty is to be even approximately followed, the need for such monetary integration will suddenly become acute. For from this year onwards, intra-Community shifts in exchange rate will theoretically be ruled out.* If at that time the United States is being forced to run a balance of payments surplus in defence of the dollar, so that Europe's supply of liquidity (in the form of Eurodollar certificates of deposit and Eurobonds)

* The Rome Treaty was, however, carefully left vague over monetary arrangements. For a valuable analysis of the *status quo* and the prospects, the reader is recommended to *Financial Integration in Western Europe*, by Professors Kirschen, Bloch, and Bassett, New York, Columbia University, 1969.

is diminishing, then enormous added pressure for a European reserve currency must be the result.

So far as Britain is concerned, a 'two bloc' approach to the world's monetary problems as part of an agreement forming a North Atlantic Free Trade Area, might seem to serve her interests well in the short, or even medium term. But the British decision to press for Common Market membership is based on much wider and longer-term considerations. In the last political analysis, the British must prefer membership in a unified Europe on whose evolution they can still have a major influence, to being part of an Atlantic entity in which greater material prosperity is bought at the price of total absorption into the American orbit. A vast majority of Europeans prefer it too. They feel the advantages not only of Britain's political maturity, her domestic market with its EFTA and Commonwealth affiliates but, by no means least, her facilities as financial intermediary with both the New and Third Worlds.

This is precisely where the financial expertise of the City of London could pay off. Britain's role as a provider of 'financial intermediary services' in channelling and marshalling Europe's vast dollar holdings has already made it pre-eminent on its side of the Atlantic as a focus for financial integration. Moreover, the City's demonstration of its willingness and ability to do business in dollars and other Eurocurrencies, as the pound has declined in its international trade-financing role, has made its formerly defensive leadership eager and ready for the challenge. As a result, it is by no means inevitable that European bankers' offers to take over Britain's sterling debts in the expectation of receiving future business of the City's traditional customers would now be turned down.

REALISM—THE VIRTUE OF SDRS

The basic difficulty in achieving monetary reform is inherent in the structure of the world monetary system. The political glue that prevents the system from working more effectively is the same substance that holds it together. Just as any attempt at decisive United Nations peace-keeping action is pre-destined to frustration without big-power accord, so any attempt at full-scale rewriting of the ground rules of world money at a time of political tension in the West, is bound to be hopeless. However, the SDR agreements have opened a way ahead. If a sufficient amount of liquidity can be created to help the Anglo-Saxons and other profligates over their balance of payments difficulties without enforcing upon them politically unacceptable deflation, or politically unacceptable inflation upon the surplus countries, this may well prove the most practical of all solutions.

In early 1969 one interesting means of deciding the rate of liquidity creation was gaining favour with a number of monetary and financial advisers and theorists. Under this approach all countries should be asked what balance of payments result they were aiming at for the year ahead. Since nearly all countries would almost inevitably say that they were aiming at a payments surplus, the answer might be that, in the words of *The Economist*, 'the world was hell-bent on running a surplus of say $8 billion a year with itself'.[3] Then it would be comparatively easy to point out that the only way that this could be done would be to provide $8 billion of new money, of which a fraction might be new gold, but the vast bulk would have to be SDRs. Under such a regime, it would be possible, with gradually increasing political acceptability, for the IMF to emerge, through its management of the mounting volume of paper gold, as the Superbank of some reformers' dreams.

MONEY TO FINANCE MAN'S SURVIVAL

In arguing the toss over a world monetary settlement, it is as well to bear in mind the fundamental political realities behind the management of money. World War II proved once and for all that provided nations are prepared to discipline their consumption, the only limit on what they can afford is what they are physically able to produce. Inflation occurs only in cases where consumption is allowed to run ahead of productivity. In fact where men show more ingenuity in creating money than in creating goods and services.

The more the world procrastinates the taking of its pleasures, the greater those pleasures can ultimately be. National price levels will vary with how much wealth a country's citizens can be persuaded to invest for tomorrow rather than consume today. The basic issue that separates Western industrial nations (as opposed to international economic groups, like farmers and industrial workers, debtors and creditors), is the extent to which their respective populations are willing to forgo immediate consumption, and the extent to which they are prepared to concentrate that investment within their national borders. A universal check upon consumption among the rich nations, combined with liberal encouragements to investment, could enable them all to grow at a quite fantastic rate, and to accumulate a surplus that could probably solve the problem of poverty in both the developed and developing world by the end of this century. For ultimately the single limitation to the creation of wealth is the availability of suitably trained manpower. Achievement of this Nirvana is today a real economic possibility. But it is still far over the political horizon.

Historically, major change in man's economic and political management comes about through revolution, war or economic collapse—in fact, when it can be resisted no longer. Today, however, such methods of changing our basic directions are luxuries which the world can no longer afford. Certainly there is no hope for solution of the scale of problems which the world now faces if new direction can only be achieved after grinding to an almost complete halt.

If we are to meet the challenge of saving humankind from poisoning his environment, while further exploiting that environment to raise the living standard of the impoverished two-thirds of his family, both human and natural resources must rapidly be mobilized on an utterly unprecedented scale; and credit to finance this mobilization must be created. This is the ultimate human imperative—the fulcrum of need around which monetary politics must increasingly come to turn. Unwillingness to contemplate the institutional reforms to meet such a new challenge was yesterday's recipe for disaster. It may be today's recipe for extinction. This is the sort of thought that should be in the minds of the world's bankers and finance ministers as they contemplate the problem of creating the means to finance change. But is it?

A Short Glossary of Terms
References
Bibliography
Index

A Short Glossary of Terms

ACCEPTANCE   The acceptance business of the City of London (and other major entrepôt centres) arose from the willingness of prominent merchants to finance other merchants' trade. Such merchants 'accepted' the use of their 'name' or credit, and would agree to BILLS OF EXCHANGE being drawn on them to finance a third party's purchase of goods. (See p. 38.)

ARBITRAGE   The process of buying something in one market for sale in another, so as to take advantage of differences in price.

BALANCE OF PAYMENTS   The difference between total payments into and out of a country during a given period of time. All items affecting the *current* income and expenditure of a country make up the balance of payments *current account*. The net result of the movement of *capital* into and out of the country is called the balance of payments, *capital account*. Both current and capital must be used to compute a country's overall balance of payments. A country in credit in any given period is said to have a favourable balance, a country in debit over a given period is said to have an unfavourable balance.

BIS   Bank for International Settlements (headquarters, Basle). (See pp. 85–6.) Since 1945, and especially in the 1960's, its operations have largely been concerned with helping to smooth out exchange fluctuations by arranging and entering into currency and gold 'swap' agreements with central banks.

BANK RATE   The official minimum rate per cent at which the Bank of England (and other central banks) will discount 'first class' commercial bills (BILLS OF EXCHANGE). Bank rate is the chief means used by central banks to control the price of credit and thus the volume of credit and the monetary situation in general. When bank rate is raised borrowing generally is made more expensive, the traditional experience being that the demand for loans then falls, and business activity generally declines. A lowering of bank rate would obviously have the opposite effect.

BANK RESERVES The money banks keep available to meet the demands of depositors.

BENELUX Belgium, the Netherlands and Luxembourg.

BILATERAL AGREEMENT One between two parties.

BILL OF EXCHANGE (Commercial Bill.) A written instruction by the person drawing the bill (drawer) to pay a particular sum either to the bearer of the bill, or a specified person (the payee). (See p. 23, for a fuller description of bills of exchange, including 'credit' bills and 'real' or 'commodity' bills.)

BILLION The American billion (= 1,000 million) is used throughout as it today has wide currency in Europe.

BULLION Gold or silver, usually in bar or ingot form, and of a recognized degree of purity.

CENTRAL BANK A bank occupying the central position in the banking system in the sense that it is the banker to both the government and other banks. Central banks manage national currencies and carry out the currency and credit policy of their country. They also control the import and export of money and monetary metals. Most central banks are now State-owned: all operate under government supervision.

CIA Central Intelligence Agency of the United States Government.

CONVERTIBILITY Originally this term referred to the free exchange of a currency for gold or silver at a fixed price (e.g. under the 'full' or 'classic' gold standard). Since the general return to convertibility in 1958, however, convertibility only applies to *foreign* holders of the domestic currency. Thus, today, if a currency is convertible, foreign earners of that currency can convert their holdings of it into gold or any other currency.

DEFLATION When the supply of money declines relative to the number of exchange transactions. If the volume of goods and services offered for sale does not fall to match the decreased supply of money, the price level falls.

DISCOUNT A discount is a deduction from the face value of a debt or price of something in return for prompt or early payment.

EEC European Economic Community or Common Market.

EPU   European Payments Union. A clearing house set up in 1950 to facilitate intra-European trade and payments in a time of great liquidity shortage.

EURODOLLAR, EUROCURRENCIES   Bank credit of extra-national origin. (See p.156.)

FIDUCIARY ISSUE   An issue of money not backed by gold or silver. (See p. 33.)

FISCAL   Concerned with public finance. Fiscal policy embraces the scope and degree of taxation, national debt, government borrowing.

FLOATING EXCHANGE   An exchange rate with no fixed parity to gold or other currencies, so that the currency's international value can float at the level determined by international supply and demand.

FOREIGN EXCHANGE   The exchange of one currency for another. The phrase is used to describe inclusively the currencies of foreign countries.

FORWARD EXCHANGE   A foreign exchange transaction designed to insure the trader against adverse changes in currency parities. A contract is made to exchange one currency for another at a fixed future date and at a fixed exchange rate. The 'forward exchange' market operates at a discount (premium) to insure traders against devaluation (re-valuation).

FROZEN   Used in contradistinction to liquid to suggest that conversion into usable money is difficult or impossible. Hence 'frozen' assets.

FUNDING   The process whereby short-term (or floating) debt is converted into long-term (or funded) debt.

GNP   Gross National Product. The total value, at current market prices, of all final goods and services produced by a nation's economy in a given period. It includes the purchases of goods and services by consumers and government plus domestic and foreign investment.

GOLD STANDARD   The measurement of values in terms of gold. The name of the monetary system that operated internationally between the 1880's and 1914 and in Britain from 1816–1914. (See pp. 37–46.)

GROUP OF TEN   The ten wealthiest western industrial countries who in the 1960's frequently met informally at Basle, London, Paris, Washington, Stockholm and elsewhere to thrash out mutual approaches to international monetary and financial problems.

HOT MONEY Money, often a part of the liquid assets of wealthy individuals but chiefly of a few very large 'multinational' companies, which is frequently moved around from currency to currency so as to earn maximum interest with minimum risk. In a currency crisis, such hot money is used to speculate on a parity change.

IDA International Development Association, affiliate of the World Bank.

IMF International Monetary Fund.

INFLATION A situation in which prices are rising. The converse of deflation, it occurs when the volume of money available for exchange transactions is not required by or followed by an appropriate expansion in the number of transactions. When this situation occurs, prices will rise.

JOINT STOCK Joint ownership of a business by a group of people. In Britain joint-stock banks gradually merged into the 'big four' commercial banks which between them today have thousands of branches all over the country and abroad.

MILLED COIN Coin with serrations stamped on its edge. (See footnote, p. 12.)

MULTILATERALISM The approach to international relations which seeks to satisfy many nations simultaneously.

NAFTA North Atlantic Free Trade Area, a grouping proposed in the 1960's by some opponents of Britain's entry into the Common Market.

OPEN MARKET OPERATIONS The buying and selling of securities in the open market by a central bank for the purpose of curtailing or expanding the volume of credit. (See pp. 171–77.)

OECD Organisation for Economic Co-operation and Development. (See footnote, p. 146.)

PARITY In connection with currencies, 'parity' indicates an agreed fixed exchange rate—'par' for a currency—around which small fluctuations are usually allowed.

PEGGING Central banks 'peg' their currencies into a narrow range around 'par'. They do this by intervening in the foreign

exchange markets, buying their own currency with their gold
and/or foreign exchange (and hence depleting their gold and
foreign exchange reserves) to support its foreign purchasing
power, or selling their currency for foreign exchange (and
hence increasing their gold or foreign exchange reserves) to
hold its exchange value down to within the pegged limits
round 'par'.

RE-CYCLING   A practice first proposed by US Treasury Secretary
Henry Fowler in 1968, whereby a country or countries
receiving large inflows of HOT MONEY as a result of a flight
from other currencies would return the speculative flows
secretly on an inter-central bank swap basis, without
revealing the extent of the inflow.

RENTIER   One who lives from money rents, whether landlord, or
bond-owner.

RESERVE CURRENCIES   In practice the pound and the dollar (and
the franc in the franc area of North Africa). To maintain a
reserve currency, the parent country must ensure that any
tendency to run recurrent balance of payments surpluses on
current account is offset by capital flows to foreign investment or other foreign expenditure. (See pp. 159–61.)

SDR   Special Drawing Right of the International Monetary Fund,
popularly referred to as 'paper gold'. (See pp. 214–16.)

SWAP AGREEMENTS   Agreements between central banks to open
'lines of credit' with each other so as to bolster the reserves
of deficit countries when their currencies come under
speculative fire.

TERMS OF TRADE   A comparison of a country's imports and exports
in terms of their prices. If a country's imports rise in price,
relative to its exports, then its terms of trade have become
unfavourable.

References

CHAPTER 1 *pp. 11–22*

1. Carlo M. Cipolla, 'Currency Depreciation in Mediaeval Europe', *Economic History Review*, No. 3 (1963), pp. 414–22.
2. John Locke, *Further Considerations*, London, 1695. Passage quoted in Sir Albert Feavearyear, *The Pound Sterling*, rev. edn., Oxford, Clarendon Press, 1963.

CHAPTER 2 *pp. 23–50*

1. Sir Albert Feavearyear, *The Pound Sterling*, Oxford, 1963, p. 102.
2. *Encyclopaedia Britannica*, see article on Bank of England.
3. George Warde Norman, *A Letter to Charles Wood, Esq., M.P.*, London, 1841, p. 34.
4. David Thompson, *Europe since Napoleon*, New York, Knopf, 1962, p. 86 *et seq.*
5. Sir Roy Harrod, *The Dollar*, New York, Norton Library, 1963, p. 16.
6. Quoted Samuel E. Morison, *The Oxford History of the American People*, Oxford University Press, 1965, p. 439.
7. Letter to *The Economist*, 20 April 1968.
8. Sir Robert Kindersley, in evidence before the Macmillan Committee on Finance and Industry, 1929. Quoted in Robert Skidelsky, *Politicians and the Slump*, Macmillan, 1967, p. 376.
9. Peter I. Lyaschchenko, *A History of the National Economy of Russia*, New York, Macmillan, 1949, pp. 561–62.
10. Sir Roy Harrod, *The Dollar*, *op. cit.*, p. 22.
11. Robert Triffin, *The Evolution of the International Monetary System: Reappraisal and Future Perspectives*, Princeton Studies in International Finance, No. 12, p. 7.

CHAPTER 3 *pp. 53–69*

1. J. M. Keynes, *A Tract on Monetary Reform*, London, Macmillan, 1923, p. 90.
2. Robert Skidelsky, 'The Grand Alternatives', *The Listener*, 29 February 1968.

3. Andrew Boyle, *Montagu Norman*, London, Cassell, 1967, p. 123. A brilliant biographical portrait on which I have relied heavily for material on the Governor.

4. *Ibid.*, p. 104.

5. Emile Moreau, *Souvenirs d'un Gouverneur de la Banque de France*, quoted Boyle, p. 198.

6. Quoted Lester V. Chandler, *Benjamin Strong, Central Banker*, Washington, The Brookings Institution, 1958, p. 270.

7. Quoted Hjalmar Schacht, *The Magic of Money*, London, Oldbourne, 1967, pp. 65–66.

8. Boyle, p. 172.

9. G. Stolper, *The German Economy, 1870–1940*, 1940, p. 176.

10. Boyle, p. 189.

CHAPTER 4   *pp. 70–102*

1. Boyle, p. 106.

2. J. M. Keynes, *A Tract on Monetary Reform*, p. 123.

3. Robert Skidelsky, *Politicians and the Slump*, p. 76.

4. *Ibid.*, p. 76.

5. Boyle, p. 196.

6. *Ibid.*

7. *Ibid.*, p. 197.

8. J. M. Keynes, 'The Economic Consequences of Mr. Churchill', *Essays in Persuasion*, New York, Norton Library, 1963, p. 270.

9. Robert Triffin, *Gold and the Dollar Crisis*, Yale University Press, 1962, p. 57.

10. Emile Moreau, quoted Boyle, p. 226.

11. *Ibid.*, p. 198.

12. Boyle, p. 224.

13. *Ibid.*, p. 204.

14. Moreau, quoted Boyle, p. 205.

15. *Ibid.*, p. 229.

16. Boyle, p. 247.

17. Paul Einzig, *The Fight for Financial Supremacy*, London, Macmillan, 1934, p. 79.

18. Boyle, p. 268.

19. *Ibid.*, p. 178.

20. *Ibid.*, p. 287.

21. Lester V. Chandler, pp. 308–316.

22. Einzig, *The Fight for Financial Supremacy*, p. 151.
23. Paul Einzig, *Behind the Scenes of International Finance*, London, Macmillan, 1934, p. 60.
24. Samuel E. Morison, p. 956.
25. Article in the *Daily Mail*, London, 3 July 1933.
26. John Morton Blum, *From the Morgenthau Diaries*, Vol. II, *Years of Crisis, 1928–1938*, Boston, Houghton Mifflin Company, 1959, p. 69.
27. Timothy Green, *World of Gold*, New York, Walker & Co., pp. 71–74.

CHAPTER 5 *pp. 103–120*

1. John Morton Blum, *From the Morgenthau Diaries*, Vol. II, p. 20.
2. Vladimir Petrov, *Money and Conquest*, Baltimore, Johns Hopkins University Press, 1968, p. 39.
3. United States Congress, Senate: 'Hearings before the Committee on Appropriations, Armed Services and Banking and Currency', 80th Congress, 1st Session, June 1947, quoted in Petrov, p. 40.
4. Sir Roy Harrod, *The Life of John Maynard Keynes*, London, Macmillan, 1951, p. 499.
5. *Ibid.*, p. 498.
6. Richard N. Gardner, *Sterling-Dollar Diplomacy*, new. edn. New York, McGraw-Hill, 1969, p. 66. I have drawn freely on this excellent standard work on wartime and post-war Anglo-American economic and financial negotiations.
7. *Ibid.*, p. 76.
8. *Ibid.*, p. 91.
9. *Ibid.*, p. 77.
10. *Ibid.*, p. 113.

CHAPTER 6 *pp. 121–135*

1. Gardner, p. 126.
2. *Ibid.*, p. 130.
3. American Bankers' Association, *Practical International Financial Organization*, 1 February 1945, quoted Gardner, p. 130.
4. Gardner, p. 139.
5. Information to author from John J. McCloy.
6. See John Morton Blum, *From the Morgenthau Diaries*, Vol. III, *Years of War, 1941–45*, pp. 295–303.

7. Gardner, p. 213.
8. Quoted, Fred Hirsch, *Money International*, London, Allen Lane, 1967, p. 356.
9. Gardner, p. 235.

CHAPTER 7 *pp. 139–158*

1. Jack Bennett, 'The German Currency Reform', *The Annals of the Academy of Political and Social Science*, Vol. 267 (January 1950), p. 44, quoted Petrov, p. 189.
2. Quoted Petrov, p. 190.
3. Petrov, p. 190.
4. This document, known as JCS1067, is analysed in detail in 'Directives for the Occupation of Germany: The Washington Controversy', by Paul Y. Hammond, *American Civil-Military Decisions*, Ed. Harold Stein, 1963, University of Alabama Press.
5. Robert Triffin, *Europe and the Money Muddle*, London, Oxford University Press, 1957, p. 161.
6. *Ibid.*, p. 164.

CHAPTER 9 *pp. 166–197*

1. For a fascinating perspective on this point, see Gordon C. Bjork, *Private Enterprize and Public Interest*, Englewood Cliffs, New Jersey, Prentice-Hall, 1968.
2. *New York Times*, 10 March 1969.
3. Rondo Cameron, *France and the Economic Development of Europe*, Princeton University Press, 1961, p. 87.
4. Herbert Feis, *Europe, The World's Banker 1870–1914*, New York, Norton Library, 1965, p. 110.
5. J. M. Keynes, *Economic Journal*, December 1914.
6. I am indebted to William Bruce Bassett for this phrase.
7. Richard Tilly, *Financial Institutions in the Rhineland*, University of Wisconsin Press, 1966, p. 137.
8. Fred Hirsch, pp. 228–29.
9. *Ibid.*, pp. 129–30.

CHAPTER 10 *pp. 198–224*

1. Robert Triffin, *Our International Monetary System: Yesterday, Today, And Tomorrow*, New York, Random House, 1968, table, p. 101.

2. Jacques Rueff, 'Sur un point d'histoire: le niveau de la stabiliz-ation Poincaré', *Revue d'Economique Politique*, Vol. 69 (1959).

3. Fred Hirsch, p. 277.

4. *New York Times*, 11 November, 1969.

5. Timothy Green, pp. 71–79.

6. *The Economist*, 23–29 December 1967.

7. J-J. Servan-Schreiber, *The American Challenge*, New York, Atheneum, 1968, pp. 18–19.

8. *Ibid.*, p. 16.

9. *Investment Dealers' Digest*, Section 2, March 1969, pp. 22–23.

CHAPTER 11   *pp. 227–248*

1. Sir Dennis Robertson, *Britain in the World Economy*, London, 1954.

2. Radcliffe Committee Report, August 1959. Cmnd. 825, paras. 739–44.

3. *Ibid.*, para. 678.

4. *New York Times*, 21 November 1967, p. 63.

5. Richard Fry, *The Banker*, March 1968.

6. David Williams, 'The Evolution of the Sterling System'. *Essays in Money and Banking*, Oxford, 1968, pp. 288–89. The reference to 'old series' and 'new series' takes account of an important break in the statistical series in 1962, when exclusion of overseas holdings of long-term government securities that had formerly been included reduced total external liabilities by £370 million, or from £3,501 million (old series), to £3,131 million (new series). See Bank of England, *Quarterly Bulletin*, Vol. III, No. 2 (June 1963), pp. 98–105, and *ibid.*, (Dec. 1963), pp. 264–78.

7. *The Economist*, 16 September, 1967, p. 1007.

CHAPTER 12   *pp. 249–264*

1. Trade figures: International Financial Statistics, May 1968, p. 34. Production figures: United States Department of Commerce, Survey of Current Business, September 1967, p. 40.

2. Christopher Layton, *Trans-Atlantic Investments*, Boulogne Sur Seine, The Atlantic Institute; quoted Harry Magdoff, *The Age of Imperialism*, New York, Monthly Review Press, 1969, p. 55.

3. Judd Polk, *Dollar Policy and International Financial Planning*, United States Council of the International Chamber of Commerce, 1 February 1967.

4. Magdoff, p. 182.
5. *Ibid.*, p. 183.
6. *Ibid.*, pp. 76–77.
7. *Ibid.*, p. 79.
8. Quoted *ibid.*, p. 184.
9. *United States Economic Policy Abroad: The Issues Before Us.* Policy statement by Hoyt P. Steele, 12 June 1968.
10 Magdoff, table, p. 188.
11. Gunnar Myrdal, *Challenge to Affluence*, New York, Vintage Books, 1965, p. 75.
12. J. K. Galbraith, 'The Balance of Payments. A Political and Administrative View': *Review of Economics and Statistics*, May 1964, p. 118.
13. Sidney E. Rolfe, *Gold and World Power*, New York, Harper and Row, 1966, p. 13.
14. Leon H. Keyserling, 'Employment and the New Economics,' *Annals of the American Academy*, October 1967, p. 108.
15. Elliot Janeway, *The Economics of Crisis*, London, Staples, 1968, p. 301. Much of Janeway's book is devoted to development of this theme.
16. *Wall Street Journal*, 4 April 1969.

CHAPTER 13   *pp. 267–282*

1. Hjalmar Schacht, *The Magic of Money*, p. 185.
2. Quoted John A. Pincus, *Trade, Aid and Development*, McGraw-Hill, 1967, p. 310.
3. *Ibid.*, p. 317.
4. Ian Shannon, *International Liquidity*, Melbourne, P. W. Cheshire, 1967, p. 103.

CHAPTER 14   *pp. 283–308*

1. *The Economist*, 30 November 1968, p. 16.
2. *Ibid*, 15 March 1969, p. 4
3. Richard N. Gardner, p. lxxxvi.

Bibliography

Both the wide historical range of this book and the different disciplines with which it deals present problems in organizing a list of suggested further readings. The headings below do not correspond exactly to the divisions of the book, but were chosen to present the reader with a minimum of overlap. Books or articles that are important to more than one of my subject-matter divisions are either included under each relevant heading, or under the 'General' heading at the end.

(M) denotes monograph or pamphlet.

ON 'PRE-PAPER' MONETARY POLITICS

Marc Bloch. 'Le Probleme de l'or au Moyen Age.' *Annuaire d'Historie Economique*, January 1933.

Carlo M. Cipolla. 'Currency Depreciation in Mediaeval Europe.' *Economic History Review*, No. 3, 1963.

G. N. Clark. *The Wealth of England from 1496 to 1760.* London: Oxford University Press, 1946.

Sir John Craig. *The Mint: A History of the London Mint from A.D. 287 to 1948.* Cambridge: Cambridge University Press, 1953.

R. De Roover. 'Money Banking and Credit in Mediaeval Bruges.' *Journal of Economic History*, supplement, December 1942.

Paul Einzig. *A History of Foreign Exchange.* London: Macmillan, 1962.

Sir Albert Feavearyear. *The Pound Sterling*, 2nd. edn., rev. by E. Victor Morgan. Oxford: Clarendon Press, 1963.

Herbert Heaton. *Economic History of Europe.* New York: Harper Bros., 1948.

Henri Pirenne. *Economic and Social History of Mediaeval Europe*, chs. 4, 5. New York: Harcourt, Brace, 1937.

M. M. Postan. 'The Rise of Money Economy.' *Economic History Review*, 1944.

R. C. Reynolds. 'In Search of A Business Class in 13th Century Genoa.' *Journal of Economic History*, supplement, December 1945.

W. A. Shaw. *The History of Currency, 1252–1894.* London: Wilson Milne, 1895.

J. W. Thompson. *Economic and Social History of Europe in the Later Middle Ages,* chs. 4, 5, 7, 9, 18, 19. London: Century, 1931.

ON THE ERA OF OLIGARCHIC MONETARY CONTROL

Walter Bagehot. *Lombard Street: A Description of the Money Market,* new edn. London: John Murray, 1931.

Rondo Cameron, Olga Crisp, Hugh T. Patrick, Richard Tilly. *Banking in the Early Stages of Industrialization.* New York: Oxford University Press, 1967.

S. G. Checkland. *The Rise of Industrial Society in England, 1815–1885.* New York: St. Martin's, 1964.

P. H. Emden. *Money Powers in Europe in the Nineteenth and Twentieth Centuries.* London: Sampson, Low, 1937.

Herbert Feis. *Europe, The World's Banker, 1870–1914.* New York: Norton Library, 1965.

Bray Hammond. *Banks and Politics in America from the Revolution to the Civil War.* Princeton University Press, 1957.

Sir Roy Harrod. *The Dollar.* New York: Norton Library, 1965.

C. K. Hobson. *Export of Capital.* London: Constable, 1914.

R. G. Hawtrey. *A Century of Bank Rate,* 2nd edn. London: Cass, 1962.

Leland H. Jenks. *The Migration of British Capital to 1875.* London: Nelson, 1963.

A. L. Levine. *Industrial Retardation in Britain, 1880–1914.* London: Weidenfeld and Nicholson, 1967.

Frederick Morton. *The Rothschilds.* New York: Atheneum, 1961.

Carl Polanyi. *The Great Transformation.* Boston: Beacon, 1957.

A. Pumphrey. 'The Introduction of Industrialists into the British Peerage: A Study in Adaptation of a Social Revolution.' *American Historical Review,* October 1959.

Robert Triffin. *The Evolution of the International Monetary System: Historical Reappraisal and Future Perspectives.* Princeton Studies in International Finance, No. 12 (M).

Joseph Wechsberg. *The Merchant Bankers.* Boston: Little, Brown, 1966.

C. R. Whittelsey and J. S. G. Wilson (eds.). *Essays in Money and Banking.* Oxford University Press, 1968.

ON THE DOWNFALL OF OLIGARCHIC MONEY

Edward Bennet. *Germany and the Diplomacy of the Financial Crisis, 1931.* Cambridge, Mass.: Harvard University Press, 1962.

John Morton Blum. *From the Morgenthau Diaries.* Vol. I: *Years of Crisis, 1928–1938.* Boston: Houghton Mifflin Company, 1959.

Andrew Boyle. *Montagu Norman.* London: Cassell, 1967.

Alan Bullock. *The Life and Times of Ernest Bevin.* Vol. I. London: Heinemann, 1960.

E. H. Carr. *The Twenty Years' Crisis.* London: Macmillan, 1961.

Lester V. Chandler. *Benjamin Strong, Central Banker.* Washington: Brookings, 1958.

Paul Einzig. *Behind the Scenes of International Finance.* London: Macmillan, 1932.

Paul Einzig. *The Fight for Financial Supremacy.* London: Macmillan, 1931.

Paul Einzig. *Finance and Politics.* London: Macmillan, 1932.

Herbert Feis. *The Diplomacy of the Dollar, 1919–1932.* New York: Norton, 1966.

Milton Friedman and Anna Schwartz. *A Monetary History of the United States, 1867–1960.* Princeton, N.J: Princeton University Press, 1960.

Sir Roy Harrod. *The Life of John Maynard Keynes.* London: Macmillan, 1951.

Herbert Heaton. *Economic History of Western Europe.* New York: Harper Bros., 1948.

Eliot Janeway. *The Economics of Crisis.* London: Staples, 1968.

J. M. Keynes. *The Economic Consequences of the Peace.* London: Macmillan, 1919.

J. M. Keynes. *Essays in Persuasion.* New York: The Norton Library, 1963.

Harold Macmillan. *Winds of Change, 1914–1939.* London: Macmillan, 1966.

Emile Moreau. *Souvenirs d'un Gouverneur de la Banque de France.* Paris: Libraire de Medicis, 1954.

Sir Harold Nicolson. *Letters and Diaries.* Vol. I (1930–1939). London: Collins, 1966.

Hjalmar Schacht. *My First Seventy-Six Years.* London: Wingate, 1955.

PM—Y

Hjalmar Schacht. *The Magic of Money.* London: Oldbourne, 1967.

Robert Skidelsky. *Politicians and the Slump.* London: Macmillan, 1967.

Michael Stewart. *Keynes and After.* London: Penguin, 1967.

Francis Williams. *A Pattern of Rulers.* London: Longmans, 1965.

ON WORLD WAR II, BRETTON WOODS AND THE
POST-WAR SETTLEMENT

Dean Acheson. *Present at the Creation.* New York: W. W. Norton, 1969.

Hanson W. Baldwin. *Great Mistakes of the War.* New York: Harper Bros., 1950.

Jack Bennett. 'The German Currency Reform.' *Annals of the Academy of Political and Social Science,* Vol. 267 (January 1950).

Elizabeth T. Bentley. *Out of Bondage.* New York: Devin-Adair, 1951.

Sir William Beveridge. *Full Employment in a Free Society.* New York: Norton, 1945.

Henry Simon Bloch and Bert F. Hoselitz. *Economics of Military Occupation.* Chicago: Foundation Press, 1944.

Arthur I. Bloomfield. *Speculative and Flight Movements of Capital in Postwar International Finance.* Princeton University Press, 1954.

James F. Byrnes. *All in One Lifetime.* New York: Harper, 1958.

John Morton Blum. *From the Morgenthau Diaries.* Vol. II: *Years of Crisis, 1938–1941;* Vol. III: *Years of War, 1941–1945.* Boston: Houghton Mifflin, 1959–67.

Lucius D. Clay. *Decision in Germany.* New York: Doubleday, 1950.

Paul Einzig. *Hitler's 'New Order' in Europe.* London: Macmillan 1941.

Herbert Feis. 'The Conflict over Trade Ideologies.' *Foreign Affairs,* Vol. xxv (1947).

Carl J. Freidrich (ed.). *American Experiences in Military Government in World War II.* New York: Reinhart, 1948.

Richard N. Gardner. *Sterling-Dollar Diplomacy,* rev. edn. New York: McGraw-Hill, 1969.

Sir Roy Harrod. *A Page of British Folly.* London: Macmillan, 1946.

Sir Roy Harrod. *The Life of John Maynard Keynes.* London: Macmillan, 1951.

Eliot Janeway. *The Economics of Crisis.* London: Staples, 1968.

J. M. Keynes. *How to Pay for the War*. New York: Harcourt, Brace, 1940.

Richard A. Lester. *International Aspects of Wartime Monetary Experience*. Princeton University Press, 1944.

Henry J. Morgenthau, Jr. 'Bretton Woods and International Co-operation.' *Foreign Affairs*, Vol. xxxiii (1945).

Henry J. Morgenthau, Jr. *Germany Is Our Problem*. New York: Harper, 1945.

Sir Harold Nicolson. *Letters and Diaries*. Vols. II (*1939–1945*) and III (*1945–1962*). London: Collins, 1968.

Vladimir Petrov. *Money and Conquest*. Baltimore: Johns Hopkins University Press, 1968.

Harry Bayard Price. *The Marshall Plan and Its Meaning*. Ithaca: Cornell University Press, 1955.

Lionel Robbins. 'Inquest on the Crisis'. *Lloyds Bank Review*, new series, No. 6 (1947).

Robert Triffin. *Europe and the Money Muddle*. London: Oxford University Press, 1957.

Arthur H. Vandenburg, Jr. (ed.). *The Private Papers of Senator Vandenberg*. Boston: Houghton Mifflin, 1952.

Harry D. White. 'The Monetary Fund: Some Criticisms Examined.' *Foreign Affairs*, Vol. xxxiii (1945).

Nathan I. White. *Harry Dexter White, Loyal American*. Waban, Mass., 1950.

John H. Williams. 'International Monetary Plans: After Bretton Woods,' *Foreign Affairs*, Vol. xxxiii (1945).

ON THE ANGLO-SAXON PROFLIGATES AND THEIR PROBLEMS

Robert Z. Aliber. 'Choices for the Dollar.' National Planning Association, Planning Pamphlet No. 127, May 1969 (M).

Peter L. Bernstein. *The Price of Prosperity*, rev. edn. New York: Vintage Books, 1966.

Gordon C. Bjork. *Private Enterprize and Public Interest*. Prentice-Hall, 1969.

Henry Brandon. *In the Red*. London: Penguin, 1967.

Sam Brittan. *The Treasury Under the Tories*. London: Penguin, 1964.

Eugene A. Birnbaum. *Changing the U.S. Commitment to Gold*. Princeton Essays in International Finance, No. 63, November 1967.

Brian Chapman. *British Government Observed.* London: Allen and Unwin, 1963.

Stuart Chase. *Money to Grow On.* New York: Harper, 1964.

William M. Clarke. *The City in the World Economy.* London: Pelican, 1967.

A. R. Conan. *The Problem of Sterling.* London: Macmillan, 1966.

William Davis. *Three Years' Hard Labour.* London: Andre Deutsch, 1968.

A. C. L. Day. *The Future of Sterling.* Oxford: Clarendon Press, 1954.

Emile Despres, Charles P. Kingleberger and Walter S. Salant. *The Dollar and World Liquidity: A Minority View.* Washington: The Brookings Institution, 1966 (M).

Peter Donaldson. *A Guide to the British Economy.* London: Penguin, 1965.

Paul Ferris. *The City.* London: Pelican, 1960.

J. K. Galbraith. 'The Balance of Payments: A Political and Administrative View.' *Revue of Economics and Statistics,* May 1964.

Lionel Gelber. *The Alliance of Necessity.* London: Robert Hale, 1966.

Herbert G. Grubel. 'The Benefits and Costs of Being the World Banker.' *National Banking Review,* 1964.

Michael Harrington. *The Other America.* Baltimore: Penguin, 1963.

Seymour E. Harris. *The Dollar in Crisis.* New York: Harcourt, Brace, 1961.

Neil Jacoby (ed.). *United States Monetary Policy.* New York: Praeger, 1966.

Eliot Janeway. *The Economics of Crisis.* London: Staples, 1968.

Sir Donald McDougall. *The Dollar Problem: A Reappraisal.* Princeton Essays in International Finance, No. 35, November 1960 (M).

Christopher McMahon. *Sterling in the Sixties.* Chatham House Essays: Oxford University Press, 1964.

Harry Magdoff. *The Age of Imperialism.* New York: Monthly Review Press, 1969.

Gunnar Myrdal. *Challenge to Affluence,* rev. edn. New York: Vintage Books, 1965.

Edward Nevin. 'Social Priorities and the Flow of Capital.' *Three Banks Review,* September 1955.

Max Nicholson. *The System*. London: Hodder and Stoughton, 1967.

Judd Polk. *Sterling—Its Meaning in World Finance*. New York: Harper, 1956.

E. T. Powell. 'Evolution of the MoneyMarket, 1385–1915.' *Financial News*, 1915.

Report of the Committee on the Working of the Monetary System (Radcliffe Committee) Cmnd. 827. London: HMSO, 1959, reprinted 1964.

Sidney E. Rolfe. *Gold and World Power*. New York: Harper, 1966.

Robert V. Roosa and Fred Hirsch. 'Reserves, Reserve Currencies, and Vehicular Currencies: An Argument.' Princeton Essays in International Finance, No. 54, May 1966.

Andrew Shonfield. *British Economic Policy Since the War*. London: Penguin, 1959.

Robert Triffin. *Gold and the Dollar Crisis*. New Haven: Yale University Press, 1960.

Arthur Seldon. 'Not Unanimous: A Rival Verdict to Radcliffe's On Money.' *IEA* 1960.

ON THE CONTINENTAL CONSERVATIVES AND EUROPEAN MONETARY INTEGRATION

Maurice Allais *et al.* 'On International Monetary Order.' Graduate Institute of International Studies, Geneva, 1968 (M).

Gabriel Almond (ed.). *The Struggle for Democracy in Germany*. Chapel Hill, North Carolina, 1948.

Rondo Cameron. *France and the Economic Development of Europe 1800–1914*. Chicago: Rand McNally, 1961.

Francis Cassell. *Gold or Credit?* London: Pall Mall Press, 1965.

William Diebold. 'Is the Gap Technological?' *Foreign Affairs* Vol. xlvi, No. 2.

European Federation of Financial Analysts' Societies, Study Group on Terminology, *List of Definitions*, 1963 (M).

Federal Trust Report (UK) No. 4. European Monetary Integration (M).

Theodore Hameron. *Restoration, Revolution and Reaction: Economics and Politics in Germany, 1815–1870*. Princeton University Press, 1958.

Fred Hirsch. *Money International*. London: Allen Lane, 1968.

Hoare and Co. (Investment Research). *The Common Market, 2, Capital Movements* (1967) (M).

Etienne-Sadi Kirschen, Henry Simon Bloch and William Bruce Bassett. *Financial Integration in Western Europe.* New York: Columbia University Press, 1969.

Miroslav A. Kritz. 'Gold: Barbarous Relic, or Useful Instrument?' Princeton Essays in International Finance, No. 60, June 1967.

Marius W. Holtrop. *Monetary Policy in an Open Economy: Its Objectives, Instruments, Limitations, and Dilemmas.* Princeton Essays in International Finance, No. 43, September 1963.

George Lichtheim. *Europe and America.* London: Thames and Hudson, 1963.

Etienne Mantoux. *The Carthaginian Peace.* Pittsburgh: University Press, 1952.

Jacob L. Riesser. *The German Great Banks and Their Concentration.* Washington: United States Government Printing Office, 1911.

Jacques Rueff. 'Sur Un Point d'Histoire: Le Niveau de la Stabilization Poincaré.' *Revue d'Economie Politique,* Vol. 69 (1959).

Hjalmar Schacht. *My First Seventy-Six Years.* London: Wingate, 1955.

Hjalmar Schacht. *The Magic of Money.* London: Oldbourne, 1967.

Claudio Segre *et al.* 'The Development of a European Capital Market.' Report of a Committee of Experts on European Financial Integration, September 1966 (M).

J-J. Servan-Schreiber. *The American Challenge.* New York: Atheneum, 1968.

Richard Tilly. *Financial Institutions and Industrialization in the Rhineland, 1815–1870.* Madison: University of Wisconsin Press, 1966.

ON MONETARY REFORM AND THE THIRD WORLD'S
MONETARY PREDICAMENT

Richard N. Cooper. *The Economics of Interdependence.* New York: McGraw-Hill, 1968.

Milton Gilbert. *Problems of the International Monetary System.* Princeton University Press, 1966.

Shigeo Horie. *The International Monetary Fund.* London: Macmillan, 1964.

Fred Hirsch. *Money International.* London: Allen Lane, 1968.

Charles P. Kindleberger. *The Politics of International Money and World Language*. Princeton Essays in International Finance, No. 61, August 1967 (M).

Fritz Machlup. *Plans for Reform of the International Monetary System*. Princeton: Special Papers in International Economics, No. 3, rev. edn., March 1964.

Fritz Machlup. *The Cloakroom Rule of International Reserves: Reserve Creation and Resources Transfer*. Princeton: Reprints in International Finance, No. 1, August, 1965.

OECD Development Assistance Efforts and Policies. Report by the Chairman of the Development Assistance Committee, 1969.

John A. Pincus. *Trade, Aid and Development: The Rich and Poor Nations*. New York: McGraw-Hill, 1966.

Robert V. Roosa. *Monetary Reform for the World Economy*. New York: Harper, 1965.

Sidney E. Rolfe. *Gold and World Power*. New York: Harper, 1966.

Ian Shannon. *International Liquidity*. Melbourne: Cheshire, 1967.

Robert Triffin *Our International Monetary System, Yesterday, Today and Tomorrow*. New Haven: Yale University Press, 1968.

Tibor Scitovsky. *Requirements of an International Reserve System*. Princeton Essays in International Finance, No. 49, November 1965 (M).

Maxwell Stamp. 'The Reform of the International Monetary System.' *Moorgate and Wall Street*, Summer 1965 (M).

United Nations Conference on Trade and Development, *International Monetary Issues and the Developing Countries* (Corea-Kahn Report). New York: United Nations, 1965.

GENERAL

Edwin Cannan. *Money—Its Connexion with Rising and Falling Prices*, 10th edn. London: Staples, 1946.

Sir Geoffrey Crowther. *An Outline of Money*, rev. edn. New York: Nelson, 1950.

Paul Einzig. *Monetary Policy: Ends and Means*, 2nd edn. London: Penguin, 1964.

Milton Friedman and Walter Heller. *Monetary Vs. Fiscal Policy*. The Seventh Annual Arthur K. Salomon Lecture. New York: Norton, 1969.

J. K. Galbraith. *A Theory of Price Control*. Harvard University Press, 1952.

Alvin H. Hansen. *A Guide to Keynes*. New York: McGraw-Hill, 1953.

Karl Helfferich. *Money* (translated from the German). London: Benn, 1927.

Harry G. Johnson. *Money, Trade and Economic Growth*, 2nd edn. Harvard University Press, 1964.

J. M. Keynes. *A Treatise on Money*. 2 vols. London: Macmillan, 1930.

J. M. Keynes. *The General Theory of Employment, Interest and Money*. London: Macmillan, 1936.

Robert Lekachman (ed.). *Keynes and the Classics*. Boston: Heath, 1964.

Arthur Nussbaum. *Money in Law, National and International*. Brooklyn: Foundation Press, 1950.

W. M. Scammel. *International Monetary Policy*, 2nd edn. London: Macmillan, 1961.

Leland Yeager. *International Monetary Mechanisms*. New York: Reinhart, 1968.

Index

Abs, Herman (Chairman of the Deutsche Bank), 192
Africa, 56
Agricultural Adjustment Act (1933), 123
Aid, to developing countries, 268–70, 271–72, 272n., 273, 274–75, 277–79, 280–81
Albania, 141n.
Alexander the Great, 15
Allied Control Council, 125
America (and United States) monetary position in, 35–36, 90, 158, 169n., 264, 298; and silver, 36, 41, 43, 46, 216; and gold standard, 37, 92, 96, 213–14, 215; over-production in, 43, 44, 46; and Europe, 47, 90, 135, 151, 153, 155, 164–65, 218–22, 223, 224, 300, 301; industry in, 48; growth of population in, 54; war debts with, 58, 60, 61, 91; role in world economy, 63, 166; gold reserves of, 77, 86, 89, 99, 101, 102, 187, 211, 212; policy towards Germany, 80–81, 139–40, 194–95; crisis in, 90, 96–97; buying and selling of gold in, 98–99, 201, 202–203, 210; Britain's investments in, 105; international trade of, 110, 135, 143, 230, 249; and the International Monetary Fund (q.v.), 114; balance of payments in, 119, 151–52, 155, 161, 168, 234, 249, 274, 275, 305; loan agreement with Britain, 128–32, 133, 134; and the European Payments Union (q.v.), 148; foreign investment of, 159, 218, 250–54, 264, 295, 300; capital ownership in, 168–69, 169n.; inflation in, 170, 170n.; Keynes Plan and, 171, 176; Italy and, 196; and South Africa, 209
American Bankers' Association, 123
Amsterdam, 188
Anglo-American alliance, 127–28
Anglo-American monetary agreement, 115, 118, 121, 145
Angola, 211n.
Arab–Israeli war, 242, 242n.
Arabs, 242, 242n.
Arbitrage, 16, 150
Argentina, 47, 239

Asia, 56
Assignats, 34, 35
Athens, 105
Atlantic Alliance, 165
Atlantic Charter, 107
Australia, 3, 47
Austria, 67, 81, 87, 89, 150n.
Austria–Hungary, 41, 54, 62

Bagehot, Walter, 28, 31n., 33
Bahrain, 201n.
Baldwin, Earl, 72, 74, 84
Bancor (bank gold), Keynes' plan for, 111–12, 114, 143
Bangkok, 201n.
Bank Act (1844), 33, 40
Bank of Amsterdam, 17n.
Bank of England, receives Charter, 19; causes inflation, 20; note issue of, 21, 31; monopoly position of, 27–30; credit control of, 31; effect of Bank Act on, 33; obliged to 'unpeg' currency, 54; raising money by, 57, 88; gold reserves of, 58, 206; and deflation, 71; dealings with Europe, 82, 85; nationalization of, 133; and the Exchange Equalization Account, 151; as agent for gold transactions, 202, 203, 204; effect of sterling crisis on, 231; controls sterling credits, 233; opposition to sale of foreign investments, 238
Bank of France, 80, 81, 82, 85, 182, 185, 206, 208
Bank of International Settlements (at Basle), 6, 7, 60, 85, 200, 201, 208, 245, 288, 304
Bank of Moscow, 75
Bank of the United States, 36, 37
Bank rate, 28, 30, 47, 83–84, 88, 174, 231, 232, 237
Banking School, 31, 31n., 32, 33, 157, 187
Banque Général (Paris), 179
Baruch, Bernard, 97
Basle. *See* Bank of International Settlements
Bassett, Professor William Bruce, 305n.
Beaverbrook, Lord, 72
Beirut, 201n.

Belgium (and Belgians), 41n., 94, 150n., 186, 198, 203, 204, 218
Benelux, 144, 212, 219
Bentley, Elizabeth, 126, 127
Berlin, 66n., 140, 142, 193
Bernstein, Bernard, 141n.
Bernstein, Edward, 287
Beveridge, Sir William (later Lord), 107, 107n.
Biddle, Nicholas (President of the Bank of the United States), 36
Bills of Exchange, 23n.–24n., 26, 26n., 30
Birch, Nigel, 232
Bloch, Professor Henry S., 305n.
Blondeau (inventor of machine for milling a coin's edge), 12n.
Blum, Leon, 95
Board of Trade, 129
Boothby, Robert (later Lord), 131
Boston Tea Party, 36
Bourges-Maunoury, M., 199
Bourse (Paris), 184, 201n.
Boyle, Andrew, 58n.
Brandon, Henry, 236n.
Bretton Woods Conference, 119, 120, 121, 123, 125, 127, 131, 143, 144, 147, 262, 270, 296, 297, 303, 304
Briand, Aristide, 79
Britain, loss of economic independence, 4–5; currency crisis in, 7; gold standard in, 35, 91; trade of, 38, 95, 108, 110, 132, 159n., 167, 247, 249; industry in, 40, 48, 56, 71, 133, 167, 276; banking in, 41, 48; foreign investments of, 47, 49, 53, 247; balance of payments of, 48, 101, 111, 161, 230–31, 239, 244, 273; inflation in, 70; gold reserves in, 78, 86, 101, 105, 131, 148, 163, 186–87, 233; economic depression in, 90; imports, 92; debts, 128, 129, 130, 135, 227, 229–30, 245, 302; dollar reserves of, 145, 163, 187, 228; investment in, 168, 232; overseas commitments of, 235–36, 240–41, 277; entrepot role of, 301, 302, 306
Brown, Rt. Hon. George, 204
Bryan, William Jennings, 44, 45
Bulgaria, 41n., 81, 141n.
Bundesbank (German Central Bank), 193–94, 237, 286
Burgess, Randolph (President of the American Bankers' Association), 122–123
Burke, Edmund, 26
Byrnes, Senator J. F. (United States Secretary of State), 126

Cailleux, M. (French Finance Minister), 84
Cairo, 129, 201n.
California, 41, 100
Callaghan, Rt. Hon. James, 238, 248
Cameron, Rondo, 184n.
Canada, 47, 58, 88, 156, 212, 264, 299, 302
Cannan, Edwin, 32n.
Carli, Guido (Italian Central Bank chief), 196
Carr, E. H., 132
Catto, Lord, 106
Central Banks, as protectors of oligarchic money, 57; code of behaviour for, 67–68, 81; effect of rule of, 90; and E.P.U. (*q.v.*), 149; role of, 150, 151; and gold, 200, 201, 202, 203, 204; and the gold crisis (1968–69), 205, 208; and the two-tier gold price, 209, 210; and America's foreign expansion, 263–64; influence of, 288–89
Central Intelligence Agency (CIA), 212
Chamberlain, Rt. Hon. Joseph, 62, 72
Chamberlain, Rt. Hon. Neville, 94
Chambers, Whittaker, 127
Charles I, 17n., 19
Charles II, 19, 25, 183
Cheron, M. (French Finance Minister), 85
Cherwell, Lord, 125
Chiang Kai-shek, 126
China, 15
Christian Democrat parties, 147, 150n.
Churchill, Winston, 69, 72, 74–75, 76, 80, 83, 84, 97, 107n., 125, 126
City, The (*see also* London), foreign trading interest of, 18; opposition to Bank of England, 27; foreign investment of, 47, 238, 247; central role of, 49, 62, 78, 127, 133, 201, 302, 306; Tories and, 56; industry and, 57; quasi-feudal hierarchy of, 58, 59, and the working man, 77, 193; and EPU, 148, 149; and sterling, 229–30, 245, 248; foreign exchange earnings of, 233
Civil War (American), 41, 172
Civil War (English), 18, 23, 34
Clarke, William, 166n. 184n.
Clearing Union, 111–12, 116, 118, 143, 279
Cloakroom rule, 157, 186
Coal Industry, 71, 75, 77
Cobden, Richard, 56
Coins, minting of, 11–12; debasement of, 12, 13–14, 13n., 16n.; variety of, 12–13, 15; milling of, 12n., 18

Cole, G. D. H., 132
Colonne (Finance Minister to Louis XVI), 35
Cominform, 142
Commodity dollar, 98
Common Market (*see also* European Economic Community), 6, 155, 164, 168, 191n., 223, 245, 263, 296, 299, 299n., 305, 306
Congress of Vienna, 34, 166n.
Conservatives (and Tories), 35, 56, 72, 94, 150, 236, 237, 247
Conservative Government, 150, 232, 236
Consols, 38, 39, 39n.
Copernicus, 13n.
Corn Law Act (1815), 35n.
Coughlin, Father, 96
Couve de Murville, Maurice, 199
'Crawling peg' (system for controlling currencies' flexibility), 293–94, 298–99
Creditanstalt of Vienna, 87
Cripps, Sir Stafford (Labour Chancellor of the Exchequer), 148
Croesus, King, 11
Cromwell, Oliver, 17, 18
Cunliffe, Lord, 57, 58
Currencies, national, 1, 45; variety of, 12–13, 15; valuation of, 60, 94, 113, 293, 298–99, 302; post-war, 105, 139–42; 'scarce currency', 118–19; reserve, 123, 169, 199, 285, 302, 306; convertibility of, 150, 153–55, 202n.; and Federal Reserve Bank's stabilization fund, 209
Currency School, 32, 32n., 186–87, 198
Czechoslovakia, 140

Daladier, Edouard, 95
Darwin, Charles, 117, 259
Davies, William, 236n.
Dawes Plan, 81, 83, 85
Deflation, effects of, 1–2, 21, 35, 37, 42, 61, 74, 92, 102, 244; Bank of England and, 71; White's Fund and, 114; Keynes and, 118; in America, 152, 170–71; in Germany, 194–95; in France, 200, 206
Depression (1930's), 97, 98, 110, 205, 253n.
Deutsche Bank, 191, 192
Devaluation, of the pound, 7, 92, 147n., 175, 204, 231, 235, 237, 242, 242n.; by Romans, 13n.; of the coinage, 20; of European currencies, 60; of the franc, 95–96, 182, 286; of the dollar, 99, 211; effect of threat of, 292, 293; 'crisis flexibility' of, 294–95

Developing countries (*see also* Third World), needs of, 268–70, 273; aid for, 274, 275–76, 303
Disraeli, Benjamin, 280
Dollars, Spanish, 36; price of, 42n., 155, 201, 209, 214, 215, 224, 299n.; and the pound, 61, 123, 130, 133, 135; world trade financed by, 77; North America and, 94; convertibility of, 96, 97, 130, 133–34, 198; devaluation of, 97–99, 210, 211, 237, 262–63; reserves, 105, 119, 131, 148; 154, 155, 163, 164, 187, 211, 250, 254, 273, 286; as the world currency, 114, 154, 156, 199, 218; crisis of (1960's), 143, 154–58, 159, 197; Marshall Aid and, 145, 146, 147; shortage of, 151, 152, 153; and sterling area, 227–28, 230, 242, 242n.; defence of, 256–59, 305; inflation of, 297; depreciation of, 298–99, 300
Dresdner Bank, 191
Dulles, John Foster (United States Secretary of State), 235
Dutch, war of 1672, 19, 41n., 167, 188

East Africa, 211n.
East Germany, 14, 192, 193
East India Company, 25, 175
Economica, 32n.
Economist, The, 28, 31n., 86, 131, 175, 215, 243, 291, 295, 307
Egypt, 128, 129, 239
Einzig, Paul, 24n., 89n.
Eire, 129
Eisenhower, President, 140, 150n.
Elizabeth I, 17, 20, 21
England (*see also* Britain), early coinage of, 12, 16, 16n., 21; trade of, 17, 37n.; paper money in, 25; prices in, 34, 54
Eurobonds, 219–20, 305
Eurocurrency, 156–58, 306
Eurodollars, 156–58, 167, 197, 233, 301, 305
Europe (*see also* Common Market and European Economic Community), currencies in, 12, 41, 60, 214; silver in, 16, 46; gold standard in, 37; protection in, 56; post World War I, 61, 63, 80, 82; post World War II, 105, 140–41, 143, 144; dollars in, 151, 153, 155, 165; American influence in, 218–23, 264, 300, 301
European Economic Community (EEC, *see also* Common Market), 212, 242–43

European Free Trade Area (EFTA), 306
European Payments Union (EPU), 146–47, 148, 149–51, 153

Federal Bureau of Investigation (FBI), 126
Federal Reserve (United States), 54, 85, 96, 101, 157, 172, 177, 194–95, 260
Federal Reserve Bank (New York), 63, 200, 201, 202, 209
Federal Reserve Board (and System), 154, 172–74, 205
Ferris, Paul, 217n.
Finland, 41n.
Fisher, Irving (American economist), 98
Ford, Henry, 279
Ford Motor Company, 218, 253
Fort Knox, 101, 154
Fowler, Henry (United States Treasury Secretary), 209, 235, 286
Franc, the, value of, 35, 41, 78, 79, 80, 82, 83, 83n., 95, 199, 206, 298; stabilization of, 86; defence of, 196; weakness of, 231
France (and the French), paper money in, 2, 25, 34–35, 179–80; devaluation in, 3–4, 96, 182; currencies in, 12, 16n., 41; trade with, 37n., 249; industry in, 48, 192; inflation in, 53, 54, 61–62, 180–82, 187; financing of World War I, 57; monetary strategy in, 78–84, 86, 87, 89, 91–92, 94, 95, 178–88, 196, 198, 199–200, 205–208, 218; gold in, 101, 102, 178, 180, 185, 211n., 212; foreign investment of, 183–84, 184n.; attitude to banking, 185, 186–87; and the London Gold Pool, 203–204; and aid to developing countries, 272–73; and the International Monetary Fund (*q.v.*), 303
Franco-Prussian war, 53
Free Trade, 18n., 38, 55, 56, 70, 72, 94, 95, 109, 131, 135, 150
Fulbright, Senator, J. W., 249
Full employment, 102, 103, 107, 132
Fullerton, John, 31n.
Friedman, Dr. Milton, 173–77, 290
Funk, Herr (German Economics Minister), 104–105, 106–107

Galbraith, John Kenneth, 169, 250n., 256, 257
Gardner, Professor Richard, N. 304
Gaulle, General de, monetary policies of, 7, 188, 199–200, 204, 205–208; concern with Anglo-Saxon inflation,

160; challenge to American leadership in Europe, 158; demands return to gold, 165, 185, 187, 214; imposes foreign investment restrictions, 218–19; opposes Britain's entry into Europe, 242, 242n., 245; attack on dollar, 272
General Agreement on Trade and Tariffs (GATT), 304
General Electric Company, 252
General Motors, Ltd., 219, 253
General Strike (1926), 75, 76
Geneva, 179
Genoa, 23
Germany (and the Germans), medieval currency in, 12; backing of mark with gold in, 41; industry in, 48, 125; France's indemnity to, 53, 53n.; reparations from, 63–64, 80, 81, 91; inflation in, 64–66, 104–105, 163, 188–89; investment in, 67; loan to, 81; trade of, 95, 249, 275; post World War II currency in, 139–42; monetary strategy of, 188–96; immigrant labour in, 192–93; reserves in, 211n., 212, 277; balance of payments, 236; aid to developing countries, 273
Gilt-edged securities, 175–76
Godfrey, Michael (Deputy Governor of the Bank of England), 27
Goebbels, Joseph, 126
Gold (*see also* Gold Standard), ratio with silver, 15–16, 25n.; reserves, 58, 61, 77, 86, 89, 101, 105, 131, 134, 148, 151, 154, 162–63, 185, 186–87, 199, 200, 204, 212, 213, 233, 276, 303; exports of, 62, 86; scarcity of, 68–69, 77, 86, 112; withdrawals of, 84–85, 90–91; hoarding of, 92, 95, 100, 178, 180, 185, 195, 285; price of, 98–99, 198, 201, 202, 209, 212, 213, 214–15, 223, 275, 276, 285; prospecting for, 100–101; drain of, 204
Gold exchange standard, 77–78, 87, 131, 153, 159, 199, 267, 270
Gold market (London), 201–203, 204
Gold Pool (London), 203–204, 204n., 208–209, 224
Gold Standard (*see also* Gold), origins of, 25; arguments concerning, 31–33; return to (1819), 35, 38; reliability of, 38, 53; becomes international, 40–44, 46–47; in Russia, 44; in World War I, 53–55; return to after World War I, 59, 67–69, 71, 74, 75–77, 83; Britain goes off, 88–89, 94, 95, 151; other countries go off, 91, 95; France and U.S. remain on, 92; United States

goes off, 96–97; Labour against, 101–102; failure of, 102; Keynes and the, 112–113, 121, 134; policy of returning to, 130–31, 147, 149–50, 153, 155, 223–24, 284, 295; restraint imposed by, 170; Friedman and, 176, 177; crisis of (1968), 205–208, 298, 299; replacement by dollar, 210–11, 214, 215–17, 218, 224
Gold Standard Act (1925), 18n., 68
Goldwater, Barry, 173, 290
Greece, 41n., 81
Green, Timothy, 216n.
Gresham, Sir Thomas, 17n.
Gresham's Law, 17, 17n.
Grimm, Privy Councillor von, 65

Hague Conference on reparations, 85
Hamilton, Alexander, 36
Hansen, Professor Alvin, 171n.
Harrod, Sir Roy, 25n., 293n.
Harte, Bret, 100
Harvey, Sir Ernest, 88
Henry I, 12
Henry VIII, 14, 17n.
Herriot, Edouard, 79
Hess, Rudolf, 65
Himmler, Heinrich, 104–105
Hiroshima, 205
Hirsch, Fred, 53n.
Hitler, Adolf, 3, 65, 95, 104, 105, 106, 129, 166, 191, 201
Holland, 25, 41, 167, 203
Holtrop, Dr (Dutch Central Bank chief), 188
Hong Kong, 201n., 239
Hoover, President, 90–91
Hopkins, Sir Richard, 106
Howe, Louis, 97
Huguenots, 179
Hull, Cordell (United States Secretary of State), 108, 110
Hungary, 81, 89, 141n.
Hurley, General Patrick, 126

Imperial preference, 94, 95, 107, 108, 110
Imperial Russian Bonds, 184
India, 25, 46, 128, 129, 217, 217n., 228, 229–30, 239, 278, 285, 304
Indonesia, 235–36, 245
Industry (and Industrialization), 26, 37–38, 43, 44, 48–49, 56, 71, 162, 167, 182, 190–91, 219, 252–53, 268–69, 276–77
Inflation, effects of, 1–2, 55, 68, 128–29; currency, 20, 21, 34, 36, 54, 57, 155, 169n., 297; in France, 61–62, 179, 206–208; in Germany, 64–66, 141,
188–89, 192, 195–96; in Britain, 70–71, 174–75; solutions for, 57, 103–104, 280–81; in Eastern Europe, 140n.–141n.; export of, 160, 161; causes of, 161–165, 187, 197, 307; in America, 170, 172, 261
International Development Association (IDA), 271, 275, 277
International Economics (Harrod), 293n.
International Monetary Fund (IMF, *see also* World Bank), Britain and the, 5, 245; authority of, 6, 287, 304; and Special Drawing Rights (*q.v.*), 24n., 32n., 262, 303; establishment of the, 118–24, 142; and the Marshall Plan, 144, 147; rules of the, 186n., 299n.–300n.; Vienna meeting of the (1961), 203; Russia and the, 213; loans by the, 275, 275n., 277, 278, 294n., 307
Italy (and the Italians), 2, 12, 13, 14, 16n., 23, 25, 41n., 54, 94, 150n., 192, 196, 198, 203, 204, 212, 272, 303

Jackson, President, 36, 37
James II, 25
Japan, 100, 156, 211n., 212, 230, 269, 272, 275, 277, 299, 302, 304
Javits, Senator, 209
Jenkins, Rt. Hon. Roy, 174, 175, 176, 231
Johannesburg, 204n.
Johnson, President, 204, 254, 259, 260, 263, 298
Joint Stock Banks, 57
Jones, Jesse (Chief of the U.S. Reconstruction Finance Corporation), 98
Joynson-Hicks, Sir William, 75
Jung, Carl Gustav, 58, 58n.

Kebak, Anthony, 127n.
Kennedy, President John F., 202, 254, 255, 256
Keynes, John Maynard, monetary ideas of, 31, 55, 71–72, 74, 76, 97–98, 99–100, 103–104, 107–109, 121–22, 129, 171–72, 174, 176–77, 185, 195, 254n., 284, 286, 287; and speculation, 79; elected to Court of Directors of Bank of England, 106; the Keynes Plan, 111–13, 115–16, 119, 128, 133, 134, 143, 146, 279; personality of, 116–18; political sympathies of, 124; and American loan, 125, 130–32; death of, 135
Keyserling, Leon H., 256
Kindersley, Sir Robert, 42, 83
Kirschen, Professor, 305n.
Kommerz Bank, 191

Korea, 153
Krishnamachari (Indian Finance Minister), 229
Krupps, 191–92
Kuwait, 201n.

Labour Government, 3, 7, 74, 132, 133, 147–48, 174, 227, 235, 236, 237, 239, 244
Labour Party, 74, 239, 247, 248
Lacour-Gayet, M., 90
Latin America, 297, 302
Latin Monetary Union, 41
Lausanne Conference, 91
Laval, Pierre, 90, 91
Law, Rt. Hon. Andrew Bonar, 57
Law, John, 179–80
Law, Richard, 115
Layton, Lord, 86
League of Nations, 60, 67, 81, 124
Lee, Jennie, 132
Lend–Lease Agreement, 108, 110, 115, 124
Lenin, 2, 54, 100
Levant, 16
Lever, Sir Hardman, 58
Liverpool, Lord, 35, 38, 56
Locarno, 60
Locke, John, 20, 21, 22, 37n.
London (*see also* City, the), banking in, 26, 33–34, 38, 160; importance of in world monetary system, 46–50, 77, 109, 123, 166–67, 168, 250, 301–302; interest rates in, 69, 87, 239; French financial attack on, 80–83, 85, 92; flight of capital from, 141–42; liquidity in, 177; gold market of, 201–204
London Monetary Conference (1932), 297
Long Island, 63
Louis XIV, 179
Louis XVI, 35
Louisiana, 179
Lowndes, William, 20, 21
Luther, Herr (German Finance Minister), 65

Macao, 201n.
MacDonald, Ramsay, 248
Mackinder, Harold, 48, 49
Macleod, Henry Dunning, 17n.
Macmillan, Lord, 106n.
Macmillan Committee on Finance and Industry, 59, 106
Magdoff, Harry, 251
Malawi, 211n.
Malaysia, 235–36, 245

Malthus, Thomas Robert, 54
Mannesman (German steel producers), 219n.
Manufacturers' Hanover Trust, 252
Mark, the, backed by gold, 41; collapse of, 63, 139–42; stabilization of, 81; revaluation of, 175, 231, 237, 291, 297, 298
Marshall, George (U.S. Secretary of State), 142
Marshall Aid, 145, 147, 149, 151, 192
Marshall Plan, 143–46, 146n., 214, 274
Martin, William McChesney (ex-Federal Reserve Board Chairman), 213
Marx, Karl, 2, 39, 44, 117
Matchlup, Fritz, 32n.
Maudling, Rt. Hon. Reginald, 237, 287
McCarthy, Senator, 126
McCloy, John J. (President of the World Bank), 270
McKenna, Reginald, 71, 74
McNamara, Robert (President of the World Bank), 271n.
Meade, Professor James, 294n.
Meyer, Eugene (President of the World Bank), 270
Mills, Wilbur (U.S. Chairman of the House Ways and Means Committee), 260
Mint, the, in history, 11–12; revenue from, 13, 16, costs of, 18, 21
Mocatta and Goldsmid (bullion brokers), 201
Moley, Raymond, 96
Molotov, Vyacheslav Mikhailovitch, 139
Money, attitude of nations to, 2–3; 'listening' aspect of, 3, 13; 'funk', 3, 33; 'hot' 3, 79, 80, 81, 87, 231, 286, 293; international control of, 7, 8, 280, 282, 288–89, 296, 300; reform of system dealing with, 7, 283–95, 301, 306–307; minting of, 11–12, 13, 16, 18; monarchical control of, 11, 16–20; milling of, 12n., 18; debasement of, 12, 13–14, 13n., 16, 16n., 21; metal for, 14–16; standard of, 14–18, 21–22, *see also* Gold Standard; oligarchic, 23–34, 41, 46, 50, 53, 57, 89; devaluation of, *see* Devaluation; deflation of, *see* Deflation; inflation of, *see* Inflation.
Moreau, Emile (Governor of Bank of France), 59, 79, 80, 81, 82–84, 85, 86
Moret, Gustave (Governor of Bank of France), 86

Morgan, J. P., 97
Morgenthau, Henry (Secretary of United States Treasury), 97, 98, 99, 104, 106, 109, 123, 124, 125, 126, 127, 130, 140, 141
Moscow, 44, 54, 140
Mosley, Sir Oswald, 94
Mun, Thomas, 18

Nagasaki, 205
Napoleon, 34, 35, 35n., 38, 41n., 166, 182
Napoleonic War, 27, 38
National Debt, 104, 130
National Government, 7, 92, 94
National Socialist Workers' Party, 65
Nationalist Chinese, 126
Neimeyer, Sir Otto, 82, 84, 85
Netherlands, 23, 94, 198
New Deal, 104, 109, 110, 115, 125, 127
'New Economics', 254, 261
New York (*see also* Wall Street), interest rates in, 69, 90; importance of in world monetary system, 77, 90, 160, 166, 177, 305; and loans, 88
Newman, Cardinal, 86
Newton, Sir Isaac, 25, 25n, 99, 118
Nixon, President, 202, 259, 290, 298
Norman, George Warde (Director of Bank of England), 32, 59n.
Norman, Montagu (Governor of Bank of England), 58; appearance of, 59; monetary ideas of, 59–62, 70, 71, 74, 75, 76, 77, 79, 82, 83, 85, 87, 88, 102, 128, 171, 188, 247; relations with Benjamin Strong (*q.v.*), 63, 67–69, 81, 82, 90, 123; opinion of Dr Schacht (*q.v.*), 66; on General Strike, 75; and Churchill, 75, 84; attitude to France, 81, 82, 83; and an international bank, 85–86
North Africa, 107
North Atlantic Free Trade Area (NAFTA), 303, 306
North Atlantic Treaty Organisation (NATO), 146n., 160

O'Brien, Sir Leslie (Governor of Bank of England), 245
Oil, 3, 208, 239, 242n.
Organization for Economic Co-operation and Development (OECD), 146n., 270n., 304
Organization for European Economic Co-operation (OEEC), 146, 146n., 148
Ottawa Conference, 94, 110

Paris, interest rates in, 84; as financial centre, 87, 89, 90, 92, 182; loans in, 88, 91; gold in, 99, 200, 201n., withdrawal of money from, 101
Pasvolsky, Dr. Leo, 109n.
Peacock, Sir Edward, 88
Peel, Sir Robert, 32
Pereires (financiers), 183
Persian Empire, 15
Persian Gulf states, 239
Peru, aid for, 278
Petrov, Vladimir, 140n.
Phillips Petroleum, 218–19
Pick, Franz, 212
Placentia Bay, Newfoundland, 107, 115
Poincaré, Raymond (President of France), 78–80, 82, 84, 199, 205
Polak, Jacques (Economic Counsellor IMF), 174
Poland, 81, 192, 201
Popular Front Government (France 1936), 169
Populist Party (America), 43, 44
Post-war credits, 104
Potsdam, 125, 126
Pound, the, fluctuations of, 62, 94, 231, 298; as reserve currency, 123, 153, 158, 187, 242, 243, 273, 302; backing of, 128, 238, 238n.; convertibility of, 130, 131, 133–34; devaluation of, 147n., 175, 235–37, 242, 243–44, 250; international role of, 154, 207, 208, 228, 230, 306; floating of, 291
Powell, E. T., 166n.
Powell, Rt. Hon. Enoch, 232, 289
Prices, politics of, 1–2, 307–308; fluctuations of, 13, 20–21, 34, 35, 39–40, 54, 55, 56, 71, 76, 98, 102, 163, 170, 196
Protection (and Protectionists), 56, 72, 92, 94, 95, 110, 121, 134, 135, 145–46, 222, 223, 268–69
Prussia (and Prussians), 53, 184, 189–190

Quebec Conference (1944), 125
Quesnay, Pierre, 82–83

Radcliffe Report, 232–34
Renaissance, 11, 13
Reuss, Henry (U.S. Chairman of the House Sub-Committee on International Exchange and Payments), 262–63
Rhineland, 41n., 189, 190
Ricardo, David, 39
Rist, Charles, 80
Robertson, Sir Dennis, 227

Rome, 13n., 15
Rome Treaty (1957), 149, 243, 305, 305n.
Roosa, Robert (U.S. Treasury Under-Secretary), 285, 287
Roosevelt, President Franklin D., 96–97, 99, 104, 107, 121, 122, 125, 129, 172n.
Rothermere, Lord, 72
Rothschilds, 50, 87, 183, 201
Rueff, Jacques (French economist), 199–200, 284
Ruhr, the, 63, 64, 75, 78, 79, 81, 83, 126
Rumania, 41n., 206
Russia (and Russians). *See* Soviet Union

Saigon, 201n., 235
Saint-Simon, Comte de, 183
Salter, Sir Arthur, 82
Sampson, Anthony, 221
Scandinavia, 41, 163
Schacht, Dr. Hjalmar (President of Reichsbank), 65–67, 81, 85, 95, 96, 107, 108, 273
Schweitzer, Pierre-Paul (Managing Director International Monetary Fund), 174, 185n.
Scitovsky, Tibor, 278, 279
Servan-Schreiber, Jean-Jacques, 164, 218, 219, 221, 251
Shaw, George Bernard, 216
Shonfield, Andrew, 234
Siberia, 41n., 100
Siegfried, André, 180n.
Silver, ratio with gold, 15–16, 25n., 43; as standard, 17, 21, 25; value of, 41, 216; American attempt to restore, 43–44, 46, 96
Singapore, 235, 245
Smith, Adam, 22, 37n.
Smoot-Hawley tariff, 92
Snowden, Philip, 74, 85, 248
South Africa, 3, 46, 101, 203, 204n., 209–210, 211
South African Reserve Bank, 203, 204n.
South Sea Bubble, 28, 36, 179
Soviet Union, gold standard, 41; over-production in, 43–44; inflation in, 54; gold prospecting in, 100; at Bretton Woods Conference, 120; policy in occupied Germany, 125, 139–41; gold production in, 211–13
Spain, 16n., 23, 41n.
Special Drawing Right (SDR), 24n., 32n., 215, 262, 275, 278, 287, 296, 303, 307
Stabilization Fund. *See* White Plan
Stalin, Joseph, 100, 125

Stamp, Maxwell, 277
Steel, Hoyt P., 253
Sterling, special role of, 48, 135, 148, 232–34, 239, 242, 302, 306; confidence in, 62; exchange rate of, 76, 94, 175; and the gold standard, 77–78, 88, 124; and the Keynes plan, 107; balances, 128–29, 130–31, 132, 239; convertibility of, 133–34, 135, 145, 201–202, 228, 236; and European Payments Union, 148; diminishing importance of, 153–54; devaluation of, 204–205, 231, 237; becomes the dollar pool, 227–28, 242, 242n., 299; India and, 229–30; crises of, 231, 231n., 232–34, 237, 243–44, 245–47, 248
Stewart, Michael, 100n.
Stilwell, General, 126
Stock Exchange (London), 168
Strakosh, Sir Henry, 83
Strong, Benjamin (Governor of Federal Reserve Bank of New York), 63, 67–68, 69, 75–76, 77, 81, 82, 85, 90, 123
Stuarts, the, 17, 23, 59
Suez, 155, 231, 235
Sukarno, President, 235
Supreme Economic Council (Versailles), 117
Sweden, 100n., 146n., 212
Switzerland (and Swiss), 33, 41n., 94, 186, 203, 204, 242n., 304

Taft, Senator, 121–22
Tariff Reform campaign, 72
Taxation, on windows, 21; in France, 78; in Britain, 103, 104; Keynes and, 171, 172; Dr Holtrop and, 188
Teheran Conference (1943), 139
Third World (*see also* Developing Countries), 268, 271, 272n., 276, 285, 304, 306
Thomas, Senator, 122
Thorneycroft, Peter, 231, 232
Threadneedle Street (*see also* Bank of England), 30, 78, 84, 87, 133, 151, 175; old lady of, 87, 151, 175, 246
Throgmorton Street, 244
Tirpitz, Admiral von, 49
Tooke, Thomas, 31n.
Tories, *See* Conservatives
Trade, international, 3, 37, 37n., 47, 77, 144, 162, 175, 189, 210, 249, 263, 267, 268, 275, 285, 291, 294, 301; medieval, 12, 13, 18; British, 25, 26, 38, 71, 92, 94, 95, 129–30, 132, 133, 159n., 162–63, 227, 230, 233, 245, 247; American, 151–52, 155, 250, 253, 255

Trades Union Congress, 75
Treasury, the, 57, 58, 74, 76, 84, 85, 89, 91, 105, 106, 129, 174, 248
Triffin, Professor Robert, 162n., 198, 287
Truman, President Harry S., 126
Turner, Frederick Jackson, 264

Unemployment, 70–71, 74–77, 79, 87, 102, 132, 146, 162, 206, 220, 222, 244, 249, 255, 255n., 256n., 258–59, 260
Union Castle Line, 204n.
United Kingdom, reserves of, 212; foreign assets of, 240–41
United Nations, 112, 115, 124; 'Development Decade', 271
United Nations Conference on Trade and Development (UNCTAD), 275–276, 304–305
United Nations Relief and Rehabilitation Agency (UNRRA), 142
United States, *see* America
United States Congress, 119, 213
United States State Department, 116
United States Treasury, 101, 106, 109, 113, 114, 115, 121, 123, 124, 127, 130, 140, 141, 142, 201, 208, 209, 215, 224, 262, 286
United States War Department, 106

Vandenburg, Senator, 143
Versailles, 60, 117
Victoria, Queen, 40, 102
Vienna, 87, 203
Vietnam, 158, 165, 170, 172, 208, 235, 251, 255, 259, 264, 290, 298
Viner, Jacob (Chicago economist), 113
Vinson, Fred (Secretary of the U.S. Treasury), 126
Vyshnegradsky (Russian Finance Minister), 44

Wages, 77, 102, 163, 175, 196, 200, 206, 255, 290, 292
Wall Street (*see also* New York), financial control by, 37, 109, 115, 127; boom on, 86, 90; depression on,

90; and the IMF, 123; and Vietnam, 262; and Development, 271
Wallis, Admiral Sir Provo, 39–40
Warren, George (economist), 98, 99
Washington, as centre of monetary power, 123; negotiations in, 125, 130, 131, 209; pressure from, 236, 242
Washington Post, 270
Waterloo, 37, 39, 40, 47
Webb, Sidney, 7
Wellington, Duke of, 35
West Germany, 150n., 192, 230, 272
White, Harry Dexter, 113–15, 116–17, 119, 121, 123, 124, 125, 126–27, 140, 141, 143, 144, 262
White Plan (or White's Fund), 113–15, 116, 118, 143, 146
Whitehall, 133, 228, 303
William III, King, 19, 20
William the Conqueror, 16n.
Williams, Professor John H., 123, 130
Wilson, Rt. Hon. Harold, 236, 237, 243, 248, 277
Wilson, James (founder of *The Economist*), 31n.
Woods, George (President of the World Bank), 272
World Bank (*see also* International Monetary Fund), 119, 120, 124, 127, 144, 270, 271, 271n., 272, 304
World Economic and Monetary Conference (1933), 96–97
World War I, reparations after, 53n., 143; inflation caused by, 54–55; War Loan, 57; war debts, 61, 84, 91; aftermath of, 102, 112, 142
World War II, Germany after, 66, 191, 194; preventing inflation during, 103–104, 261, 307; War Bonds, 104; war debts, 128–29, 130, 135, 143; aftermath of, 129, 161, 191, 227, 229, 230, 231

Yalta, 126
Young plan, 85, 86, 95

Zurich, 58, 179, 201 n.